Discovering Jesus' Disciples

DISCOVERING JESUS' DISCIPLES

Who They Were, What They Believed, and What They Achieved

James Allen Moseley

RESOURCE *Publications* • Eugene, Oregon

DISCOVERING JESUS' DISCIPLES
Who They Were, What They Believed, and What They Achieved

Copyright © 2024 James Allen Moseley. All rights reserved. Except for brief quotations in critical publications or reviews, no part of this book may be reproduced in any manner without prior written permission from the publisher. Write: Permissions, Wipf and Stock Publishers, 199 W. 8th Ave., Suite 3, Eugene, OR 97401.

Resource Publications
An Imprint of Wipf and Stock Publishers
199 W. 8th Ave., Suite 3
Eugene, OR 97401

www.wipfandstock.com

PAPERBACK ISBN: 979-8-3852-2336-7
HARDCOVER ISBN: 979-8-3852-2337-4
EBOOK ISBN: 979-8-3852-2338-1

VERSION NUMBER 06/11/24

Unless otherwise noted, Scripture quotations are from *The Holy Bible, English Standard Version*, copyright © 2001 by Crossway Bibles, a publishing ministry of Good News Publishers. They are used by permission, in accordance with the "License Agreement for Bible Texts—English Standard Version," http://bibleabc.net/site/translation_esv.htm. All rights reserved or from The Holy Bible: New International Version. © 1996. Grand Rapids: Zondervan. Used in accordance with the publisher.

To Madlene, my wife, my children Natalie, Christopher, Jamie, and Anastasia, and my grandchildren James and Mason.

CONTENTS

Chronology | 1
Who Were the Apostles? | 3
What Are Apostles? | 16
The Apostles' World | 21
Biographies of the Apostles
    Simon Peter, the Rock | 33
    Andrew, the First-Called | 72
    James, Son of Thunder | 85
    John, the Apostle of Love | 91
    Philip, Apostle to Ethiopia | 114
    Nathanael Bartholomew, Apostle to Armenia | 130
    Thomas the Twin | 134
    Matthew Levi, the Tax Collector | 144
    James, Son of Alphaeus, "the Less" | 153
    Judas Thaddaeus Lebbaeus, "Dear Heart" | 155
    Simon the Zealot | 160
    Judas Iscariot, the Traitor | 163
    Matthias, the Thirteenth Disciple | 177
    Saul of Tarsus, or Paul | 182

About the Author | 237
Bibliography | 239

CHRONOLOGY

THE MANY EXACT DATES that I give in my writings on biblical theology are not guesses. They are the result of rigorous and meticulous research. The Bible and early Christian literature are so rich in harmonious time markers that given enough dedicated effort, the puzzles always work out. In the study of chronology, proof mainly depends on four things: primary textual evidence, astronomical data, math, and persistence. For over seventeen years, I have made a study of biblical chronology. My method was as follows.

First, I identified every chronological marker in the Bible. Then I plotted the certain dates on a spreadsheet. Next, I plotted all the dates relative to the certain dates. Then, I developed parallel timelines of the Hebrew, Babylonian, Seleucid, Julian, and Gregorian calendars. This required taking careful account of all leap years and intercalary months and relating days of the week to days of the month. I then tested whether these dates agreed with or contradicted the dating of the narrative of the entire canon, from Genesis to Revelation. Wherever discrepancies arose, I worked to resolve them, which was never impossible and was most often due to a simple math error, such as overlooking a leap year or an intercalary month. I then compared these dates to dates proposed in other scholarly chronological studies. Where there were variances, I examined whether a rational argument supported the variant dates or whether they were just guesses. The mere guesses I set aside. The rational arguments I plotted in my spreadsheet, and I accepted them when they were sound and rejected them when they proved flawed. I then tested dates geographically, by which I mean that if, for example, Paul set out from one city to another city, I would use Google Maps to measure the time required to walk from the first city to the second and compare the results to the chronological markers in the Bible. The Bible proved gratifyingly accurate time and again. Finally, I compared my results to extrabiblical historical records and astronomical data, which also proved surprisingly supportive of the biblical record.

It is nothing short of miraculous that the biblical authors, without the aid of computers, calendars, and atomic clocks, got their chronology so perfectly right. Even when their chronological markers seem complex and problematic, close inspection reveals them to be precisely correct. If they had been inventing the Scriptures, they might have "sanitized" or "generalized" chronological markers or left them out altogether.

I was recently asked why my results seem so much more consistent and defensible than other scholarly chronological studies. First, in my opinion, this is a neglected area of study. There are not many scholarly studies of biblical chronology. Second, many chronological studies simply accept the dates in previous studies without working them out by means of primary research. Third, some scholars seem not to care deeply about chronological problems. For example, the generally proposed (and erroneous) dating of Jesus' birth in 4 BC is almost universally understood to be problematic, but it is usually accepted and glossed over. My approach has always been to dig into a problem like stubbornly mining for gold until the nugget can be found. Fourth, many other chronological studies focus on only a segment of biblical history without taking the whole into account. This is like looking at history through a straw. For example, enthusiasts of a late date for the Exodus usually fail to grapple with the fact that such dating throws the whole chronology of the subsequent biblical canon wildly off track. Valid chronology cannot work for one part of the Bible and blow up the rest, especially if a rational, harmonious solution can be found. Finally, I studied pre-med and in the course of those studies, I acquired training in advanced math and science. Thus, my approach to biblical chronology starts with math and science and develops theses on that basis. By contrast, it appears to me that many scholars in this area may be equipped with an excellent philosophical, historical, or theological education but they seem to appeal to math and science as a secondary resource.

My resulting spreadsheet, if printed, would be over 8,500 pages long. I hope to complete my Ph.D. dissertation in the Fall of 2025 and propose to entitle it *Just in Time: The Perfect Chronology of the Bible*. For more details, please visit the Chronology section of my website, www.thebiblehistoryguy.com, through which you can also send me emails.

WHO WERE THE APOSTLES?

"I AM AN AMBASSADOR in chains," wrote Paul (Eph 6:20).[1] He also wrote:

> I think that God has exhibited us apostles as last of all, like men sentenced to death, because we have become a spectacle to the world, to angels, and to men. We are fools for Christ's sake, but you are wise in Christ. We are weak, but you are strong. You are held in honor, but we in disrepute. To the present hour we hunger and thirst, we are poorly dressed and buffeted and homeless, and we labor, working with our own hands. When reviled, we bless; when persecuted, we endure; when slandered, we entreat. We have become, and are still, like the scum of the world, the refuse of all things (1 Cor 4:9–13).

Who were Jesus' apostles? Were they rich or poor? Educated or illiterate? Related to Jesus and to each other or random strangers? Did they live long and travel far or die young in their hometowns? Did they die as martyrs or in peace?

Apostle means ambassador. These ambassadors did not wear luxurious clothes, travel in style, eat as honored guests at banquets, and retire with government pensions. They bore the Cross in pain and joy across the world.

For two centuries, Christians were a persecuted minority. There was no worldly reward for being Christian, and being a follower of Christ took courage. The twelve apostles and their first-century co-workers suffered tribulation and often death as they fulfilled the Great Commission

---

1. Unless otherwise noted, all Scripture references are from *The Holy Bible, English Standard Version, ESV* (Wheaton, Illinois: Crossway, Good News Publishers, 2001).

Jesus had given them (Matt 28:19–20). They turned an iron empire upside down and changed our world forever.

In AD 100, about when the apostle John died, there were perhaps one million Christians in the world, probably only 0.3 percent of the global population at that time. Today, about 2.5 billion people profess Christianity, or about thirty-two percent of the world's population. So, about 107 times more people, in relative terms, profess Christ today than at the close of the Apostolic Age. These ambassadors in chains fulfilled their mission with surprising effect. This book tells their little-known stories, drawn mainly from the ink on the pages of Scripture, where they have lain in plain sight for over nineteen centuries.

DISCIPLES AND APOSTLES

All apostles were disciples. Not all disciples were apostles. Disciples (Greek: *mathetes*) were pupils, hence, followers. Apostles (Greek: *apostolos*) were ambassadors, hence, leaders. Many disciples followed Jesus, witnessing the Gospel in the context of their normal lives. The apostles followed Jesus as full-time servants of the Lord and took his Word to the world. Jesus had many disciples, but of them, he chose only twelve principal apostles (although he also chose Paul, the Holy Spirit chose Matthias to replace Judas, and Scripture calls Barnabas and James the Just apostles).

THE CALLING OF THE APOSTLES

While some of Jesus' Twelve Disciples followed him part-time from the start of his ministry, they only became full-time followers in phases. On Wednesday, October 17, AD 29, at Bethany by the Jordan River, Andrew and John stopped following John the Baptist and began following Jesus. Andrew called his brother Peter to Jesus that same day. This was during the Feast of Tabernacles in the autumn of AD 29. The next day, Nathanael and Philip were called (John 1:43–45).

These five disciples accompanied Jesus to the Wedding at Cana on October 21, after which they all went, with Jesus' whole family, for a lakeshore holiday by the Sea of Galilee (John 2:1–12), probably staying in James' and Peter's capacious homes. They were not, however, yet in full-time ministry.

Not until May 1, AD 30, did Jesus call the four fishermen, Peter, Andrew, James, and John, into full-time ministry. This was 197 days, more than six months, after they first began following him (Matt 4:18–22, Mark 1:16–20). So, Jesus did not appear as a stranger and say, "Follow me, and I will make you fishers of men." Peter, Andrew, James, and John did not rise up and follow someone they did not know. They not only knew him from the previous year, but they probably also had grown up with him from childhood. Jesus of Nazareth was not new to them. Jesus the Messiah was.

Jesus called Matthew toward the end of June AD 30, about two months after calling the four fishermen (Matt 9:9, Mark 2:14). On August 19, AD 30, Jesus selected the full complement of the Twelve. This was 352 days after his baptism in the Jordan and was 111 days after calling the four fishermen (Matt 10:1–4, Mark 3:16–19, Luke 6:13–16).

DUAL NAMES AND LANGUAGES

Why did so many of the apostles have two names, like Simon Peter and Matthew Levi? This was common in ancient Judaea, partly because it was a multilingual province. The language spoken in Judaean families was Aramaic.[2] The language of worship was Hebrew[3] (the primary language of the Old Testament). The language of trade and government was Greek, the legacy of Alexander the Great's conquests.

Judaea's Roman rulers from Italy spoke Latin, but few people in the Eastern provinces did, so Roman officials had to be educated men, that

---

2. Aramaic was the language of ancient Assyria, Babylon, and Persia. It was named after Aram, the son of Shem (son of Noah), whose descendants are the "Shemites" or Semites, including Jews, Arabs, Assyrians, Babylonians, Carthaginians, Phoenicians, and Ethiopians.

3. Hebrew may derive its name from Eber, a great-grandson of Shem and ancestor of Abraham. Eber's name means "one from beyond" or "outsider," so this quintessential insider of the covenant community was the ultimate outsider of secular culture. Jewish tradition says that Eber refused to participate in building the Tower of Babel, and so his language, Hebrew, remained pure while God confused the languages of all others. The Jews teach that Hebrew was, therefore, the original language of mankind (Gen 11:1), suggesting that God spoke to Adam in Hebrew and Adam named the animals in Hebrew. This is possible, but as with so much Jewish lore, it lacks biblical support. Moses, who wrote Genesis, was born 2,371 years after Eden. He wrote Pentateuch in Hebrew but that does not necessarily mean that Hebrew was the language that original humanity spoke. What does seem undeniable is that the Hebrew Bible is the oldest and most reliable complete history of antiquity.

is, fluent in Greek.[4] Roman soldiers in Judaea would have been Greeks, Egyptians, Gauls, Spaniards, Scythians, Armenians, Italians, and others, but if they or Pontius Pilate had spoken Latin, few people would have understood them. Worse, most people would have scorned them, rather as Parisians today disdain tourists who ask directions in English. It was one thing to be a Roman governor in barbarian Britain; one could speak Latin and use an interpreter. Why should a cultured Roman need to speak Celtic or Gallic? But if a Roman were posted to Greece, Asia (Turkey), Syria, Judaea, or Egypt, anyone boorish enough not to be schooled in the language of Homer, Sophocles, and Plato would earn pity and contempt. So, in this polyglot society, Jews often had dual names. Matthew had two Hebrew names, Matthew and Levi. Some had one Hebrew and one Geek name, such as John Mark and Saul Paul. And Jesus' followers often had nicknames. Jesus called James and John "the Sons of Thunder." He called Simon "Peter" or "Cephas," which means "the Stone" or "the Rock"—"Rocky." Andrew and Philip had only one recorded name each, only in Greek (perhaps testifying to their evangelical work among Gentiles).

SCRIPTURAL LISTS OF THE DISCIPLES

All four gospels record that Jesus chose an inner group of only twelve disciples. The lists of the Twelve in Scripture appear in three groups of four, probably to assist easy memorization in those cultured days when the mind was the library of mankind.

Group One consists of the three men who were always in Jesus' inner circle (Peter, James, and John), plus Andrew, who was one of the only four present for the Olivet Discourse (Matt 24, Mark 13, Luke 21). The names in Group One are consistent, listing the two pairs of brothers (and business partners), the sons of Jonah and the sons of Zebedee. Only the order of the names changes.

Group Two always starts with Philip. The names in Group Two are also consistent, changing only in order. These are the disciples of whom Scripture gives more details; they are the second best-known men after those in Group One.

Group Three always starts with James, son of Alphaeus, and concludes with Judas Iscariot (except in Acts, by which time Judas had

---

4. When Julius Caesar was assassinated, he did not say *et tu Brute*, as Shakespeare wrote, *but kai su teknon* (and you, child?) in Greek. If a man cries out in Greek upon dying, he is either intimately familiar with that language or he is an awful snob.

betrayed Jesus and had committed suicide). Group Three consists of the disciples of whom we know the least. Judas of James has only one "speaking part" in Scripture (John 14:22), while the Bible records no speeches by Simon the Zealot or Jude of James (Judas Thaddaeus Lebbaeus). We know Judas Iscariot only in the context of his treachery.

Group 1

Mt 10:2–4	Mk 3:16–19	Lk 6:14–16	Acts 1:12
1 Simon Peter	1 Simon Peter	1 Simon Peter	1 Peter
2 Andrew, his brother	2 James, son of Zebedee	2 Andrew, his brother	2 John
3 James, son of Zebedee	3 John, brother of James	3 James	3 James
4 John, his brother	4 Andrew	4 John	4 Andrew

Group 2

Mt 10:2–4	Mk 3:16–19	Lk 6:14–16	Acts 1:12
5 Philip	5 Philip	5 Philip	5 Philip
6 Bartholomew	6 Bartholomew	6 Bartholomew	6 Bartholomew
7 Thomas	7 Thomas	7 Thomas	7 Thomas
8 Matthew	8 Matthew	8 Matthew	8 Matthew

Group 3

Mt 10:2–4	Mk 3:16–19	Lk 6:14–16	Acts 1:12
9 James, son of Alphaeus	9 James, son of Alphaeus	9 James of Alphaeus	9 James of Alphaeus
10 Thaddaeus	10 Thaddaeus	10 Simon the Zealot	10 Simon the Zealot
11 Simon the Cananean	11 Simon the Cananean	11 Judas (Jude) of James	11 Judas (Jude) of James
12 Judas Iscariot	12 Judas Iscariot	12 Judas Iscariot	

Only Group Three contains apparent inconsistencies. Matthew and Mark list Simon the Cananean, and Luke lists Simon the Zealot. They are the same person. "Zealot" is a translation into Greek (*zelotes*) of the Aramaic word for "zealous" or "jealous" (*ganana*). In English, it is rendered as "Cananean." The Zealots were a Jewish faction dedicated to expelling the Romans from Judaea by force. They sparked the Jewish War with Rome (AD 66–73), which ended in the destruction of the Jerusalem Temple in AD 70 and the mass suicide of the last Jewish resistors at Masada in AD 73. Jesus had no difficulty pairing a rebel, Simon the Zealot, with Matthew, the tax collector, a despised collaborator with Roman power. His gospel would embrace the world.[5]

Matthew and Mark list Thaddaeus, whereas Luke lists Jude of James. Since several of the disciples had more than one name or nickname, there is no reason why Judas Thaddaeus should not have had two names. In fact, he had three: Judas Thaddaeus Lebbaeus. Both Thaddaeus (Greek) and Lebbaeus (Aramaic) translate into "beloved" or "dear to the heart"—"dear heart." Since three other disciples had the name Judas (Judas Iscariot, Judas Thomas Didymus, and Judas Simon the Zealot), it is reasonable that Matthew and Mark would distinguish Judas Thaddaeus by calling him Thaddaeus only.

Luke lists the same names in his gospel as he does in his book of Acts, but in a different order. Possibly, he wished to show their later status in the Church. In his gospel, he lists James and John in birth order. In Acts, he lists John, who had become a pillar of the Church (Gal 2:9), before James, his older brother, who had died a martyr early in Church history (Acts 12:1–2).

THE FULL ROSTER OF THE ORIGINAL TWELVE

1. Simon Peter Cephas bar Jonah
2. Andrew, his brother (no nickname or Hebrew name)
3. James, son of Zebedee, son of Thunder, the Elder
4. John, his brother, son of Zebedee, son of Thunder, the disciple Jesus loved
5. Philip (no nickname or Hebrew name)

---

[5] This is even more startling when one considers that Matthew and Simon may have been brothers.

6. Nathanael Bartholomew
7. Judas Thomas Didymus (the Twin)
8. Matthew Levi, son of Alphaeus
9. James, son of Alphaeus, the Younger, the Less
10. Judas Thaddaeus Lebbaeus, son of James
11. Judas Simon the Zealot, the Cananean
12. Judas Iscariot, son of Simon

WHY TWELVE?

Jesus chose the Twelve to correspond to the twelve tribes of Israel. He made this clear when he told the disciples:

> "Truly, I say to you, in the new world, when the Son of Man will sit on his glorious throne, you who have followed me will also sit on twelve thrones, judging the twelve tribes of Israel. And everyone who has left houses or brothers or sisters or father or mother or children or lands, for my name's sake, will receive a hundredfold and will inherit eternal life. But many who are first will be last, and the last first (Matt 19:28–30).

In Revelation, John saw that the New Jerusalem would have twelve foundation stones, and on them would be the names of the Twelve Apostles of the Lamb (Rev 21:14). John thus saw his own honorific in this vision. The Twelve would have an eternal place in the New Creation. The twelve patriarchs of Israel would also be there. The sons of Jacob (Israel) fathered the chosen people with whom God made the Old Covenant. The Twelve Apostles spiritually fathered the Church (the *ekklesia* or "people who are called" or the "chosen people") with whom God made the New Covenant.

Both sets of twelve give rise to the people of God. The 144,000 witnesses of Revelation (Rev 14:1) are rich in symbolism. Their number possibly indicates the 12 patriarchs x the 12 apostles x 1,000 believers (a multitude) = 144,000. The sense is that Israel multiplied by the Gospel multiplied by large numbers of converts (symbolized by 1,000) equals the eternal body of Christ, the kingdom of heaven. Jesus said that the Twelve Apostles would judge the Twelve Patriarchs, meaning that the New Covenant is superior to the Old (Heb 8:13).

Paul explained that faith merges Gentile and Jewish Christians into one body, using the metaphor of a cultivated olive tree, Israel, into which God grafts wild olive shoots, Gentile Christians (Rom 11:17). The Bible teaches that God has only ever had one chosen people, namely those people who choose God. Israel was the standard bearer, but many non-Israelites, like Ruth and Rahab, were Gentiles whose faith put them in the ancestry of Jesus, the Messiah. Israel was meant to be a light to the Gentiles (Isa 49:6, Acts 13:47). The Gentiles, by following the Light, Jesus, would join the community of God (John 1:9).[A]Records of the Apostles

The written history of the apostles is scanty. The apostles were, for the most part, too busy making history to write it. They also did not consider themselves to be celebrities. Jesus was their whole focus (1 Cor 3:4–11). If the apostles believed that Jesus might return in their lifetimes, they might have felt there was great urgency to convert the world and make new disciples, but there was little point in writing history for future generations that might never arise to read it.

Luke's Acts of the Apostles is not a history of the apostles but an account of the transformation of the Church from an obscure Jewish sect into a worldwide religion. Since Acts tells the story of the emerging Church, not of the apostles, it seems almost like a book in two parts: (1) the Acts of Peter and (2) the Acts of Paul. Readers may feel tantalized by the abrupt ending of Acts, wondering, "What happened to Paul and Peter then?" But it never was their story. Acts ends with the arrival of Christianity at the imperial capital of Rome because that is the tale: the Gospel's journey from the Mount of Olives to Vatican Hill.[6]

THE LITERACY OF THE APOSTLES

Sermons frequently refer to the apostles of Christ as poor, uneducated tradesmen. Probably, this verse chiefly leads to that conclusion:

> "Now when they [the Sanhedrin] saw the boldness of Peter and
> John and perceived that they were uneducated, common men,

---

6. Christianity reached Rome before Paul first arrived there in AD 57. He wrote his letter to the Roman Church from Corinth in AD 54, so there was already a church in Rome by then. Peter probably founded the church in Rome in AD 43. Jewish believers from Rome were present at the birth of the Church during Pentecost in Jerusalem (Acts 2:10), and so Christianity reached Rome as early as AD 33. Luke, the author of Acts, used the arrival of the Apostle Paul to illustrate the astonishing events that led to the conversion of the empire from within its imperial heart.

they were astonished. And they recognized that they had been with Jesus" (Acts 4:13).

The Greek word in this passage for "uneducated" means "unlettered." But three of the Twelve, Matthew, John, and Peter, wrote some of the world's all-time best-selling literature. They were thus far more "lettered" than the snobbish Sanhedrin, who felt that only people who had studied under them and had accepted the same twisted teachings of Scripture that they professed were educated. In fact, the scholarship of the first-century elite leadership was wobbly at best and false at worst. As just one of many examples, the Jewish elite did not think that any prophet could come from Galilee (John 7:52), whereas Jonah did (2 Kings 14:25). What affronted the Jewish leaders was that these so-called "unlettered" men were so bold. The apostles were not rabbis, but they had built businesses, had established respectable positions in society, and spoke more persuasively than any group of men in history. They lacked the trappings of the Jewish rulers and yet had more influence. They exasperated the upper class.

SCRIBES IN THE NEW KINGDOM OF HEAVEN

The apostles were more than just literate; Jesus called them scribes "who [had] been trained for the kingdom of heaven . . . like a master of a house, who brings out of his treasure what is new and what is old" (Matt 13:52). It would be surprising if the disciples ignored this and failed to take notes during Jesus' ministry. Consider, for example, that Matthew was not present at the Sermon on the Mount, yet only Matthew recorded it. Either Jesus or the only disciples present, Peter, James, and John (Matt 4:18–22, 5:1), gave Matthew the text.[7] These apostolic scribes would bring out of their treasure what is new, the New Covenant, and what is old, the Old Covenant promises that Jesus fulfilled.

Jesus' ministry lasted 1,350 days, spanning five calendar years (AD 29–33), fifty calendar months, and 44.36 months (calculated as being of 30.5 days' average duration). The gospels have gaps in their narratives in which Jesus disappears from the pages of history. The gaps total 770 days, which is about two years, representing fifty-seven percent of Jesus'

---

7. The Holy Spirit could have given Matthew the text, of course, but it is difficult to see why He would do so when Jesus could have done in during the over 1,000 days that Matthew spent following Jesus as a disciple.

total ministry time. No wonder John wrote, "Jesus did many other signs in the presence of the disciples, which are not written in this book" (John 20:30) and "There are many more things that Jesus did. If all of them were written down, I suppose that not even the world itself would have space for the books that would be written" (John 21:25).

It is plausible that Jesus used these private times to rehearse his disciples in all his teaching and that they, as scribes, wrote their notes and checked them with Jesus for accuracy. In this way, when Jesus ascended and the disciples became apostles, they would have been well equipped with sermon notes that would empower them to take the gospel to all nations, as the Great Commission required (Matt 28:19–20). When Matthew, Mark, Luke, and John composed their gospels, it is also plausible that they would have had access to the sermon notes of all the other apostles, who would doubtless have been happy to share them for the purpose of creating a verified account of Jesus and his ministry.[8]

THE ALLEGED POVERTY OF THE APOSTLES

> "Peter said [to Jesus], 'See, we have left everything and followed you. What then will we have?'" (Matt 19:27).

> If the disciples had been poor, leaving everything to follow Jesus would have had little merit.

> "Peter said, 'I have no silver and gold, but what I do have I give to you. In the name of Jesus Christ of Nazareth, rise up and walk!' (Acts 3:6).

Peter might have meant simply that he had no cash on hand, not that he was broke. Or he might have simply been making the point that what he was about to bestow through the power of Christ had "a price above pearls" (Job 28:18).

In the third year of Jesus' ministry (32 AD), a curious event occurred regarding the payment of the tax to support the Jerusalem Temple.

> When they came to Capernaum, the collectors of the two-drachma tax went up to Peter and said, "Does your teacher not pay the tax?" He said, "Yes." And when he came into the house,

---

8. John may even have been the first to compose his gospel, which he may have carried around with him as sermon notes, much as Paul carried notes (2 Tim 4:13). So perhaps John wrote his gospel before Mark, Matthew, and Luke wrote theirs, but he published his gospel last of all.

Jesus spoke to him first, saying, "What do you think, Simon? From whom do kings of the earth take toll or tax? From their sons or from others?" And when he said, "From others," Jesus said to him, "Then the sons are free. However, not to give offense to them, go to the sea and cast a hook and take the first fish that comes up, and when you open its mouth, you will find a shekel. Take that and give it to them for me and for yourself" (Matt 17:24–27).

This story does not necessarily imply that Peter lacked the money to pay for himself and Jesus. It does imply that Jesus, as the true King of Creation and the New Temple, was not subject to the tax, nor was Jesus' chosen disciple, Peter. Poignantly, Jesus did not ask Peter to take money out of the disciples' moneybag (John 13:29) to pay the tax. Jesus sent Peter to catch a fish, where he found coins enough to pay for both Jesus and himself. Jesus produced the money from a supernatural source, emphasizing that he was sovereign over all resources.

The apostles all traveled hundreds, and some traveled thousands of miles proclaiming the Gospel. This cost a lot of money. As the Gospel spread, they could probably rely on donations from an increasing number of believers. But at the start, they must have relied on their own funds. Then, as now, spreading the Gospel incurred expenses. As Margaret Thatcher once said, the Good Samaritan could not have been the Good Samaritan if he had not had some money in his purse.

The disciples were, most likely, rather well off. Peter and Andrew were business partners of James and John (Luke 5:7, 10). James and John, under the supervision of their father, Zebedee, ran a fishing business wealthy enough to employ multiple hired men (Mark 1:19–20). John apparently had a house in Jerusalem, as well as in Galilee, because when Jesus, from the Cross, consigned Mary, his mother, to John's care, the Bible states that John took Mary into his house that same hour (John 19:26–27). That would be impossible, if John's only house were in Galilee, since John could not have transported Mary from Jerusalem to Galilee in one hour. It is possible that the Bible was using the word "house" figuratively, meaning that John took Mary into his household that very hour. But there is another piece of evidence suggesting that John owned a house in Jerusalem.

When Nicodemus met Jesus, he came secretly at night to someone's house (John 3:2). Jesus did not have a house. He said that the birds had nests and foxes had dens, but the Son of Man had no place to lay his head

(Matt 8:20, Luke 9:58). And since Nicodemus came to Jesus, and not the other way around, the place cannot have been Nicodemus' house. The meeting was private, so presumably, Nicodemus and Jesus were alone, except for the only gospel writer who recorded that meeting: John. This does not prove that John owned a house in Jerusalem, but together with the statement about his taking Mary into his house, it is suggestive. If so, he was a man of means, and yet another clue supports this.

When Peter was unable to enter the building where the Jewish leaders were trying Jesus on the night before the Crucifixion, John was able to gain entry for Peter because John was "known to the High Priest" (John 18:15–16). If John, an ally of Jesus, whom Ananias (Annas) the High Priest hated, could still call in a high priestly favor, and, of all favors, that of giving a pass to Jesus' chief disciple, who had just cut off the ear of the High Priest's servant, Malchus (Matt 26:51, Mark 14:47, Luke 22:50, John 18:10), John must have been a man of influence. How does one gain influence with a High Priest? Be a major donor.

One other clue about the affluence of disciples is that Andrew and John were followers of John the Baptist before they became disciples of Jesus (John 1:35–40). To enroll as disciples of Jesus' radical, Nazirite cousin, the Baptist, both John and Andrew must have been young men able to afford some time off from work. They cannot have been merely subsistence fishermen.

Matthew, of course, was a tax collector and, as such, was flat-out wealthy and educated. Yet the others also were probably not poor. Jesus' statement that it is easier for a camel to pass through the eye of a needle than for a rich man to pass into heaven provoked a yelp from the disciples (Matt 19:24, Mark 10:25, Luke 18:25). They asked who then might be saved? If they had considered themselves poor, they would not have asked that question. Jesus told them that while with men this would be impossible, with God all things are possible.

Paul, who was once one of the Jewish ruling class (Acts 23:6, Phil 3:5), must have been somewhat wealthy to be able to afford to travel from Tarsus to reside in Jerusalem and take up advanced studies under the famous rabbi, Gamaliel. His sister also lived in Jerusalem with Paul's nephew, for it was Paul's sister's son who warned Paul of the Jews' intention to ambush and kill him (Acts 23:16).

If the disciples were rich or at least comfortable financially when they began following Jesus, their faith was more remarkable, not less. They left comfort behind to store up their treasure in heaven (Matt 6:20).

THE WITNESS OF THE APOSTLES

The testimony of the apostles is some of the most compelling evidence for the truth of the Resurrection. That a band of persecuted men would willingly suffer and even go to grisly deaths rather than break down and confess something that every one of them knew to be a lie stretches credulity beyond the breaking point. If Jesus' Resurrection had been a fraud, the apostles, of all people, would have known it. While a fanatic might die for a lie he thought to be true, only a lunatic would die for a claim that he knew to be false. Yet even the apostles' enemies knew that they were far from mad; they marveled that such untutored fishermen were so erudite (Acts 4:13).

All the apostles suffered arrest and torture, and most suffered martyrdom for refusing to deny the Resurrection of Christ. ("Martyr" is the Greek word for "witness.") Materially and socially, they had everything to lose. There was no rich legacy of money or honor or power for these martyrs to leave to their families if the Resurrection was a hoax. Until the Edicts of Toleration in AD 311–337, a Christian in the Roman Empire was a despised outlaw.

From AD 33, on Good Friday[9] through the following Sabbath day,[10] the apostles were whimpering, broken fugitives. After Resurrection Sunday,[11] they were lions who revolutionized the world. What caused this astonishing change? After watching Jesus undeniably die, the apostles saw, touched, and ate with the risen Lord, not once, but many times for over forty days. The fact of the Resurrection demonstrated to them (and demonstrates to us) that Jesus is God; and if he is God, his teaching is true. Only the realization of that could have been worth more to the apostles than their lives.

---

9. April 1, AD 33.
10. Saturday, April 2, AD 33.
11. Sunday, April 3, AD 33.

WHAT ARE APOSTLES?

PROOFS OF AN APOSTLE

MANY HAVE CLAIMED TO be apostles, such as Mohammad and some religious leaders today. Are they? One way to know is to see how many biblical precedents of apostleship they meet. These apply to most of those whom Scripture calls "apostles:"

- They saw the Lord Incarnate.
- Jesus called them in person.
- The Holy Spirit worked through them.
- They taught God's word, not their own philosophy.
- God worked miracles through them.

The Apostles Saw the Lord Incarnate

When Peter urged the apostles to choose a replacement for Judas Iscariot after his suicide, he described a direct relationship with Jesus during his earthly mission as an indispensable criterion. He said the replacement should be: "One of the men who have accompanied us during all the time that the Lord Jesus went in and out among us, beginning from the baptism of John until the day when he was taken up from us—one of these men must become with us a witness to his Resurrection" (Acts 1:21–22). When Paul defended his status as an apostle, he said, "Am I not an apostle? Have I not seen Jesus our Lord?" (1 Cor 9:1). So, an apostle must have seen Jesus face-to-face.

Jesus Christ Called Them in Person

Jesus personally called the Twelve into a unique, lifelong mission: "And when day came, he called his disciples and chose from them twelve, whom he named apostles" (Luke 6:13). Jesus told them: "You did not choose me, but I chose you and appointed you that you should go and bear fruit and that your fruit should abide, so that whatever you ask the Father in my name, he may give it to you" (John 15:16). Paul described himself as: "An apostle—not from men nor through man, but through Jesus Christ and God the Father, who raised him from the dead" (Gal 1:1). So, an apostle must be someone whom Jesus appointed in person.

The Holy Spirit Worked Through Them

Jesus ordained the apostles to bring the Word to the world. God guaranteed the accuracy and success of their mission through the guidance of the Holy Spirit. Jesus told the apostles, while he was still with them: "The Helper, the Holy Spirit, whom the Father will send in my name, he will teach you all things and bring to your remembrance all that I have said to you" (John 14:26). The apostles knew that their wisdom and miracles were of God, not the fruit of their own talents. As Paul wrote,

> These things God has revealed to us through the Spirit. For the Spirit searches everything, even the depths of God. For who knows a person's thoughts except the spirit of that person, which is in him? So also no one comprehends the thoughts of God except the Spirit of God. Now we have received not the spirit of the world, but the Spirit who is from God, that we might understand the things freely given us by God. And we impart this in words not taught by human wisdom but taught by the Spirit, interpreting spiritual truths to those who are spiritual. The natural person does not accept the things of the Spirit of God, for they are folly to him, and he is not able to understand them because they are spiritually discerned. The spiritual person judges all things but is himself to be judged by no one. "For who has understood the mind of the Lord so as to instruct him?" But we have the mind of Christ (1 Cor 2:10–16).

So, the Holy Spirit empowered the apostles.

They Taught God's Word, Not Their Own Philosophy

Paul wrote to the Thessalonians, "And we also thank God constantly for this, that when you received the word of God, which you heard from us, you accepted it not as the word of men but as what it really is, the word of God, which is at work in you believers" (1 Thes 2:13). Peter wrote: "No prophecy of Scripture comes from someone's own interpretation. For no prophecy was ever produced by the will of man, but men spoke from God as they were carried along by the Holy Spirit" (2 Peter 1:20–21). So, apostolic teaching is directly from God, not produced by man.

God Worked Miracles through Them

God endorsed the mission of prophets and apostles through signs and wonders. A true miracle is not merely an inexplicable event. Many inexplicable events are so commonplace we hardly notice them. For example, the ability to conceive the thought that your finger should move, to command your finger to move, and to see it move as you intended is fundamentally inexplicable. Physiology can trace some of the mechanisms by which the brain translates an idea into electricity, which traverses the nerves, leaps synapses, and stimulates the finger's muscles to react. But what originally causes the brain to give birth to the idea to set these events in motion is a profound mystery. We can describe why the sun seems to rise and many of the properties of light, but why the sun should exist at all or have the characteristics it does—let alone why its rays should renew hope in a soul which, the night before, lay prostrate in despair—the wise cannot explain. A miracle is an event that God causes to highlight his message to mankind and to inspire faith in his chosen messengers.

Jesus performed miracles that confirmed his identity as Messiah. God worked miracles through the apostles to confirm their authority to preach God's Word to the world. After Jesus' Ascension, the apostles "went out and preached everywhere, while the Lord worked with them and confirmed the message by accompanying signs" (Mark 16:20). In the early days in Jerusalem, "many signs and wonders were regularly done among the people by the hands of the apostles" (Acts 5:12). Paul assured the Church at Corinth that they could trust his message, because "the signs of a true apostle were performed among you with utmost patience, with signs and wonders and mighty works" (2 Cor 12:12). So, the apostles worked verifiable miracles through the power of God.

TESTS OF APOSTLESHIP

There has never been a shortage of false apostles, even in the first century. They fall into two categories: (1) those who deceive others and (2) those who deceive others and themselves. Of those who deceive others, Paul wrote:

> What I do I will continue to do, in order to undermine the claim of those who would like to claim that in their boasted mission they work on the same terms as we do. For such men are false apostles, deceitful workmen, disguising themselves as apostles of Christ. And no wonder, for even Satan disguises himself as an angel of light. So, it is no surprise if his servants, also, disguise themselves as servants of righteousness. Their end will correspond to their deeds (2 Cor 11:12–15).

Of those who deceive others and themselves, Jesus said:

> You will recognize them by their fruits. Not everyone who says to me, "Lord, Lord," will enter the kingdom of heaven, but the one who does the will of my Father who is in heaven. On that day many will say to me, "Lord, Lord, did we not prophesy in your name, and cast out demons in your name, and do many mighty works in your name?" And then will I declare to them, "I never knew you; depart from me, you workers of lawlessness" (Matt 7:20–23).

Discerning Christians should ask these Scriptural questions of anyone claiming to be an apostle:

- Has he seen Christ face-to-face?
- Has Jesus personally called him?
- Is the Holy Spirit empowering him?
- Is he teaching God's Word and not his own philosophy?
- Is he working confirmed miracles through the Holy Spirit?

Only if these things are true of someone can Christians be quite sure that such a person is an apostle. The likelihood of an apostle, in the original, biblical sense, appearing today is, therefore, slight. Of course, God can do anything through anyone at any time, but given these criteria, it is probably safe to regard the Apostolic Age as past.

BIBLICAL EXCEPTIONS

Luke calls Barnabas an apostle (Acts 14:14), and Paul calls James the Just an apostle (Gal 1:19). James the Just was the half-brother of Jesus. He certainly knew Jesus face to face, and Jesus called him personally. Whether these two criteria were true of Barnabas is unknown. It is, however, possible. Barnabas was a wealthy Jew from Cyprus who was resident in Jerusalem and was a follower of Jesus in the early days of the Church. He may have known the incarnate Jesus personally. Perhaps the Holy Spirit called Barnabas in a way that qualified him especially to be called apostle. The inescapable fact is that the Bible calls him an apostle and calls no one else by that title other than the Eleven, Matthias, Paul, and James the Just.

The fact that Scripture never calls Luke, Mark, Timothy, or Titus apostles probably means that we should not bestow the title of apostle on anyone lightly. The office is clearly a special one, for Paul writes, "[Christ] gave the apostles, the prophets, the evangelists, the shepherds and teachers to equip the saints" (Eph 4:11), and "God has appointed in the church first apostles, second prophets, third teachers, then miracles, then gifts of healing, helping, administrating, and various kinds of tongues" (1 Cor 12:28). This latter verse reveals that an apostle ranks even higher in God's kingdom than a prophet, so even higher than Moses or Isaiah. Probably, this is because Old Testament prophets foretold the mission of Christ, while Jesus' apostles witnessed and testified to it. Jesus told the Twelve, "For truly, I say to you, many prophets and righteous people longed to see what you see, and did not see it, and to hear what you hear, and did not hear it" (Matt 13:17). The apostles were messengers of Christ especially ordained in the first century to proclaim the Gospel to the world. Although many good disciples proclaim the Gospel to the world today, to call them apostles is probably a stretch.

THE APOSTLES' WORLD

THEIR FAMILY TIES

GOD USED THE TWELVE Patriarchs of Israel, all brothers, to form the Old Covenant community of God. God used the Twelve Apostles, all Galileans (except possibly Judas Iscariot), to form the New Covenant community of God. Their family ties may have been surprisingly tight. Peter and Andrew were blood brothers (Matt 4:18). James and John were blood brothers (Matt 4:21). Peter, Andrew, James, and John were partners in the fishing business (Luke 5:7, 10). Matthew Levi, James the Less, and Simon the Zealot may have been brothers. James, John, James the Less, Matthew, Judas Thaddaeus, and Simon the Zealot may have been Jesus' cousins and thus nephews of Jesus' mother, Mary. Simon the Zealot may have been the groom at the Wedding in Cana.

In any case, all the apostles came from Galilee, except perhaps Judas Iscariot, whose name means "from Kirioth," a town in Judaea. Yet even he may have been a Galilean, for his father, Simon Iscariot (John 6:71, 13:2, 26), may have moved to Galilee and raised Judas there. If so, his identifier, Iscariot, would have made sense, marking him as someone whose family was originally from outside Galilee. Paul was born in Gischala in Galilee. When Quirinius annexed Galilee to the Roman province of Judaea in AD 7,[1] Paul's family moved to Tarsus in Cilicia (modern Turkey).[2]

Galilee was a small place, and so all the apostles except Paul undoubtedly knew each other growing up, even if they were not related by

---

1. Josephus, *Antiquities*, 18:2:1.
2. Jerome, *On Illustrious Men*.

blood. They surely traveled together on the yearly family pilgrimages to Jerusalem to celebrate Passover in Spring, Pentecost in Summer, the High Holy Days in Fall, and Chanukah in December.

THEIR APPEARANCE

Paintings of Jesus with long hair and a full beard and of first-century Jews in Persian turbans and Bedouin robes are fantasies of later artists. The Hellenistic world created by Alexander the Great was remarkably homogeneous in style. From Britain to North Africa, from Spain to India, people affected Greek manners. The earliest painting of Jesus depicts him as the Good Shepherd with short hair, no beard, and wearing a knee-length tunic.[3] This is probably far more what Jesus looked like than the paintings we know and love. The apostle Paul admonished men not to let their hair grow long (1 Cor 11:14), which he would hardly have done if the other apostles or the Sanhedrin had worn their hair long; he certainly would not have written that if Jesus had worn his hair long.

The Caesars were all clean-shaven until the emperor Hadrian made a short beard fashionable, which he only did to cover his badly blemished skin. The Sadducees, who were the Hellenized rulers of the Jews, and the overtly Romanized Herodians, were certainly clean-shaven, in imitation of their Latin overlords. Do not let shaggy Medieval and Renaissance portraits of Herod the Great deceive. Look at the smooth ancient busts of Herod; it is hard to distinguish him from a noble Roman. Most of the apostles would have presented themselves in the same way, retaining the services every three days of professional barbers, who used iron razors to keep beards trim. Women wore head coverings and let their hair grow to shoulder length.

People in Jesus' day wore Greek tunics, which were like loose dresses with elbow-length sleeves and a belt. The cloth was wool in winter and linen in summer. The hem of the tunic reached below the knee, although in Greece it often fell above the knee, both for men and women. Over the tunic, men and women wore a cloak, which was a simple, rectangular poncho with a hole for the head and neck. For poor people, the simple cloak might also serve as their only blanket at night. In the Eastern Empire, people did not wear togas. The toga was the ornamental dress of the nobility in Rome.

3. Caldwell, "Three of the Oldest Images of Jesus."

GALILEE

Galilee was the most fertile and productive part of Israel. Josephus, the first-century Jewish historian, wrote that the region consisted of two hundred villages. It was about the size of Rhode Island or about one-tenth the size of California. He described Galilee in this way:

> Thanks to the rich soil, there is not a plant that does not flourish there, and the inhabitants grow everything . . . walnuts . . . flourish in abundance, as do palms . . . side by side with figs and olives . . . not only does it produce the most surprisingly diverse fruits; it maintains a continuous supply. Those royal fruits, the grape and fig, it furnishes for ten months on end.[4]

The Sea of Galilee, also called Lake Tiberias, the Sea of Gennesaret,[5] or Lake Kinneret,[6] is only thirteen miles long and eight miles wide, with a maximum depth of about 130 feet. It is about one percent the size of Lake Ontario, the smallest of the Great Lakes. At over six hundred feet below sea level, it is the lowest freshwater lake in the world.

Galilee had an important Jewish population, but the majority of its residents were Gentile.[7] Other Gentile populations also surrounded Galilee—Syrian Phoenicians to the north and west, Samaritans (Assyrian-Hebrew half-castes) to the south, Greeks in the Decapolis,[8] and nomadic Arabs to the east. The Jewish Galileans were independent, resourceful, worldly, and proud of their heritage.

---

4. Josephus, *Jewish War*, 3:10:8.
5. Which means "a garden of riches."
6. Referring to a nearby town, Kinnereth, allotted to the tribe of Naphtali (Josh 19:35)
7. The word Gentile is generally used to indicate non-Jewish people groups. The Greek word is ἔθνος (*ethnos*, from which we get the English word ethnic). The Hebrew word is גוי (*goy*). Curiously, before there were any Israelites (descendants of Israel/Jacob) or any Jews (descendants of Judah), God said he would make a great *goy* (nation) of Abraham, and through him, all the families of the earth would be blessed (Gen 12:2–3).
8. Decapolis means "Ten Cities" in Greek. It was a league of Hellenistic cities established by Pompey the Great in 63 BC and governed by Rome. The ten cities were Philadelphia (Amman, Jordan), Gerasa (Jerash, Jordan), Gadara (Umm Qais, Jordan), Pella (Tabaqat Fahl, Jordan), Dion (Tell Ashari, Syria), Raphana (Ar-Rafi'ah, Syria), Scythopolis (Bet She'an, Israel), Hippos (Sussita, Israel), Canatha (Qanawat, Syria), and Damascus.

THE IMPORTANCE OF JUDAEA

Judaea was not a forgotten backwater in the Roman world. Jews represented about ten percent of the population of the Western Empire and about twenty percent of the population of the Eastern Empire. By comparison, Jews represent only about two percent of the population of the United States today. Never, since the fall of Judah to Babylon in the sixth century BC until the twentieth century, had Jews comprised so large a part of any body politic. The Herods, as faux "kings of the Jews," were on friendly, familiar terms with several Roman emperors, and Roman law initially recognized Judaism as a tolerated religion, despite its frequent friction with the state cult of emperor worship.

Egypt, to the south of Judaea, was Rome's breadbasket. Rome relied on the dependable harvests of the Nile Valley for grain to feed its legions. Alexandria in Egypt was the second largest and richest city in the empire, after Rome. Syria, to the north of Judaea, was a thriving commercial territory and a bulwark against Rome's only Asian enemy, Parthia (Persia). Antioch in Syria was the third largest and richest city in the empire. Judaea was the lynchpin between these two vital provinces. The great resources Rome spent defeating the Jewish Revolt of AD 66–73 is a measure of Judaea's political, military, and economic importance.

THE JEWISH SECTS

Josephus identified four main Jewish sects.[9] (1) The Sadducees or Zadokis, named after David's priest, Zadok (2 Sam 8:17), meaning "righteous," were the Roman-friendly, ruling class who did not believe in an afterlife, angels, or the supernatural. They were the most numerous and powerful Jewish leaders. They believed that only the Torah (first five books of the Bible) was canonical. The High Priests Ananias (Annas) and Joseph Caiaphas were of their number (2) The Pharisees, whose name means "set apart," believed in the supernatural, the resurrection of the dead, and angels, and they counted Paul and Gamaliel among their number. (3) The Essenes, "secret or sacred," were a strict, holy order of Jewish ascetics who lived a life of work, prayer, and celibacy in wilderness communities. (4) The Zealots (Hebrew: *kanai*, meaning an ardent follower), objected to Roman emperor worship, Roman taxation,

---

9. Josephus, *Jewish War*, 2:8:2–14, 7:8:1, *Antiquities of the Jews*, 13:5:9, 18:1:2.

and the Roman-supported Herodian kings. They aimed to drive Rome from the Promised Land under the leadership of a monarch from the line of Judah (the anticipated Messiah, whom they were prepared to follow zealously, hence their name).

ROME

The Roman Empire extended from Britain to North Africa and from Spain to Russia and Parthia (Persia). It was a somewhat dysfunctional family of nations, forged by military conquest and held together by Roman law and legions. This was the iron part of Daniel's dream statue. The people of the empire spoke many languages and worshiped diverse gods. The Eastern Roman Empire never adopted Latin as its common tongue. Greek was the language of culture and trade. The elite considered Latin vulgar. For this reason, the New Testament was written in Greek and its later translation into Latin by Jerome was called the Vulgate Version, a rendering into the vulgar or common tongue. The empire's cultural diversity was the clay in Daniel's dream statue (Dan 2:40–43).

Rome is the city of seven hills (cf. Revelation 17:9). The seven hills are the: (1) Aventine Hill (*Aventinus*), (2) Caelian Hill (*Caelius*), (3) Capitoline Hill (*Capitolinus*),[10] (4) Esquiline Hill (*Esquilinus*), (5) Palatine Hill (*Palatinus*), (6) Quirinal Hill (*Quirinalis*), and (7) Viminal Hill (*Viminalis*). The Vatican Hill was not one of the traditional Seven Hills. It is north of the river Tiber, outside the ancient city walls. The word "Vatican" comes from the Latin "*vates*," meaning "seer, soothsayer." Vaticanus was an Etruscan god, and his temple sat on the Vatican Hill. The Church of Rome moved its seat to the Vatican Hill in the fourteenth century (after the awkward interlude of the Avignon Papacy, during which, at one point, no fewer than three Popes claimed Peter's tiara.)

Pagan historians mainly ignored Christianity in its early days. Plutarch's famous history was called *Lives of Noble Greeks and Romans*. The Church Fathers were neither noble, Greek, nor Roman and therefore little worth noting. The apostles were born in the reign of Caesar Augustus, from 27 BC to AD 14. This was the era of the *Pax Romana* or Roman

---

10. The American Capitol is spelled with an -ol rather than an -al in imitation of Rome. The U.S. capital ("head" from Latin, *capus*) city is Washington, D.C. The U.S. Congress is on the Capitol (or Capitoline) Hill, because the Founders considered the American Republic a "New Rome." They even pretentiously named Goose Creek, a tiny tributary of the Potomac River, the Tiber, in strained emulation of the Eternal City.

Peace. The endless civil wars were over and would not resume until AD 69. Travel was relatively easy and safe over the Roman network of roads, and the government was tolerant of different religions.

After Augustus, Tiberius reigned from AD 14 to 37.[11] Tiberius was the emperor who appointed Pontius Pilate procurator of Judaea. Caligula followed Tiberius from AD 37 to 41. Caligula started well but then went mad. His praetorian guards assassinated him. He attempted to install a statue of himself as a god in the Jerusalem Temple, an abomination that certainly would have caused desolation (Dan 12:11, Matt 24:15, Mark 13:14). The Jews were outraged, but before the ship carrying the statue could reach Caesarea, news of Caligula's death preceded it, and the statue was never installed. Claudius followed Caligula from AD 41 to 54. Although apparently a drooling, stumbling fool, he was savvier than he seemed, and he restored stability to the empire. He had his promiscuous wife, Messalina, executed for plotting against him. Irritated at the squabbling between Christians and Jews, whom he probably could not bother to distinguish from each other, he expelled all Jews from Rome in AD 49. This caused the Roman church to become Gentile-led. When Claudius' edict lapsed, and the Jewish Christians returned to Rome, they were aghast to find that the church had abandoned Jewish traditions. To bridge this gap between Jewish and Gentile Christians, Paul wrote his epistle to the Romans. Claudius married his niece, Agrippina, and adopted her son, Nero, as his heir. In AD 54, Claudius died at a feast, probably from eating mushrooms poisoned by Agrippina so that her son Nero could become emperor. Nero ruled from AD 54 to 68. Like Caligula, he started well but degenerated into a tyrant of bestial cruelty, persecuting Christians terribly for three and a half years, from mid-AD 64 until his suicide in mid-AD 68.

Nero's Persecution of Christians

In AD 64, a great fire destroyed ten of Rome's fourteen districts. Rumors circulated that Nero had started the fire to clear the city of commoners and make space for his planned Golden Palace (*Domus Aureus*). The rumors were dubious, but to deflect the erupting anger of the Roman mob, Nero accused the Christians of arson. He began a persecution of epic

---

11. Finegan, *Handbook*, 339. Finegan's chart is a little confusing, but a close inspection reveals that Finegan means Tiberius' first regnal year was from August 19, AD 14, to August 18, AD 15.

proportions, lasting three and a half years, until his death in AD 68. The Roman historian Tacitus wrote this account of what Christians, whom he personally despised, suffered:

> Neither human resources nor imperial generosity nor appeasement of the gods eliminated the sinister suspicion that the fire had been deliberately started. To stop the rumor, Nero made scapegoats—and punished with every refinement the notoriously depraved Christians (as they were popularly called). Their originator, Christ, had been executed in Tiberius' reign by the Procurator of Judaea, Pontius Pilatus. But in spite of this temporary setback, the deadly superstition had broken out again, not just in Judaea (where the mischief had started) but even in Rome. All degraded and shameful practices collect and flourish in the capital. First, Nero had the self-admitted Christians arrested. Then, on their information, large numbers of others were condemned—not so much for starting fires as because of their hatred for the human race. Their deaths were made amusing. Dressed in wild animals' skins, they were torn to pieces by dogs, or crucified, or made into torches to be set on fire after dark as illumination. . . . Despite their guilt as Christians, and the ruthless punishment it deserved, the victims were pitied. For it was felt that they were being sacrificed to one man's brutality rather than to the national interest."[12]

Suetonius also wrote, "[after the Great Fire] . . . punishments were also inflicted on the Christians, a sect professing a new and mischievous belief."[13] Ironically, Nero's gardens, where so many Christians suffered, were on the Vatican Hill, the future site of the Church of Rome, which would outlive and replace the dynasty of the Caesars. How many Christians died under Nero is unrecorded, but the Neronian persecution was probably not confined to Rome, and throughout the empire, it probably claimed the lives of a large number of believers. Christians who were Roman citizens, by law, were exempt from torture. Thus, Paul was beheaded because he was a citizen, while Peter was crucified because he was not. Subsequent emperors (Domitian, Valerian, and Diocletian) imitated Nero's persecution of Christians. They, like the philosopher-king Marcus Aurelius, scorned Christianity. Finally, the emperor Constantine's Edict of Toleration in AD 313 allowed anyone in the empire to observe the Christian religion freely and openly.

12. Tacitus, *Annals* 15:44.
13. Suetonius, "Nero," *Lives of the Twelve Caesars*.

Under Roman persecution, the Church grew through suffering, and it eventually conquered Rome. Under Rome's persecution, the Jewish Temple and sacrificial system perished utterly.

Jesus' Prophecy Fulfilled

The Old Covenant ended with the baptism of Christ in AD 29. Rome destroyed Jerusalem and the Temple in AD 70. The last vestige of national Israel perished in AD 73. (There would be two second-century revolts, one from AD 115–117 and another from AD 132–136 that would attempt a restoration of Jewish independence, but the Romans would crush them mercilessly.) So, Jesus' generation indeed had not passed away until not one stone of the Temple was left standing upon another and until the universal reign of Christ had replaced the rule of Jewish priests (Matt 24).

A NEW COVENANT FOR THE WORLD

The missionary labors of the apostles pre-dated the much-prophesied end of the Old Covenant. Pentecost, Sunday, May 22, AD 33, was an international experience. Hundreds of thousands, if not over two million, visiting Jews came from many nations to Jerusalem.[14] After hearing Peter's sermon, many took the Gospel home to Parthia, Media, Elam, Mesopotamia, Cappadocia, Pontus, Phrygia, Pamphylia, Egypt, Libya, and Rome (Acts 2:9–11). In AD 33, Philip witnessed to an Ethiopian eunuch, who brought Christianity to Africa (Acts 8:27–39). In AD 37, God directly told Peter to bring the Gospel to a Roman centurion, Cornelius, and his family at Caesarea, proving that Christ's salvation was for Gentiles as well as for Jews. Eusebius wrote that the apostles divided the inhabited world into regions of influence for evangelism: Thomas to Parthia (Persia), John to Asia Minor, Peter to Pontus (the south coast of the Black Sea in northern Turkey) and Rome, and Andrew to Scythia (Central Asia).[15] Paul planted churches in Asia Minor (modern Turkey), Macedonia (northern Greece), and Greece from AD 44–54.

Luke finished his book of Acts by AD 59, the year Nero released Paul from his first imprisonment at Rome. The book covered a period

---

14. Josephus, *Jewish War*, 6:9:3.
15. Eusebius, *Church History*, 3:1.

of twenty-six years. Probably all the apostles had traveled far and wide by the end of Acts.

THE CHRISTIAN EMPIRE

The Flavius Valerius Constantinus "Constantine" (AD 285–337) first contended for the title of emperor when fighting his rival, Maxentius, at the Battle of the Milvian Bridge (October, AD 312) at Milan, Italy. Before the battle, Constantine had a dream in which he saw the sign of Christ in the sky (the Greek letters X and 'P, equivalent to "Ch" and "R," the first two letters in the title Christ or "Anointed One"). Constantine thought this vision presaged his victory, and he became a Christian. After spending the next twelve years defeating his enemies, he became sole emperor in AD 324. He outlawed pagan sacrifices, and Christianity became Rome's official religion. On 8 November AD 324 (after trying several other sites), he founded the great city of Constantinople[16] ("Constantine's City") and made it the imperial capital. While Rome retained its ancient honors, the population and wealth of the empire were greater in the eastern, Greek-speaking provinces. Italy was now far from the political center of gravity.

Whether Constantine was a true believer is debatable. He built the Church of the Twelve Apostles in Constantinople with the idea of finding and exhuming the bodies of the Twelve, burying them in his church, and choosing a place in their midst for his own tomb as the Thirteenth Apostle. To this end, the emperor set about searching for the remains of the Twelve. He did not get far. He dedicated the church on Easter of AD 337 and died on May 22 of the same year. So, he was buried among the apostles' tombs, as planned, but all except his sepulcher were empty.

THE TRAIL OF RELICS

Still, the official search for the remains of the Twelve Apostles continued for centuries, stimulating the quest for venerable relics. This gave rise to many stories about where the apostles lived and died. These hagiographies (biographies of saints) were a mixture of truth and legend. In the

---

16. When the Turks conquered Constantinople in AD 1453, they renamed it Istanbul, which is a mispronunciation of the Greek words "*sti poli*" or "*to the city.*" Even today, Greeks refer to this great city as "The City" or "*i poli.*" The Turks pronounced "*sti*" as "*istan*" and "*poli*" as "*bul*," hence "Istanbul."

Middle Ages, Christians were a bit too eager to believe all legends. Possibly today, we are a bit too eager to dismiss them. There is, undoubtedly, truth mixed with fantasy in many of them.

Any parts of the apostles' bodies, or pieces of wood or nails from the True Cross, or the cup from which Jesus served the wine of the Last Supper (the Holy Grail)[17] were considered sacred. Superstition attributed holy powers to relics. Churches claiming to house relics became important pilgrim and tourist destinations (raking in donations). Of course, many relics were false. Probably if all the pieces of the "true" Cross were put together, one could reconstruct Noah's ark.

FULFILLING THE GREAT COMMISSION

The problem with tracking down the apostles' relics was that the apostles took Jesus' command in Acts 1:8 seriously. The Lord told them to go to Judaea, Samaria, and the farthest parts of the world, and off they went. They mostly died in distant mission fields, making recovery of their relics difficult. Nevertheless, the apostles were not aimless wanderers. They had a strategy. They first went to major cities that had a Jewish synagogue (a Greek word that simply means "assembly"). The Jews lived in cities all over the Roman world. There were about 120 synagogues throughout the empire in the first century. In these, the new Jewish Christians planted churches. And the apostles did not aim simply to make single converts. They wanted to convert congregations, carry out the Great Commission, and inspire new Christian communities to found other faithful congregations. In this way, Christianity spread by the testimony of a few dedicated men who bore astonishing hardships and died mainly as martyrs.

---

17. Grail is from Old French, *graal*, which is from Latin *gradalis*, which is from Greek, *krateros*, or cup, referring to the Cup of Blessing that Jesus used to drink the wine at the Last Passover Supper.

BIOGRAPHIES OF THE APOSTLES

SIMON PETER, THE ROCK

Peter was the first in the list of apostles. Peter's original name was Simon (Hebrew: "God has heard"), son of Jonah ("Dove" in Hebrew). Andrew was his brother. He was born in Bethsaida (John 1:44), a small town at the north end of the Sea of Galilee. Bethsaida means "House of Fish." A better English translation of Bethsaida might be Fish Town, and it was probably from life in this fishing village that Peter and Andrew derived their profession. Perhaps fishing was a generational business, accounting for Peter's father's name being Jonah, a wryly appropriate name for a seafaring man.

Philip the apostle was also born in Bethsaida (John 12:21), so Philip, Simon Peter, and Andrew probably knew each other growing up, and perhaps they were friends prior to becoming disciples. Simon Peter and Andrew made their home in Capernaum (Mark 1:29), a larger, nearby town on the northwest shore of the Sea of Galilee. Capernaum means "Town of Nahum." Possibly, it takes its name from the prophet Nahum, although Nahum means "Comfort," so it also is possible that the place name means "Comfort Town."

Peter and Andrew had a fishing business and possessed their own boat (Luke 5:3). Peter spoke to Jesus more than any other disciple, and Jesus spoke more to Peter than to anyone else. Peter lived with his mother-in-law in a house he owned with his brother (Mark 1:29–30, Matt 8:14, Luke 4:38). He was married (obviously), and according to Clement of Alexandria, he had children.[1] Peter took his wife with him on missionary

---

1. Clement of Alexandria, *Stromata*, 3:6:52

journeys (1 Cor 9:5). Clement wrote that Peter's wife, like her husband, eventually died as a Christian martyr.[2]

PETER'S APPEARANCE

The earliest known portrait of Peter is on a bronze medallion in the Roman catacombs.[3] It dates from the late second or early third century, about 130 years after Peter's death. This portrait might have been copied from earlier portraits and might bear a resemblance to Peter. Or it might be just an artist's impression. In any case, this image of Peter looks resolute, far-seeing, fearless, long-suffering, and distinctive, like a real person who has lived a real life, not like a mere icon.

Painters often portray Peter as burly and old. This is questionable. No doubt Peter was physically fit. All the disciples walked hundreds of miles with Christ, and most walked many thousands more on their missionary journeys after the Resurrection. Peter walked on water (until his faith failed). He cut off a man's ear with his sword (he probably missed his main target). And he dove into the Sea of Galilee to swim to Jesus when Jesus called to him from shore. Yet he was not as fast a runner as John, who beat Peter to the empty tomb. In any case, there is no reason why Peter could not have been younger than Jesus. The only person we can assume Peter was older than is Andrew, since the Bible always lists Andrew second after Peter, suggesting that Andrew was the younger of the two brothers. If Peter were approximately the same age as Jesus, he would have been about thirty-one when Jesus was baptized and about seventy when Nero executed him in AD 68. The dramatic Ford Maddox Brown painting (1856) of Jesus washing an ancient, graying Peter's feet is delightful but probably unrealistic. In that painting, Peter appears to be in his sixties. If he were in his sixties in AD 33, Peter would have been 95 or older at his death. This is improbable and not based on Scriptural evidence.

---

2. Clement of Alexandria, *Stromata*, 7:11

3. Catacombs are subterranean sepulchral vaults in Rome, of which about forty have been excavated. During the centuries when Christianity was illegal, Roman Christians dug these tunnels out of soft volcanic rock so they could bury their dead and hold funeral services in secret. Pagan Romans cremated their dead. Christians preferred to entomb their dead in expectation of the final, bodily resurrection. Some of the catacombs are several kilometers in length and consist of four stories or floors. They are an important source of early Christian art, which adorns their walls.

Peter and all the disciples probably looked very similar—a bunch of Jewish boys from Galilee of about the same age. If they did not all look rather alike, the Temple guards might not have needed Judas to point out Jesus at night in the Garden of Gethsemane.

PETER'S HOME

As his Galilean ministry headquarters, Jesus returned to Peter's house often. Around Wednesday, May 1, AD 30, Jesus called Peter, Andrew, James, and John to drop their nets and follow him (Matt 4:19–20, Mark 1:16–18, Luke 5:5–11). Jesus made Peter's house his base of operations in Galilee. On the Sabbath of May 18, Jesus taught in the Capernaum synagogue and exorcised a demon-possessed man (Mark 1:23–26). That same day, Jesus found Peter's mother-in-law at home, lying sick with fever (Matt 8:14, Mark 1:30, Luke 4:38). The people spoke to Jesus about her, Jesus raised her up, and the fever left her. Then Jesus healed many who were ill, and he cast out demons, forbidding the demons from saying who he was—for they knew. Jesus did these miracles all through the night until sunrise. At dawn on Sunday, he rose and went to a secluded place and prayed (Mark 1:35).

We can deduce from all of this that Peter's house was large, since Jesus spent the night there with two extended families, healing a crowd of people. Also, despite the house being filled with Peter, his wife, his mother-in-law, Andrew, and two other disciples, Jesus was able to sneak out in the morning without tripping over and waking any of them. However, the house could not have been a palace because "the whole city was gathered at the door" (Mark 1:33); apparently, they could not all get inside at once.

WALKING ON WATER

After feeding the five thousand (Matt 14:21, Mark 6:44, Luke 9:14, John 6:10), Jesus told the disciples to coast their boat along the Sea of Galilee shore and shelter at Bethsaida. Disobeying, they instead attempted to make an evening crossing back to Capernaum—where Peter and Andrew had their comfortable house and where Peter's wife and mother-in-law would no doubt serve them a warm meal. After sending them and the crowds away, Jesus went to the hilltop where he had fed the multitude to pray, alone.

A strong wind arose against the disciples in the boat. The sea became rough; they made painfully slow headway. Beaten by waves, the storm blew them far offshore. Against a contrary wind, sailing was useless, so the disciples dropped canvas and took to rowing. The Sea of Galilee is only about five miles wide, and the disciples had rowed about three-quarters of the way across. It was now between 3 and 6 a.m.[4] Since the disciples had launched around sunset, they had been toiling at the oars for an exhausting nine to twelve hours.

At this time, Jesus walked across the water to overtake the Twelve in the boat. He had to cross three to four miles of storm-tossed water to catch up to them. When the disciples saw the figure approaching, they were terrified. They cried, "It is a ghost!" But Jesus said, "It is I. Do not be afraid." Peter cried, "If it is you, command me to come to you on the water." Jesus said, "Come!" and Peter got out of the boat and walked to him. But seeing the wind, he lost heart, began to sink, and cried out, "Lord, save me!" Jesus took hold of his hand and said, "You of little faith, why did you doubt?" Jesus brought Peter into the boat, and immediately the storm ceased. The disciples worshiped him and said, "You certainly are God's Son" (Matt 14:22–33).

TRANSFIGURATION

In AD 31, Jesus took his disciples north to Caesarea Philippi near Syria. There he foretold his death. Peter affirmed that Jesus was the Christ. Jesus called Peter blessed. Then Peter wanted to forbid that Jesus should suffer and die. Jesus rebuked Peter, even saying to him, "Get behind me, Satan!" (Matt 16:23, Mark 8:33) and saying that Peter was a stumbling block to him, focused on the things of men, not of God. Few have received such high praise and so sharp a rebuke in the course of a few minutes.

On about Tuesday, April 29, Jesus took Peter, James, and John to nearby Mount Hermon, where he was transfigured before them. His face shone like the sun, and his clothes became as white as light. Moses and Elijah appeared to them, talking to Jesus. Peter cried out, "Lord, it is good for us to be here. If you wish, I will make three tabernacles here,

---

4. The Bible says this was the "fourth watch of the night." Night was considered to consist of twelve hours. Dividing it into four watches yielded four three-hour periods: 6 p.m.–9 p.m., 9 p.m.–12 a.m., 12 a.m.–3 a.m., and 3 a.m.–6 a.m.

one for you, one for Moses, and one for Elijah." While Peter was speaking, a bright cloud overcame them, and a voice said, "This is My beloved Son, with whom I am well pleased. Listen to him." This was one of three times, Jesus' Baptism, the Transfiguration, and Palm Sunday, when the Father spoke from heaven with Jesus present (Matt 3:17, 17:5, Mark 1:11, 9:7, Luke 3:22, John 12:28, 2 Peter 1:18, revealing a manifestation of the Trinity. The three disciples fell to the ground, terrified. Then Jesus touched them, saying, "Get up. Do not be afraid." And when they arose, they saw no one there but Jesus, who said, "Tell no one about this until the Son of Man has risen from the dead" (Matt 17:1–9). That same day, coming down the slope of Mount Hermon, they met the other nine disciples who were trying, without success, to drive a demon from a boy. Jesus told them that such a demon comes out only with prayer and fasting, and then he exorcised it himself (Matt 17:15–21).

THE TEMPLE TAX

Coming back to Capernaum, the Temple tax collectors challenged Peter about Jesus, asking if his rabbi had failed to pay the two-drachma tax. This was not a Roman tax, but a tax imposed on Jews by Jews for the support of the Levitical priesthood that ran the Temple. Peter defended Jesus, telling them yes, Jesus did pay it. But when Peter came home, before he could say anything, Jesus told him that kings collect taxes from strangers, not from their sons. Therefore, Jesus, God's Son, was exempt from the Temple tax. Jesus could have tapped the disciples' money bag, which Judas Iscariot kept, to pay the tax. Instead, Jesus told Peter, so as not to offend anyone, to go throw a hook into the Sea of Galilee and pull up the first fish he caught. That fish would have a shekel in its mouth. A shekel was worth four drachmas or about four days of a skilled laborer's wages. Peter was to take the money and pay the tax for Jesus and himself (Matt 17:24–27).[5] In all his life of fishing, Peter doubtless found many strange things inside fish, but Jesus surely was amusing both himself and Peter by using this uniquely personal method of prophecy, fulfillment, and teaching.

---

5. Only Matthew, the professional tax collector, recorded this account.

FORGIVENESS AND WEALTH

Peter was the disciple who asked Jesus how many times he should forgive a brother who sinned against him, and Jesus told him not seven times, but seventy times seven (Matt 18:21–22). When Jesus told the disciples that it was easier for a camel to pass through the eye of a needle than for a rich man to enter the kingdom of God, they were distressed. Peter and Andrew, with their big house, the sons of Zebedee with their fishing fleet, servants, and Jerusalem residence, and Matthew Levi, the tax collector, were certainly not poor. They asked, dismayed, "Who then can be saved?" Jesus replied that with man it would be impossible, but with God all things are possible. Peter pressed the point. "We have left everything and followed you. What then will there be for us?" If they had been poor, leaving everything would probably not have meant as much to them, even though Jesus taught them that the poor woman who gave her little all had given more than the rich who had given only some of their wealth (Mark 12:41–44, Luke 21:1–4). Jesus told him that in the regeneration, when the Son of Man should sit on his glorious throne, they would sit upon twelve thrones, judging the twelve tribes of Israel and would inherit eternal life (Matt 19:28). By this Jesus revealed that the apostles would represent the New Covenant, which was superior to the Old Covenant, represented by the twelve Israelite tribes (Heb 8:13).

PASSION WEEK

On Tuesday, March 29, AD 33, Jesus took only Peter, Andrew, James, and John (the sons of Zebedee) to the Mount of Olives and predicted his death by Friday, as well as the future destruction of the Jerusalem Temple (Matt 24). On Thursday, March 31, Jesus sent only Peter and John from Bethany to Jerusalem to prepare the Last Supper. Normally, preparing for the Passover would have been a happy task. This year it was grim and foreboding. His disciples already knew Jesus expected this to be his last meal with them; two days before, he had told them he would be dead by Friday. Jesus told Peter and John that they would meet a man carrying a pitcher of water, who would lead them to a house with a large, furnished Upper Room. They found everything as Jesus foretold (Luke 22:8–13). This must have increased their sense of impending doom. If Jesus were right about these things—as, indeed, he was right about everything—surely tomorrow he would die.

THE LAST SUPPER

When Jesus washed his disciples' feet before the Last Supper, he came first to Peter, who protested that he should be the one to wash Jesus' feet. Jesus declared that if Peter did not submit, Peter would have no part in him. Peter cried, "Lord, not only my feet but also my hands and my head" (John 13:9).

After singing hymns at the end of the meal, Jesus warned that all the disciples would fall away because of him that night but that Jesus would be struck down, raised, and go ahead of them into Galilee. This must have been thoroughly baffling. How could he die tomorrow and also go ahead of them, back home, safe to Galilee? Peter protested, "Even though all may fall away because of you, I will never fall away." But Jesus told Peter, "This very night, before a rooster crows twice, you will deny me three times." Peter insisted, "Even if I have to die with you, I will not deny you." All the other disciples said the same (Matt 26:30–35). Peter asked John, who was reclining near Jesus, to ask Jesus who he thought would betray him. Jesus told John that it was the man to whom he would give a morsel of food. Jesus gave that morsel to Judas Iscariot (John 13:24), who then left the room on his treasonous mission.

The setting of the Last Supper was not as most paintings depict it. In Jesus' day, three tables at a banquet were arranged in a U-shape. The arrangement was called a triclinium. The guests reclined on couches set at right angles to the three tables. Jesus, as the host, sat on the long end of the U on the right, with John on his right (at the table's edge) and Judas on his left. Peter, as the first of the disciples, sat across the open space of the U at the long end of the U on the left and on the table's edge, opposite John. So John and Peter were looking at each other across the open area in the middle of the U. When Jesus said that one of the disciples would betray him, John was reclining to Jesus' right—on a couch, not leaning on Jesus. Since John was next to Jesus when he said this, Peter motioned across the open space to John to ask who the traitor would be. This was not the sort of question Peter would shout across the room.

John, leaning back against Jesus, said to him, "Lord, who is it?" Jesus answered, "It is he to whom I will give this morsel of bread when I have dipped it." Jesus obviously said this softly to John. When he had dipped the morsel, he gave it to Judas. This was not a visible gesture to most of the disciples on their couches arrayed around the triclinium. For those who could see it, it was an unremarkable and natural gesture since Judas was seated at Jesus' left, and dipping in the bowls together was a normal part of the Passover ceremony. Given their positions, however, and the fact that they were looking for a signal, it was a gesture easy for both John and Peter to recognize. Even so, the disciples did not really comprehend what Judas was going to do. After Judas had taken the morsel, Satan entered into him. Jesus said to him, "What you are going to do, do quickly."

GETHSEMANE

That night, Jesus went to the Garden of Gethsemane (which means the Garden of the Olive Press) with his disciples. He told eight of them to sit aside, but he took Peter and the sons of Zebedee with him to an isolated place, where he began to grieve and feel great distress. He asked the three disciples to keep watch with him and went to a place a little beyond. After praying in anguish, Jesus returned to find them sleeping. He asked Peter, "Could you not keep watch with me one hour? Keep watching and praying that you might not enter into temptation, for the spirit is willing but the flesh is weak." Then he went and prayed a second time and came back and found them sleeping again. He went and prayed again for the Father's will, not his, to be done. He came back to the three disciples and said, "Are you still sleeping? Get up, let us go. Behold, the one who betrays me is at hand" (Matt 26:36–46).

When the Temple soldiers (not Romans) seized Jesus, Peter cut off the ear of Malchus, servant of the High Priest—meaning the servant of Ananias (Annas), the defrocked High Priest who was the real power behind Joseph Caiaphas, the actual High Priest at the time. Obviously, Peter had prepared for this abortive attempt to defend Jesus' life. Peter knew from Jesus' rebuke at Caesarea Philippi two years ago that Jesus expected to be killed. Prophecy had to run its course. More than that, Jesus had called Peter Satan for wishing to defend Jesus from death. Peter must have assumed that he could arm himself with a weapon and defend Jesus even against his will. So, Peter procured a sword. In fact, at the Last Supper, the disciples showed Jesus that they had two swords, to which Jesus replied, "It is enough." Jesus would say later that night that he could call on the Father for twelve legions of angels, if he wanted to.

When the time came to use his sword, Peter missed. He sliced off Malchus' ear. It is hard to believe that is what Peter was aiming at. He was not trying to warn Malchus off. He was trying to defend Jesus, and that meant killing Malchus, along with anyone else who threatened his rabbi. He was doubtless aiming at Malchus' skull. Jesus told Peter to put away his sword, saying that those who live by the sword die by it. Then, astonishingly, Jesus healed Malchus' ear (Luke 22:51).

IN THE COURTYARD OF THE HIGH PRIEST

At Jesus' trial, Peter was sitting outside in the courtyard of the High Priest's home. A servant girl eyed Peter closely and said to the people standing by, "This man also was with him." Then she said directly to Peter, "You also were with Jesus, the Nazarene. You are not also one of his disciples, are you?" Peter replied, "I neither know nor understand what you mean. I am not." And the rooster crowed the first time.

When Peter went out to the entrance of the courtyard, another servant girl saw him, and she said to the bystanders, "This man was with Jesus of Nazareth. This man is one of them." Then she said directly to Peter, "You also are one of them." But Peter denied it with an oath, saying, "I do not know the man." Then, one of the servants of Ananias (Annas), a relative of Malchus, the man whose ear Peter had cut off, asked, "Did I not see you in the garden with him?"

The other bystanders crowded around Peter, saying, "Certainly, you too are one of them. Your accent betrays you. You are a Galilean." Peter began to invoke a curse on himself and to swear, "I do not know the man of whom you speak." And the rooster crowed a second time.

Then Peter remembered how Jesus had said to him at the Last Supper: "Before the rooster crows twice, you will deny me three times." Peter had done just that. As the mob led Jesus out of the High Priest's house, Jesus turned and looked at Peter. Their eyes met. Peter went out and wept bitterly (Matt 26:69–75, Mark 14:66–72, Luke 22:54–62, John 18:15–18).

Judas sold Jesus. Peter denied Jesus three times, cursing and swearing. Both were guilty and felt guilty, but Judas did not seek God's forgiveness. He committed suicide. Peter confessed, repented, sought forgiveness, and received it.

THE ROOSTER

Jesus said to Peter:

> "Truly, I tell you, this very night, before the rooster crows, you will deny me three times" (Matt 26:34).
>
> "Truly, I tell you, this very night, before the rooster crows twice, you will deny me three times" (Mark 14:30).
>
> "I tell you, Peter, the rooster will not crow today until you have denied three times that you know me" (Luke 22:34).
>
> "Truly, truly, I tell you, before the rooster crows, you will deny me three times" (John 13:38).

These are not contradictory accounts but various ways of describing the same events. In the courtyard of the High Priest, Jesus denied Peter once, and the rooster crowed the first time (Mark 14:68). This should have struck a chord with Peter. It was an omen that Jesus' prediction was about to come true. The rooster's first crowing might have warned him not to deny Jesus two more times. But he did deny Jesus two more times, and the rooster crowed a second time (Matt 26:74, Mark 14:72, Luke 22:60, John 18:27).

So, the statement of Matthew was correct. Before the rooster crowed (albeit for the second time), Peter denied Jesus three times. The statement of Mark was correct. Before the rooster crowed twice, Peter denied Jesus three times. And the statements of Luke and John are correct. Although the rooster did crow once, he stopped crowing and would not crow again until Peter had denied Jesus the second and third time.

THE EMPTY TOMB

On Resurrection Sunday, Mary Magdalene ran to Peter and John with news of the empty tomb. John outran Peter and reached the tomb first. He stooped to look in but did not enter yet. Peter boldly entered first and saw the linen shrouds lying there and Jesus' facecloth rolled up by itself.

This may not mean, as some assert, that Jesus or an angel calmly folded the shrouds after Jesus' Resurrection to show that God is in no haste. Jesus' Resurrection body, which later that evening would pass through closed doors, probably also passed through these mummy-like winding sheets. They remained folded, that is, wrapped, but empty. This is an additional testimony that Jesus' body was not stolen. Thieves would either have taken the winding sheets with them or torn them off in their haste to escape detection by the guards, whose duty it was to arrest or kill anyone violating their watch.

John then entered the tomb and believed, but what did he believe? The Bible says the disciples did not yet understand that Jesus must rise again from the dead. John believed that the tomb was empty and that God was somehow at work, but he did not comprehend in what way. Peter and John went back to where they were staying, probably the Upper Room at John Mark's house, leaving Mary Magdalene to be the first to meet the risen Lord (John 20:1–18).

THE RISEN LORD APPEARS TO PETER

The risen Jesus met Peter privately, sometime between morning and evening on Resurrection Sunday. Mark, Luke, and Paul all recorded this, but they gave no details of the encounter (Mark 16:7, Luke 24:34, 1 Cor 15:5). This appearance to Peter is significant. Probably Jesus knew how deep Peter's grief was at having denied him three times. The intimate appearance of Jesus to Peter allowed Peter to experience Jesus' kindly mercy, to know that he was forgiven, and to understand that his mission in Christ had only just begun.

EMMAUS AND THE UPPER ROOM

Late in the afternoon on Resurrection Sunday, Jesus appeared to two followers, one named Cleophas and his companion, on the road to a village called Emmaus. They broke bread with Jesus at sunset. Only then did they recognize him. Then he vanished from their presence. Cleophas and his companion hurried back to Jerusalem to meet the eleven disciples, only to find them in a state of great excitement, for the risen Lord had already met Peter. Thomas left the room. As Cleophas and everyone else were still speaking, Jesus appeared to the ten disciples, to Cleophas and his companion, and to others assembled in the Upper Room that Resurrection Sunday evening. The following Monday, Jesus appeared again to the eleven disciples with Thomas present (John 20:26).

BACK TO GALILEE

Then seven disciples (Peter, Thomas, Nathanael, the sons of Zebedee, and two others) went back to Galilee. Peter said, "I am going fishing." His friends went with him. They fished until daybreak but caught nothing. Jesus stood on the beach, but they did not recognize him. He said, "Boys, you do not have any fish, do you?" They said no. Jesus said, "Cast the net on the right side of the boat, and you will have a catch." So, they did and could not haul in the net because of the great number of fish they caught. John said to Peter, "It is the Lord." Peter put on his outer garment and plunged into the sea. Why did he get dressed to swim? Because the Bible says he was *gymnos* or naked. (A gymnasium was a place where athletes exercised naked). The outer garment, an *ependítis* in Greek, is a blouse or a tunic, not a coat, as some Bibles translate it. So, Peter was probably wearing a loincloth, our equivalent of shorts, while fishing. When he saw Jesus, out of respect, he threw on a shirt and went swimming to meet him.

The others followed ashore, bringing the boat and its net full of fish. They found Jesus tending a charcoal fire, with fish and bread already on it. Jesus, who could feed five thousand out of two fishes and five loaves, did not need their catch to make breakfast for his friends. But graciously, Jesus said, "Bring some of the fish you caught." Peter, the consummate fisherman, not only brought them, but carefully counted 153 large fish[6] and noted that even with such a big haul, the net was not torn (John 21:1–11). One can imagine Jesus enjoying his friends' very human enthusiasm as they counted the fish and inspected the net. This was the third time the resurrected Jesus appeared to the disciples.

In one of the most moving dialogs of Scripture, Jesus compassionately echoed Peter's three denials.

> When they had finished breakfast, Jesus said to Simon Peter, "Simon, son of John, do you love me more than these?" He said to him, "Yes, Lord; you know that I love you." He said to him, "Feed my lambs." He said to him a second time, "Simon, son of John, do you love me?" He said to him, "Yes, Lord; you know that I love you." He said to him, "Tend my sheep." He said to him the third time, "Simon, son of John, do you love me?" Peter was grieved because he said to him the third time, "Do you

---

6. Still today, a type of tilapia, *Sarotherodon galilaeus galilaeus*, known as St. Peter's Fish, is harvested in the Sea of Galilee and is popular in local markets and restaurants.

love me?" And he said to him, "Lord, you know everything; you know that I love you." Jesus said to him, "Feed my sheep" (John 21:15–17).

The Greek words John used to record this conversation add meaning to the passage. Greek commonly uses four words to mean love: *agápe* (love), *philía* (friendship), *storgí* (affection), and *éros* (lust). The first and second times Jesus asked Peter, "Do you love me?" he used the Greek word *agapás*, referring to the noblest form of love. The third time Jesus asked Peter, "Do you love me?" he used the Greek word *phileís*, meaning "Are you my friend?" Jesus' choice of words was touchingly personal, but also echoed what Jesus had said about himself (recorded by John): "Greater love has no one than this, that he lay down his life for his friends" (John 15:13). Jesus was saying, "Do you love me, do you love me, do you really love me enough to give your life for me?" Then Jesus revealed that Peter would give his life as that kind of friend.

> Truly, truly, I say to you, when you were young, you used to dress yourself and walk wherever you wanted, but when you are old, you will stretch out your hands, and another will dress you and carry you where you do not want to go." (This he said to show by what kind of death he was to glorify God.) And after saying this he said to him, "Follow me" (John 21:18–19).

Realizing Jesus was foretelling a martyr's death, Peter wanted to know how John would end.

> Peter turned and saw the disciple whom Jesus loved [John] following them, the one who had been reclining at table close to him and had said, "Lord, who is it that is going to betray you?" When Peter saw him, he said to Jesus, "Lord, what about this man?" Jesus said to him, "If it is my will that he remain until I come, what is that to you? You follow me!" So the saying spread abroad among the brothers that this disciple was not to die; yet Jesus did not say to him that he was not to die, but "if it is my will that he remain until I come, what is that to you?" This is the disciple who is bearing witness about these things, and who has written these things, and we know that his testimony is true. Now there are also many other things that Jesus did. Were every one of them to be written, I suppose that the world itself could not contain the books that would be written" (John 21:20–25).

THE GREAT COMMISSION

There were only seven disciples present at the lakeshore breakfast in Galilee. After that, all eleven met in Galilee, reclining at a table with Jesus. He rebuked them for their unbelief and hardness of heart because they had not at first believed those who saw him after he had risen. He said to them:

> Go into all the world and proclaim the gospel to the whole creation. 16Whoever believes and is baptized will be saved, but whoever does not believe will be condemned. And these signs will accompany those who believe: in my name they will cast out demons; they will speak in new tongues; they will pick up serpents with their hands; and if they drink any deadly poison, it will not hurt them; they will lay their hands on the sick, and they will recover (Mark 16:15–18).[7]

The Eleven also went with Jesus to a mountain in Galilee, possibly Mount Eremos, where Jesus had delivered the Sermon on the Mount. There they worshiped him, but some still doubted. He said to them:

> All authority in heaven and on earth has been given to me. Go therefore and make disciples of all nations, baptizing them in the name of the Father and of the Son and of the Holy Spirit, teaching them to observe all that I have commanded you. And behold, I am with you always, to the end of the age (Matt 28:16–20).

PETER'S LEADERSHIP

Peter was present at Christ's Ascension on Sunday, May 13, AD 33. He, with the other ten apostles, heard the angel say that Jesus would return in the same way that he ascended (Acts 1:9–11). Then Peter assumed leadership of the Eleven in the Upper Room, where they were praying with Mary, the mother of Jesus, and with Jesus' half-brothers (which surely included at least James and Jude). After Jesus' Ascension and before Pentecost, that is, between May 13 and May 21, AD 33, Peter proposed the selection of someone to replace Judas Iscariot. Guided by the Holy Spirit, the apostles chose Matthias (Acts 1:12–26).

---

7. Some manuscripts end the gospel of Mark at verse 16:8, so possibly this was not part of Mark's original book. That does not necessarily mean, however, that it is not a faithful account of what happened.

PENTECOST

On Sunday, May 22, AD 33, the day of Pentecost, a noise like a rushing wind filled the house where the apostles were gathered, tongues of fire appeared above their heads, and they began speaking in all the tongues of Africa and the Middle East. Visitors from those countries were astonished to hear Galileans speaking their languages. Some mocked them, thinking they were drunk. Peter rose and rebuked the joke. Far from drunk, they were fulfilling prophecy. In a powerful sermon, Peter showed from Scripture how Jesus, whom the Jews had crucified, was Lord and Christ. Cut to the quick, the congregation asked what they should do. Peter told them to repent and be baptized in the name of Jesus Christ for the forgiveness of their sins, so that they might receive the gift of the Holy Spirit. Three thousand people became followers of Jesus. On that Sunday, the Church was born (Acts 2). When these pilgrims returned to their homes, they brought their faith with them, so that churches were planted all around the empire and in Rome long before the apostles' missionary journeys.

The Church witnessed the apostles perform many signs and wonders, becoming a community of believers, with others daily added to their numbers. It grew at an astonishing rate. The assembly in the Upper Room after the Ascension was probably about twenty people. The assembly when choosing Matthias was about 120 people (Acts 1:15)—up 600 percent. The assembly at Pentecost was about 3,000 people (Acts 2:41)—up 2500 percent!

HEALING THE LAME MAN

One day, at about 3 p.m., Peter and John were going up to the Temple for the afternoon prayer[8] when they saw a man lame from birth being carried to the Beautiful Gate where he could beg for alms. He asked Peter and John for money. Peter fixed his gaze on him and said, "Look at me! I do not possess silver and gold, but what I do have I give to you. In the name of Jesus of Nazareth—walk!" The lame man leaped up and entered the Temple, praising God. All the people were amazed, and Peter took the opportunity to preach a second sermon about Jesus (Acts 3). About five thousand believed (Acts 4:4).

---

8. Observant Jews still pray at the time of the morning sacrifice, in the afternoon around 3 p.m., and at sunset.

FIRST ARREST

The priests, the captain of the Temple guard, and the Sadducees arrested Peter and John for their public "heresy," keeping them in jail overnight. The next day, Ananias (Annas), the defrocked ex-High Priest, Caiaphas, the current High Priest (Ananias' son-in-law), and all the Jewish elders placed Peter and John on trial.

Ananias was the first High Priest appointed by Rome in AD 6, which made him illegal from the start since he succeeded to the office by the order of a Gentile power, not by being a descendant of Aaron. God had told Moses, "You shall appoint Aaron and his sons, and they shall guard their priesthood. But if any outsider comes near, he shall be put to death" (Num 3:10). Therefore, Ananias, who pushed for Jesus' execution, was himself under a death sentence according to God's law. The Roman procurator Gratus deposed Ananias in AD 15 for subjecting a heretic to capital punishment, which was Rome's sole prerogative. Ananias was presiding when the twelve-year-old Jesus questioned the Temple elders in AD 10 (Luke 2:41–52). Although out of office, Ananias exercised control through his five sons and son-in-law, Joseph Caiaphas, who were his puppet High Priests. He presided semi-officially over the trial of Jesus through Caiaphas, who was High Priest from AD 18 to 36. Ananias was assassinated in AD 66 for advocating peace with Rome at the outbreak of the tragic Jewish Revolt.

PETER'S DEFENSE

Peter, filled with the Holy Spirit, spoke boldly before Ananias and Caiaphas. He asked if he and John were on trial for healing a sick man. He told them that Jesus, whom they had crucified, God had raised from the dead, and that "there is no other name under heaven that has been given to men by which we must be saved" (Acts 4:12). The Council was amazed that these uneducated men could reason so powerfully from the Scriptures. By uneducated, they did not mean that Peter and John could not read or write; obviously, they could and did. They meant that they had not completed formal religious training. They were not rabbis, like John the Baptist, son of a Levite (John 3:26), Jesus (John 1:38), and Paul (Acts 22:3, Gal 1:14, Phil 3:5).

CIVIL DISOBEDIENCE

The Council warned the apostles to speak no more about Jesus. But Peter replied that they would listen to God and not to men and could not keep quiet about the truth. The Council threatened them further but released them because they found that the crowd was praising God for the miracle of the lame man healed. Then Peter and John went to the other apostles and told the story. They all rejoiced and prayed to the Lord to give them strength to keep witnessing and performing God's works. They were filled with the Holy Spirit and spoke God's word with boldness (Acts 4). This was around May 27, AD 33.

Writing around AD 59, twenty-six years later, Peter seemed to contradict himself when he said, "Be subject for the Lord's sake to every human institution, whether it be to the emperor, as supreme, or to governors as sent by him to punish those who do evil and to praise those who do good. For this is the will of God" (1 Peter 2:13–15). Paul seemed to agree, for he wrote, "Let every person be subject to the governing authorities . . . whoever resists the authorities resists what God has appointed" (Rom 13:1–2). Daniel, however, flouted the authority of Babylon's ruler, Belshazzar, saying, "let your gifts be for yourself and give your rewards to another . . . God has numbered the days of your kingdom . . . you have been weighed in the balances and found wanting" (Dan 5:17–28). So, should a believer obey civil authorities or not? There is no moral contradiction in these biblical accounts. The abiding principle is that believers should obey civil authorities when they are aligned with the will of God and should disobey them when they oppose God's will.

ANANIAS AND SAPPHIRA

Around May 30, AD 33, Joseph Barnabas, the Levite Cypriot cousin of John Mark, sold a plot of land and gave the proceeds to the Church (Acts 4:36–37). Another couple, Ananias and Sapphira, imitated him. They sold a plot of land but kept part of the proceeds for themselves. Ananias, with his wife's full knowledge, pretended to bring all the proceeds, but laid only a portion of it at the apostles' feet. Peter saw through him. He asked Ananias why Satan had filled his heart with the desire to lie. Peter said that the land was his; no one had asked him to sell it or give any part of the money to the Church. But now he had lied not to men but to God. As he heard these words, Ananias breathed his last. The young men present carried him off and buried him. After about three hours, Sapphira came to Peter and told the same lie. Peter replied, "Why have you agreed together to put the Spirit of the Lord to the test? The feet of those who have buried your husband are at the door, and they will carry you out as well." She, too, fell dead, and great fear spread over the whole Church, as the apostles performed many signs and wonders. People from all around Jerusalem brought the sick and lame and demon-possessed, and the apostles healed them all, as the Church continued to grow, sharing everything in common (Acts 5:1–11).

SECOND ARREST

The priests and the Sadducees were greatly annoyed that Peter and John continued in their defiant ministry. Around June 6, AD 33, the Temple captain threw them in jail a second time. During the night, an angel came and released them, telling them to return to the Temple to preach. At daybreak, Peter and John entered the Temple and resumed teaching. When the Council met again, they called for the prisoners, but the officers reported that, although the prison was still securely locked, they were gone. Someone came and reported where Peter and John were: in the Temple. The authorities dragged the apostles back before the Council, but gingerly, as the crowd seemed like they were inclined to stone the arresting officers. The Council reminded Peter and John that they were not to teach in Jesus' name, but the apostles boldly answered that they must obey God and not men. They then testified that Jesus is the Savior.

The Council wanted to put Peter and John to death, but Gamaliel, Paul's mentor, advised letting them alone. "If this plan or action is of men," he said, "it will be overthrown, but if it is of God, you will not be able to overthrow them; or else you even may be found fighting against God." So, the Council flogged the apostles, warned them once more to stop preaching Jesus, and released them. Peter and John rejoiced that they had been found worthy of suffering for Jesus and continued to preach (Acts 5).

THE MARTYRDOM OF STEPHEN

After this, probably on December 26, AD 33,[9] Stephen was stoned, and Saul began persecuting the Church. Possibly, in his rampage, Saul

---

9. This is the Catholic Feast of St. Stephen, which is as good a date as any and which

personally persecuted Peter and the other apostles. Certainly, he persecuted people whom Peter knew and loved. There would be quite a wound to mend between these two men. Yet they became close fellow workers in Christ.

SAMARIA AND SIMON MAGUS

Between December AD 33 and March AD 34, Saul (Paul) was ferociously persecuting Christians in Jerusalem. This may have prompted Philip to go to Samaria and convert Samaritans. Paul's persecution probably did not drive Philip (or Peter or John) out of Jerusalem because the Bible says that Saul's persecution caused all except the apostles to scatter (Acts 8:1). It also says that those who had been scattered preached the Gospel wherever they went (Acts 8:4). Therefore, Paul did not frighten the apostles away. Their evangelistic work in Samaria, on the Gaza Road, and in Antioch was simply obedience to Jesus' statement that the disciples would be his witnesses in Jerusalem, Judaea, Samaria, and to the ends of the earth (Acts 1:8).

All this evangelistic outreach right after the stoning of Stephen must have seemed like an epidemic of Christianity to Paul. Like a general seeking to outflank his enemy, he applied for a priestly commission to head the Christian heretics off at Damascus, north of Samaria. Paul, of course, met with an utterly unexpected result, becoming a convert to Christ on the Damascus Road.

Meanwhile, Philip reached the city of Samaria (today's Nablus) and proclaimed Christ. Between January 1–15, AD 34, he preached, healed the lame, and cast out unclean spirits. Many believed in Jesus and were baptized, including a sorcerer named Simon Magus, who followed Philip's miracles with amazement.

The other apostles in Jerusalem heard that hostile Samaria, of all places, had received the word of God. They sent Peter and John to investigate. John had once asked Jesus for permission to bring heaven's fire down on the Samaritan villages to destroy them (Luke 9:54). Now John and Peter laid hands on the Samaritans, and they received the Holy Spirit. When Simon Magus saw this gift of the Holy Spirit, he offered the apostles money to give him the power. Peter rebuked him, saying:

---

sufficiently fits the chronology of Acts.

May your silver perish with you because you thought you could obtain the gift of God with money! You have neither part nor lot in this matter, for your heart is not right before God. Repent, therefore, of this wickedness of yours, and pray to the Lord that, if possible, the intent of your heart may be forgiven you. For I see that you are in the gall of bitterness and in the bond of iniquity. Simon Magus answered, "Pray for me to the Lord, that nothing of what you have said may come upon me" (Acts 8:20–24).[10]

Simon Magus seemed to be a seeker, but inwardly he was not right with God. Irenaeus recorded that the apostles cast him out and that he went to Rome, where he became a famous magician. The emperor Claudius honored him with a statue. Peter followed him to Rome and overthrew his scam.[11]

FOUNDING THE ANTIOCH CHURCH

Jerome says Peter founded the church in Antioch, Syria.[12] If so, January 15–22, AD 34 was probably the time when Peter did it. Scripture mentions some Jewish Christians from Jerusalem (probably led by Peter) who were preaching the Gospel to Jews in Antioch (Acts 11:19). Since Peter was already in Samaria, he could have made the trek to Antioch in about ten hours. It was a convenient time for him to plant a church in the third-largest city in the Roman Empire. The Patriarchate of Antioch confirms this date, saying that AD 34 was the year of the church's founding.[13]

Once the church was established, it became a hotbed of activity. Jews from Cyprus and Cyrene (Libya) descended on Antioch and began preaching and converting many Gentiles (Acts 11:20). Then the Jerusalem church sent Barnabas to Antioch, between March 29 and April 2, AD 34 (Acts 11:22–24). In Antioch, the followers of Christ were first called "Christians" (Acts 11:26). Tradition says that the evangelist Luke was from Antioch, and he may have become a Christian around this time.

---

10. Simon's request is the origin of the word simony, which means attempting to sell grace for money.

11. Irenaeus, *Against Heresies*, Book I, Chapter 23.

12. Jerome, *On Illustrious Men*.

13. "The Patriarchate of Antioch: Founded by Saints Peter and Paul," *Antiochian Orthodox Christian Archdiocese of North America*.

MEETING PAUL

In AD 37, after his withdrawal to Arabia, Paul returned to Damascus and preached the Gospel fearlessly. The Jews of the city plotted to kill him, so he escaped when friends let him down the city wall in a basket. Full of conviction, Paul went to Jerusalem, from about April 22–26, AD 37. Remembering how he had ravaged the Church, the Jerusalem Christians feared Paul. Barnabas, however, approached him and mended fences between Paul and the apostles. Paul saw Peter over a period of fifteen days. He also saw James, the half-brother of Jesus. He met no other apostles there at that time (Gal 1:18–19).

Paul preached boldly in Jerusalem. The Jewish leaders, aghast that their agent in Damascus had returned a traitor, plotted to kill him. Paul's friends helped him escape to Caesarea. From there, Paul retreated to his hometown of Tarsus and remained there in obscurity for six years until about May 19, AD 43, during all of which time he had a bounty on his head in both Damascus and Jerusalem.

TO LYDDA

In June AD 37, Peter traveled thirty miles from Jerusalem to Lydda. There, he healed a man named Aeneas, who had been paralyzed and bedridden for eight years. All the people in Lydda and Sharon saw the miracle and turned to the Lord (Acts 9:32–35).

RAISING TABITHA IN JOPPA

Then Peter went to nearby Joppa, the same port from which the prophet Jonah sailed away from God's command to preach at Nineveh. Jonah was the name of Peter's father, but this son of Jonah was far more obedient to God's commands than the Jonah of old. Some disciples in Joppa had sent for Peter because a kindly woman named Tabitha (Aramaic for "gazelle") or Dorcas (Greek for "gazelle") had died. Tabitha had done many acts of kindness. When Peter came to where her body lay, he sent all the weeping widows from the room, knelt, prayed, and said, "Tabitha, arise." She opened her eyes, saw Peter, and arose. The miracle became known all over Joppa, and many believed in the Lord (Acts 9:36–43).

CORNELIUS

Up the coast toward Syria was the seaport of Caesarea, the seat of Roman power in Judaea. Cornelius, who resided there, was a centurion of the Italian cohort, an army unit consisting of about 5,120 troops. A centurion commanded about one hundred soldiers and was an important man in the Roman government of Judaea. The procurator, Marcellus, who had just replaced Pontius Pilate, would have known Julius personally, met him from time to time, and relied on him as a key subordinate. The *gens* or tribe of Cornelius was one of the most distinguished patrician family names in Rome. This man either was someone important or was related to someone important.

Cornelius and his whole household feared God, gave alms to the Jews, and prayed to God continually. One day at about 3 p.m., Cornelius clearly saw an angel of God, who came to him and called his name. Staring at the angel in terror, Cornelius asked, "What is it, lord?" By calling the angel "lord," Cornelius was showing deference and respect for the heavenly apparition. He was as yet untutored in Christian theology, and so he was not addressing the angel as the risen Jesus. It is unlikely, however, that Cornelius mistook the angel for a pagan, Roman god. His prayers to "God," not "the gods," and his almsgiving to Jews suggest that he embraced Jewish monotheism. He was certainly a spiritual seeker, and perhaps he already had a yearning to know about the burgeoning Church. The angel replied that God had answered the Roman's prayers and that he should send to Joppa for Simon Peter. Cornelius dispatched a soldier and three servants.

The next day at about noon, Peter was praying on the housetop of his host, a man named Simon the Tanner. Peter grew hungry, and then he saw a vision of the sky opening and a great sheet descending, lowered by four corners to the ground. In it were all kinds of animals and birds. A voice said, "Get up, Peter. Kill and eat!" Peter answered, "By no means, Lord, for I have never eaten anything unholy and unclean." The voice replied, "What God has cleansed, no longer consider unholy." The vision recurred three times. Then Cornelius' messengers arrived, and the Holy Spirit urged Peter to go with them without misgivings, for God was sending him on this mission.

The next day, he and some of the other Christians left Joppa. Since the journey to Caesarea was one of forty-two miles, Peter's party probably spent the night somewhere along the way. Then they entered Caesarea the next day, probably June 11, AD 37. The centurion was waiting for him with all his relatives and close friends. Peter entered the house of Cornelius, who fell at Peter's feet. Peter made him rise, saying, "I, too, am just a man." Peter told the Roman family that they knew how unlawful it was for him, a Jew, to visit a foreigner but that God had shown him through visions that he should not call any man unholy or unclean.[14]

Cornelius told Peter of the angel's visit, and Peter realized that God was sending salvation not only to the Jews but also to the Gentiles. Peter preached the Gospel, and the Holy Spirit fell on all who were listening. Peter baptized the entire household in the name of Jesus Christ. He then stayed with his new flock for several days (Acts 10).

Interestingly, Paul had fled from Jerusalem to Caesarea to escape a Jewish death threat a month earlier. Why did God not choose Paul, the apostle to the Gentiles, who was available in Caesarea at just the right time, to convert Cornelius and his family? The Bible does not say. It tells us only that God chose Peter instead. If Paul was aware of all this, perhaps he felt discouraged and overlooked.

BACK IN JERUSALEM

Around June 19, AD 37, Peter returned to Jerusalem. The other apostles criticized him. "You went to uncircumcised men and ate with them," they said. But Peter told them the whole story, saying that if God gave to the Gentiles the same gift he gave to Jews who believed in Jesus Christ, Peter could not stand in God's way. Then, the other apostles glorified God, affirming that he had granted to the Gentiles the repentance that leads to life (Acts 11:1–18).

---

14. Peter was not referring to Mosaic Law because it nowhere prohibited Jews from visiting Gentiles. It does prohibit Jews from adopting Gentile pagan practices (Lev 18:24–30) and from marrying Gentiles (Deut 7:3, Ezra 9:12), but only because of the risk of foreign wives leading Hebrew men away from the worship of Yahweh (Num 25:1–2, 1 Kings 11:1–2). The Bible condones the marriage of Boaz and Ruth, for example, even though Ruth was a Gentile (Ruth 1:4). Moreover, God told the Jews they would be a "light to the Gentiles, and [they would] bring [God's] salvation to the ends of the earth" (Isa 49:6). The Jews of Peter's Day had twisted the commands of God into ethnic snobbery.

PETER IN ASIA MINOR

Peter and Mark went on wide-ranging missions, preaching to Jews in Pontus, Galatia, Cappadocia, Asia, and Bithynia between AD 41 and 43. Reading Acts, one may easily get the impression that Paul was the first to bring the Gospel to these parts of the world. In fact, Peter and Mark preceded him.

FOUNDING THE CHURCH IN ROME

Jerome wrote that Peter first traveled to Rome in the second year of the reign of the emperor Claudius, AD 43.[15] When Paul first arrived in Rome in AD 57, he found many Christians already there (Acts 28:15), so somebody had to found the Roman church before then. In AD 49, Claudius expelled all the Jews from Rome because of squabbles between non-Christian and Christian Jews (Acts 18:2),[16] so there were Christians in Rome as early as that.[17] This evidence supports the tradition that Peter founded the church in Rome in the year AD 43. Undoubtedly, Jews who heard Peter's sermon on Pentecost in Jerusalem in AD 33 had already brought Christianity back to Rome (Acts 2:10, 41). The fact that Peter's sermon converted the Roman Jews visiting Jerusalem in AD 33 may qualify Peter as the founder of the Roman church. At any rate, when he visited Rome in AD 43, ten years later, he may have built on that foundation to found the Church in the Eternal City formally.

THE BATTLE WITH SIMON MAGUS

Simon Magus, after Peter rebuked him in Samaria in AD 34, traveled to Rome, where he gained such fame as a sorcerer that the emperor Claudius honored him as a god with a statue.[18] Eusebius wrote of this as follows:

    15. Jerome, *On Illustrious Men*.

    16. This caused Aquila and Priscilla to leave Rome and migrate to Corinth, where they ultimately met Paul.

    17. Suetonius, "Tiberius Claudius Drusus Caesar," *Lives of the Twelve Caesars*, Cassius Dio in his Roman History, 60:6:6, says that Claudius did not expel the Jews but ordered them not to hold meetings. Since this meant a closure of synagogues, the Jews probably left Rome in consequence, which is why Suetonius said that Claudius expelled them. Jewish Christians also left Rome, while Gentile Christians felt no compulsion to do so.

    18. Eusebius, *Church History*, 2:13:3.

For immediately, during the reign of Claudius, the all-good and gracious Providence, which watches over all things, led Peter, that strongest and greatest of the apostles, and the one who, on account of his virtue, was the speaker for all the others, to Rome against this great corrupter of life. Clad in divine armor like a noble commander of God, He carried the costly merchandise of the light of the understanding from the East to those who dwelt in the West, proclaiming the light itself and the word that brings salvation to souls and preaching the kingdom of heaven.[19]

PETER'S GOSPEL OF MARK

Eusebius quoted Clement of Alexandria as follows:

As Peter had preached the Word publicly at Rome and declared the Gospel by the Spirit, many who were present requested that Mark, who had followed him for a long time and remembered his sayings, should write them out. And having composed the Gospel, he gave it to those who had requested it.[20]

John Mark's name is unusual: half Jewish (John) and half Latin (Marcus). Marcus, like Cornelius, is a singularly Latin name. Many Jews in Roman Judaea had Jewish and Greek names, like Simon Peter, but having a Latin name was uncommon. Roman officials of the Eastern Empire spoke Greek, not Latin. John Mark's name suggests that he may have had a Roman father and a Jewish mother. He may have been raised with a Western Roman education. Perhaps John Mark spoke Latin, which Peter and the other apostles perhaps did not. John Mark was thus the perfect assistant to accompany Peter to Rome and translate Peter's Aramaic or Greek into Latin. This fits well with Eusebius' account that Mark's gospel evolved because, on this same trip to Rome with Peter, the Romans appealed to Mark to write down Peter's sermons so that "he would leave them a written monument of the doctrine which had been orally communicated to them."[21] This means that Mark completed and published his gospel in AD 43.

Jerome wrote that Peter held the sacerdotal chair in the Roman church for twenty-five years,[22] which would be until AD 68, the most

---

19. Eusebius, *Church History*, 2:14:6.
20. Eusebius, *Church History*, 6:14:6.
21. Eusebius, *Church History*, 2:15:1.
22. Suetonius, "Tiberius," *Lives of the Twelve Caesars*.

likely year of Peter's execution by Nero. Since, however, the next time marker in Acts places Peter in Jerusalem in AD 44, when the Jewish leaders arrested him for the third time, Peter cannot have remained in Rome without interruption for all twenty-five years. Therefore, Peter arrived in Rome in AD 43,[23] founded the church, opposed and brought down Simon Magus, and returned to Jerusalem by AD 44 (Acts 12:3). He would return to Rome later, and he would remain there until his death.

Peter and John Mark probably remained in Rome for one hundred days until August 13, AD 43. The ancient sailing season in the Mediterranean "commenced either in March or April and spanned the summer months before drawing to a close in October or November."[24] So, because of the dangerous winter sailing weather, they would not have wished to sail after Yom Kippur in AD 43 or before Passover in AD 44. So, they probably set sail for Caesarea around September 1, AD 43, arriving home before Yom Kippur.

AGABUS PREDICTS A FAMINE

While Peter was in Rome, Barnabas went to Tarsus in May AD 43 and brought Paul back to Antioch, where Paul began ministering for one year. A prophet named Agabus traveled from Jerusalem to Antioch. He predicted that a great famine would devastate Judaea. The Antioch church sent Barnabas and Saul to Jerusalem with famine relief (Acts 11:30). The prophesied famine occurred between AD 45 and 46.[25] Thus, the famine relief trip had to occur before AD 45, which fits with the date of AD 44.

THIRD ARREST

In AD 44, during Passover, Herod Agrippa I, son of Aristobulus and grandson of Herod the Great, killed James, the son of Zebedee. When he saw that this pleased the Jews, he also arrested Peter on April 1, 16 Nisan, the third day of Passover (Acts 12:3–4). Herod put a guard of sixteen soldiers over

23. Finegan, *Handbook*, 382.

24. Bereford, *The Ancient Sailing Season*, 9.

25. Josephus, *Antiquities*, 20:2. As foretold by the prophet Agabus and recorded by Josephus, famine raged in Judaea under the procurator Cassius Fadus (AD 44–46). Orosius, in his *Histories Against Pagans*, 7:6:9, 12, placed it in the fourth year of Claudius' reign, which began on January 24, AD 41; so his fourth year began on January 24, AD 45.

Peter, probably remembering Peter's former miraculous deliverance from jail and hoping to prevent a repeat of that event. He intended to display Peter to the mob during the days of Unleavened Bread.

The night before Herod planned to present him, Peter was sleeping chained between two soldiers, with other soldiers also guarding the prison door. An angel of the Lord appeared and illuminated the cell. He struck Peter's side. Peter's chains fell away, and the angel led Peter off, as if in a dream. They passed the first and second guards and came to the outer iron gate, which opened by itself. They went out into the city street, where Peter found himself suddenly alone.

Coming to his senses, Peter went to the house of Mary, the mother of John Mark. Many were gathered there, praying. This would have been natural, both because they were concerned for Peter and because it was Passover week. Peter knocked at the gate, and a servant girl named Rhoda came to answer. She recognized Peter's voice, but from joy ran back to tell everyone without letting him in. They said she was out of her mind, but she kept insisting until they thought it must be Peter's angel. Peter kept knocking, and when they opened and saw him, they were amazed. He made a sign for them to keep silent, and then he described how the Lord had rescued him. Peter told them to report everything to James, Jesus' half-brother, and the other apostles, and then he went to another place (Acts 12:17).

This account is another indicator of the wealth of some of Jesus' followers. First, John Mark's mother had a servant girl, Rhoda. Second, the house was large enough that those within could not hear the voice of Peter beyond the outer door; this was not a modest hovel.

The next day Jerusalem was in an uproar at Peter's escape. With as many as 2.7 million pilgrims in town for the Passover,[26] the miracle could not have occurred at a more dramatic time. Herod executed the guards, and Peter returned to Caesarea. Shortly afterwards, at the height of his arrogance, Herod died a grisly death by parasitic worms, while the word of the Lord continued to grow and multiply (Acts 12). Then Paul and Barnabas returned to Antioch, taking Barnabas' cousin John Mark with them (Acts 12:25).

Paul, Barnabas, and John Mark embarked on their first missionary journey around May 25, AD 44 (Acts 13:1–4). They completed this and returned to Antioch around September 6, AD 44 (Acts 14:26–28). They

---

26. Josephus, *Jewish War*, 6:9:3.

reported to the church in Antioch how the Holy Spirit was working among the Gentiles.

CONFIRMING PAUL

The predicted famine struck Judaea from AD 45–46. Then fourteen years after Paul's conversion, in AD 47, Paul and Barnabas returned to Jerusalem. Paul took the Greek Christian Titus with him. Paul said that this trip was "because of a revelation," referring to Agabus' prophecy, meaning that Agabus had prophesied the famine, the famine had occurred, and now Paul, Barnabas, and Titus were traveling to Jerusalem to inspect the famine's aftermath and the efficacy of the relief funds the church in Antioch had sent.

Since Titus was a Greek Christian, he was uncircumcised. Some "false brothers" spied on Titus and verified the fact. They argued that he must be circumcised. Paul and Barnabas, however, did not submit to this. But some "who seemed to be influential" in the Jerusalem church recognized that Paul "had been entrusted with the Gospel to the uncircumcised, just as Peter had been entrusted with the Gospel to the circumcised." James (Jesus' half-brother), Peter, and John, who seemed to be "pillars" of the Church, perceived the grace given to Paul by Jesus, and they agreed with Paul about Titus. They gave Paul and Barnabas the right hand of fellowship and sent them off to the Gentiles, while reserving to the other apostles the mission to the circumcised (the Jews). James, Peter, and John only asked Paul and Barnabas to remember the poor, which Paul said was the very thing he was eager to do (Gal 2:1–10).

This did not mean that Paul was to minister only to Gentiles and Peter was to minister only to Jews. Peter had already proclaimed the Gospel to Gentiles. He had ministered in Samaria (Acts 8:14), to Cornelius and his family (Acts 10:25), to Antioch, and to the Romans. Paul's customary practice was to preach about Jesus in synagogues, and thus to Jews, before preaching to Gentiles (Acts 9:20, 14:1, 26:11). Moreover, Jesus had told Peter and the other eleven apostles to "make disciples of all nations" (Matt 28:19), not some, and to be his witnesses in Jerusalem, Judaea, Samaria and to the end of the earth (Acts 1:8). The job of all the disciples was to proclaim the Gospel to both Jews and Gentiles. Therefore, the meaning of Paul's statement in Galatians 2:7–8 is not absolute but focuses on three things: (1) Paul's authority regarding Titus,

(2) Paul's recent first missionary journey (Acts 13-14), and (3) Paul's upcoming second missionary journey (Acts 15-18).

PAUL'S REBUKE OF PETER

Paul, Barnabas, and John Mark returned to Antioch in AD 47 and remained there for some time. Around March 49, some Christian Jews came to Antioch from Jerusalem and taught that only those circumcised according to the Law of Moses could be saved. Paul and Barnabas had seen God open the door of faith to the Gentiles, and they disputed with the Judaizers.

At this time, Peter visited Antioch (Gal 2:11). He probably remained over Passover, which ran from April 3-11. Some friends of James, Jesus' half-brother, arrived from Jerusalem and advised Peter to keep aloof from the Gentiles, because they were afraid that he would alienate the Jewish Christians. Probably they were thinking that celebration of the Passover meal should be a non-Gentile event. Surprisingly, since Peter had ministered to the Gentile Cornelius in his house, had already evangelized in Rome, and had agreed with Paul that Titus did not need to be circumcised, Peter did as the Judaizers advised. Other Jewish Christians at Antioch, including Barnabas, followed his lead. Probably Peter and Barnabas, although they both had had experience proclaiming the Gospel to Gentiles, thought that only Jewish Christians would really want to celebrate the Passover anyway.

Paul, however, thought Peter was not being straightforward about the truth of the Gospel. He rebuked Peter in the presence of all, saying, "If you, being a Jew, live like the Gentiles and not like the Jews, how is it that you compel the Gentiles to live like Jews? . . . a man is not justified by the works of the Law but through faith in Jesus Christ" (Gal 2:14-15). Evidently, Peter accepted this rebuke with humility, and fellowship resumed between Jewish and Gentile Christians. Peter then returned to Jerusalem.

Paul's words suggest that the Jewish Christians of the first century "lived like Gentiles," perhaps meaning that they did not strictly observe Mosaic law. For example, they probably felt free to travel on the Sabbath and eat food prohibited to Jews (but not food polluted by idol worship). They still observed Jewish holidays (Acts 20:16) and frequented the Temple (Acts 21:26), but evidently with a sense of newfound freedom in Christ.

THE JERUSALEM COUNCIL

The vexing question of whether believers had first to become Jews before becoming Christians still burned. The Antioch church decided that Paul and Barnabas should go to Jerusalem and lay the matter before the apostles and elders there. They struck out in May, AD 49. At the Council of Jerusalem, which probably convened from June 21–23, some Christian Pharisees (Acts 15:5)[27] stood up and stated that Gentile Christians should be circumcised and should observe Mosaic Law. After much debate, Peter arose and reminded them how he had preached to the Gentiles and how God had given them the Holy Spirit, making no distinction between them and Jews and cleansing their hearts by faith. Peter asked why the Pharisees wanted to place a yoke on the necks of the Gentiles which the Jews themselves had been unable to bear.[28] Both Jews and Gentiles were saved not by obeying the Law, but by God's grace. Then the people listened in silence as Paul and Barnabas related the signs and wonders that God had worked through them among the Gentiles. Finally, James, the half-brother of Jesus, stood up and agreed with Peter and Paul. He advised that they give Christian Gentiles only four prohibitions: (1) to abstain from things sacrificed to idols, (2) to abstain from sexual immorality, (3) to abstain from blood, and (4) to abstain from strangled animals.

These four prohibitions seem to have been designed mainly to separate Gentiles from pagan practices. Paul wrote that idols were not real gods and so eating animals sacrificed to idols was not really a problem, except that the practice might lead people without mature theological knowledge to stumble into the trap of idolatry (1 Cor 8:1–13). As for sexual immorality, Leviticus 18 detailed what sexual practices are sinful. In the Ancient Near East temple prostitutes had sex with worshipers to unite the devotee with the spirit of the god. Paul probably had this in mind when he wrote "Do you not know that he who is joined to a prostitute becomes one body with her? . . . or do you not know that your body is a temple of the Holy Spirit? . . . you are not your own, for you were bought with a price" (1 Cor 6:15–20). Leviticus 17 forbade the Israelites, and the foreigners living among them, to consume blood. This prohibition

---

27. Even Pharisees, who as a group had so vigorously opposed Jesus, were becoming Christians.

28. Despite becoming Christians, these Pharisees still tended to lay burdens on others that they themselves could not bear, as Jesus had told them before (Matt 23:3–4).

might be related to the prohibition against strangled animals, for such victims die with their blood still in them, in contrast to animals sacrificed by a knife (the practice of Romans, Greeks, and Jews), whose blood drains out of the carcass. Believers in the apostolic age would encounter animals sacrificed to idols by strangulation, for Herodotus wrote that Scythians sacrificed animals in this way.[29] In any case, the main thrust of the apostles' prohibitions cannot have been against eating non-kosher foods, because God had specifically told Peter that it was lawful to eat all kinds of animals (Acts 10:9–16). The point was to prompt new, Gentile converts to leave their idolatrous paganism behind. The Jerusalem Council wrote a letter to this effect, entrusting Paul, Barnabas, a certain Judas Justus Barsabbas, and Silas (Silvanus) to bring the welcome news to the Gentile converts at Antioch (Acts 15:1–35).

PETER'S TRAVELS

Probably from AD 49 to 59, Peter made a wide missionary journey that ended in Rome. Hippolytus, a third-century Christian author, wrote that, "Peter preached the Gospel in Pontus, and Galatia, and Cappadocia, and Betania, and Italy, and Asia."[30] He probably also visited Bithynia, on the south shore of the Black Sea, because 1 Peter was written to Christians there. He also visited the church in Corinth,[31] which Paul had planted between January 26, AD 50 and August 24, AD 51. Paul was in Corinth, Ephesus, and Caesarea in this period, returning to Jerusalem in September, AD 51. So, it is possible that the paths of Peter and Paul crossed. Peter took his wife with him on his travels, as we learn from Paul, who wrote, "Do we not have the right to take along a believing wife, as do the other apostles and the brothers of the Lord and Cephas" (1 Cor 9:5).

---

29. Herodotus, *Histories* 4.

30. Hippolytus, *List of the Apostles and Disciples*. Hippolytus is an early source, but his facts are not ironclad. For example, by his calculation, Nero would have had to execute Paul in AD 69, a year after Nero died. Hippolytus' information is always worth considering, but when comparing it to other biblical and extra-biblical evidence, one should always be prepared to reach for a pinch of salt.

31. Eusebius, *Church History*, 2:25:8.

ROME AGAIN

When Peter wrote his first epistle, Mark and Silas were with him. Silas acted as Peter's scribe (1 Peter 5:12–13). This writing probably was from Rome between AD 59–68, and not during Peter's first trip to Rome in AD 43, because the letter was to Bithynia (the southern coastline of the Black Sea), and that was too early a date for the establishment of a church there since Paul was planning to evangelize that region in AD 49 (Acts 16:7). The fact that Peter sent Mark's greeting to a number of churches in Bithynia implies that Mark must have been widely known and respected there. Since Mark was with Barnabas in Cyprus in AD 49 (Acts 15:39), was with Paul in Rome during his first incarceration there from AD 57 to 59 (Col 4:10) and was back in Asia Minor in AD 68, when the Romans arrested him in Troas (2 Tim 4:11–13), Mark must have joined Peter on his missionary journeys after AD 49 and must have left Rome for the east before Peter's martyrdom in AD 68. Peter was probably on his missionary journeys at the same time that Paul was on his second, third, and fourth missionary journeys, and again, their paths may have crossed. Since both Luke and Mark were in Rome during Paul's first imprisonment (Col 4:10, 14), probably Peter and Mark arrived together in Rome prior to Paul's first acquittal in AD 59.

PETER'S DEATH

Eusebius says that Peter and Paul died in Rome.[32] Jerome says that they died on the same day in AD 68.[33] Nero began persecuting Christians after the Great Fire of Rome in July, AD 64. Tradition says Nero kept Peter in chains for nine months in the Mamertine dungeon.[34] Possibly Nero's reason for detaining Peter for nine months was that his agents were scouring the empire for that other notorious Christian, Paul, so that Nero could celebrate a double execution.

Nero committed suicide on June 9, AD 68, so Peter and Paul must have died before that date. It is possible that Nero arrested Peter around July, AD 67. He probably arrested Paul in Troas around March, AD 68, so Paul probably reached Rome in April. Late church tradition says that a

---

32. Eusebius, *Church History*, 3:1:2.
33. Jerome, *On Illustrious Men*.
34. De Montor, *The Lives and Times of the Roman Pontiffs*, 26.

spring flowed miraculously up from the depths of the Mamertine prison and that Peter used its water to baptize his jailers and fellow prisoners. Peter's wife was with him, for she also died a martyr's death in Rome. Clement of Alexandria wrote:

> The blessed Peter, on seeing his wife led to death, rejoiced on account of her call and conveyance home, and called very encouragingly and comfortingly, addressing her by name, "Remember thou the Lord." Such was the marriage of the blessed and their perfect disposition towards those dearest to them.[35]

Paul, as a Roman citizen, died in a noble way, by the sword, while Peter, who was not a citizen, died a criminal's death, on a cross. Saying he was unworthy to die in the same way as his Lord, Peter asked his executioners to hang him on a cross upside down, which they did, and he died in that way. Jesus had foretold the manner of Peter's death:

> "Truly, truly, I say to you, when you were young, you used to dress yourself and walk wherever you wanted, but when you are old, you will stretch out your hands, and another will dress you and carry you where you do not want to go." (This he said to show by what kind of death he was to glorify God.) And after saying this he said to him, "Follow me" (John 21:18–19).

These last two words to Peter, "Follow me," echoed, movingly, those that the Lord had used in first calling Peter to be a fisher of men.

NERO'S LAST DAYS

Nero's execution of Peter and Paul was among the last angry acts of a cornered animal. The emperor knew he was in fatal danger. In March, AD 68, one of Nero's governors in Gaul rebelled against his tax policies. Another loyal governor put down the rebellion at the Battle of Vesontio in May. Support was growing to replace Nero with Galba, a senator and the governor of Spain. In a draft speech, Nero considered running away to a distant, loyal province, running away to Parthia, throwing himself on Galba's mercy, or begging the people of Rome to forgive him. If they would not consent to let him remain emperor, perhaps they would let him retire as the prefect of Egypt. Nero never delivered that speech, for fear that the mob would tear him to pieces before he could reach the Forum.

---

35. Clement of Alexandra, *Stromata*, 7:11, Eusebius, *Church History*, 3:30:2.

One night, Nero awoke to discover that the palace guard had abandoned him. Terrified and traveling in disguise, Nero and four loyal followers escaped to a villa four miles outside Rome. He ordered his followers to dig a grave for him. Learning that the Senate had declared him a public enemy, he paced back and forth, muttering, "What an artist dies in me!" Lacking the fortitude to kill himself, he asked one of his followers to set the example by committing suicide first. Then the sound of approaching cavalry drove him to beg one of his followers, Epaphroditus, to do the deed. Epaphroditus struck the regicidal blow. When one of the calvary broke into the villa, he tried to staunch the flow of Nero's blood, but to no avail. Nero's last words were, "Too late! This is loyalty!" If Nero's end had come just a bit sooner, the lives of Peter and Paul might have been spared.

Peter was crucified on Vatican Hill, probably around May 5, AD 68. He was originally buried there. His body was then removed to a cemetery along the Appian Way until the emperor Constantine moved it back to the Vatican and enlarged the Vatican Church in the apostle's honor. Peter's head is now supposed to be in the cathedral of Saint John Lateran.

DID JESUS FOUND HIS CHURCH ON PETER?

There are two views on this question: the Catholic view and the Protestant view. The reader must decide which to embrace. Both should be considered, as Peter said, with gentleness and respect (1 Peter 3:15).

The Catholic View

The Catholic Church teaches that Jesus gave special authority to Peter. They teach that the Pope, the bishop of Rome, derives his authority as leader of the true Church from Peter. Peter was the first Vicar of Rome, so the Pope is Peter's heir. Catholics say that Jesus built his Church on the Rock of Peter, and so the papacy is the foundation of Christ's Church. Jesus gave Peter the keys to the kingdom of heaven, which means that Peter (and his successors, the popes) exercise unique power over the community of God. This teaching is based on the following verses:

> Now when Jesus came into the district of Caesarea Philippi, he asked his disciples, "Who do people say that the Son of Man is?" And they said, "Some say John the Baptist, others say Elijah, and others Jeremiah or one of the prophets." He said to them,

SIMON PETER, THE ROCK

"But who do you say that I am?" Simon Peter replied, "You are the Christ, the Son of the living God." And Jesus answered him, "Blessed are you, Simon Bar-Jonah! For flesh and blood has not revealed this to you, but my Father who is in heaven. And I tell you, you are Peter, and on this rock, I will build my Church, and the gates of hell shall not prevail against it. I will give you the keys of the kingdom of heaven, and whatever you bind on earth shall be bound in heaven, and whatever you loose on earth shall be loosed in heaven." Then he strictly charged the disciples to tell no one that he was the Christ" (Matt 16:13–20).

The title pope comes from the Latin *papa*, meaning father. The Pope's official title is Holy Father, and the correct way to address the Pope is "Your Holiness." Rome, of course, was the capital of the Roman Empire, and the Romans ethnocentrically considered their empire to be the whole world. We read, for example, in Luke that: "In those days a decree went out from Caesar Augustus that all the world should be registered" (Luke 2:1). By "all the world," Augustus had Rome in mind. He definitely knew of Persia, Ethiopia, Arabia, India, Russia, and China, but he had no illusions of having the authority to register people there. He certainly had no plans to register the Apaches, Aztecs, Incas, Zulus, Maoris, or Eskimos, people who existed but of whom he knew nothing. Rome thought itself to be the only "world" worth considering. Even today, in Italy, Romans smugly say, "*Noi siamo romani. Noi mangiamo, e gli altri lavorano.*" ("We are Romans. We eat. Others work.") When Christianity took root in Rome, Romans assumed that Rome's Church would lead the world.

The Pope first used the title *Vicarius Christi* (the representative of Christ) in the eighth century; before that he used the title Vicar of the Prince of Apostles or *vicarius principis apostolorum*. The Prince of the Apostles was Peter. Since Jesus said he would build his Church on Peter the Rock and give Peter the keys to the kingdom of Heaven, and since Peter founded the Roman Church, died in Rome, and bequeathed his authority to his successor Roman bishops, or popes, the Catholic Church teaches that the Pope is the true heir to Christian leadership.

The Protestant View

Jesus' play on words in Scripture is clear in Greek but lost in Latin (and in English). Jesus said that Peter was a *pétros* (stone), but that upon this *pétra* (boulder), Jesus would build his Church. In pre-New Testament

Greek, Heraclitus coined the phrase "leave no stone (*pétros*) unturned." Since one can turn a *pétros*, it is a rock that can be rolled or thrown. It is a movable stone. The word in Aramaic for a movable stone is *kepha*, which was, in fact, Peter's Aramaic nickname: Cephas. A *pétra* is a foundation stone, a boulder, or a cliff. It is a large, unmovable rock. The corresponding Aramaic word for *pétra* is *shua*. Where the New Testament elsewhere calls Jesus a rock, the Greek word is *pétra*, an immovable rock. For example, Paul wrote, "All drank the same spiritual drink. For they drank from the spiritual Rock that followed them, and the Rock (*pétras*) was Christ" (1 Cor 10:4).[36] In Matthew 7:24, the reference to the man who built his house upon a rock rather than upon sand uses the word *pétra* for that immovable rock. In Matthew 27:60, Joseph of Arimathea's tomb was hewn out of rock (*pétra*); the large stone that was rolled over the entrance was a *lithos* in Greek, a movable marker stone.

Catholic scholars counter this by saying that Jesus had to call Peter a *pétros*, because that is the masculine form of *pétra*, and Peter was a man. In Greek, adjectives must agree with the gender of the noun they modify, but when one makes a simile, likening one noun to another, the gender of each side of the simile need not conform. To use an approximation in English, if one calls a man an "old woman," he means he is effeminate in behavior, not that his gender is female.

Catholics also say that if Jesus made his declaration in Aramaic, he would not have made a distinction between *pétros* and *pétras* since he would have used *kepha* in both parts of the statement, i.e., "You are *kepha*, and on this *kepha*, I will found my Church." The problem is that no one can guess what words Jesus might have used in Aramaic. The only gospel manuscripts we have are in Greek. Furthermore, Aramaic does have two distinct words, like Greek, for a movable stone (*kepha*) and an immovable rock (*shua*). Since the gospel writers chose Greek as their language of communication (not Aramaic), they must have been comfortable in either language. In a multi-lingual society, such as Judaea was and Israel still is, there is no reason why Jesus may not have chosen to make this statement originally in Greek, especially if he wanted to employ the pun which the Greek preserves for us. In multi-lingual countries and families, it is normal for people to intermix phrases from

---

36. The image of drinking from a rock refers to the story of Moses, at God's command, twice struck a rock, causing water to gush from it to slake the thirst of the Israelites in the wilderness (Exod 17:1–6, Num 20:10–11).

whichever language makes the point best. This is especially true of dramatic or humorous remarks.

If Jesus had not meant to make a distinction between himself, the foundation of the Church, and Simon, a tile in the Church's mosaic, he could have used the same word: "Simon, you are a *pétra,* and on this *pétra* I will build my Church." Yet Matthew takes pains to retain the exact emphasis Jesus made: "You are *pétros* and on this *pétra* I will build my Church." Jesus basically was saying, "Simon, you are a pebble, but I am the rock on which I will build my Church. You are a chip off the old block." Peter echoed this interpretation of his own and Christ's roles when he wrote:

> As you come to him, a living stone rejected by men, but in the sight of God chosen and precious, you yourselves, like living stones, are being built up as a spiritual house, to be a holy priesthood, to offer spiritual sacrifices acceptable to God through Jesus Christ. For it stands in Scripture: "Behold, I am laying in Zion a stone, a cornerstone chosen and precious, and whoever believes in him will not be put to shame." So, the honor is for you who believe, but for those who do not believe, "The stone that the builders rejected has become the cornerstone," and "A stone of stumbling, and a rock of offense." They stumble because they disobey the word, as they were destined to do. But you are a chosen race, a royal priesthood, a holy nation, a people for his own possession, that you may proclaim the excellencies of him who called you out of darkness into his marvelous light (1 Peter 2:4–9).

Paul removed any doubt about who is the Church's one foundation when he wrote, "for no one can lay a foundation other than that which is laid, which is Jesus Christ" (1 Cor 3:11). Moreover, Jesus did not give exclusive control over the keys to the kingdom of heaven to Peter (which is the basis of making Peter, and his successor popes, uniquely authoritative). Speaking to all his disciples, Jesus said:

> Truly, I say to you (ὑμῖν, you, plural), whatever you (ὑμῖν, you, plural) bind on earth shall be bound in heaven, and whatever you (ὑμῖν, you, plural) loose on earth shall be loosed in heaven. Again I say to you (ὑμῖν, you plural), if two of you (ὑμῖν, you, plural) agree on earth about anything they ask, it will be done for them by my Father in heaven. For where two or three are gathered in my name, there am I among them (Matt 18:18–20).

Peter was a prominent apostle but not uniquely powerful. Peter did use the keys Christ gave him to open the door to heaven in some special ways, namely, (1) through the first great sermon at Pentecost, (2) by leading Cornelius and his Gentile household to Christ, (3) by preaching in Samaria, Antioch, Bithynia, and Rome, and (4) by his many other inspired and miraculous acts. His leadership was outstanding. But the other apostles did similar work for the Lord, and the Protestant view is that there is no Scriptural basis for the apostolic transmission of unique authority from Peter down through the popes.

Peter's Personality

Peter was impetuous, emotional, and assertive. When Jesus invited Peter to follow him, he decisively dropped his net. When Jesus walked on water, Peter stepped over the side of the boat and did so, too. Jesus spoke more to Peter than to any other disciple. Jesus praised Peter more than any other disciple. "Blessed are you, Peter, son of Jonah" (Matt 16:17). Peter was the only disciple who dared to rebuke Jesus. When Jesus said he would go to Jerusalem and be killed, Peter cried, "God forbid it, Lord! This shall never happen to you" (Matt 16:22). Jesus rebuked Peter more sharply than any other disciple. "Get behind me, Satan! You are a stumbling block to me; for you are not setting your mind on God's interest, but man's" (Matt 16:23). In the Garden of Gethsemane, Jesus rebuked Peter for sleeping while Jesus suffered fatal anguish (Mark 14:37). Peter was the loudest in vowing loyalty to Jesus before his arrest; he even armed himself with a sword and cut off Malchus' ear. Yet he abandoned Jesus, cursing and swearing. When Jesus looked at Peter during his trial, Peter wept in bitter shame. After the Resurrection, Peter charged first into the empty tomb and later leaped into the Sea of Galilee to join Jesus on shore. Peter rebuked Simon the Magician. Peter worked miracles, including raising the dead. Peter led Romans to Christ. Peter graciously accepted a rebuke from Paul. Peter defended the rights of Gentile Christians at the Jerusalem Council. Peter demanded to die on an upside-down cross because he refused to believe he was worthy to die in the way his friend, Savior, and Lord had perished.

Peter's Epistles

Peter wrote 1 and 2 Peter, two inspired letters that are part of the New Testament. A minority of scholars dispute Peter's authorship, but the majority, dating from the earliest Church Fathers, affirms it. Peter's first letter encouraged Christians who were suffering for Christ. It promised that suffering is not eternal; Heaven is the real home of Christians because of God's grace. He seems to have written the letter from Rome since he wrote that he was in "Babylon" (1 Peter 5:13). Babylon was code for two apostate cities: Jerusalem and Rome. Peter addressed the letter to Christians who were "elect exiles of the dispersion in Pontus, Galatia, Cappadocia, Asia, and Bithynia" (1 Peter 1:1). He also mentioned that Silvanus and Mark were with him at the time of writing. Silvanus appears to have acted as Peter's scribe on this occasion (1 Peter 5:12–13). There were probably few, if any, churches in Asia Minor prior to Paul's first missionary journey in AD 44. So, Peter probably did not write this letter on his first trip to Rome with Mark in AD 43. He probably composed 1 Peter around AD 59.

The books of Jude and 2 Peter are similar in content. In his second letter, Peter urged his readers to be stronger Christians, to shun false teachers, to hold fast to sound doctrine, and to be ready for Christ's return and for the final judgment of the wicked. He probably also wrote this from Rome between AD 59 and 68. Probably he wrote it toward the end of this period, when the Neronian persecution of Christians (AD 64–68) and the Roman-Jewish War (AD 66–73) were raging. That would explain Peter's emphasis on the truth of the Gospel (2 Peter 1:16), his warning against false teachers, who were abundant in Judaea during the Roman-Jewish conflict (2 Peter 2), and his apocalyptic vision of the Day of the Lord (2 Peter 3:1–13).

ANDREW, THE FIRST-CALLED

ANDREW WAS VARIOUSLY THE second or the fourth in the list of apostles. His name, Andreas, means "manly" in Greek. The Bible records no Hebrew or Aramaic name for him. He was born in Bethsaida, "Fish Town," at the north end of the Sea of Galilee. Later, he lived with his brother, Simon Peter, in Capernaum. The fact that Scripture lists him after Peter suggests that he was Peter's younger brother, but given Peter's prominence as the leader of the apostles, it is also possible that Peter was younger but more important, as was the case with Isaac (the younger half-brother) and Ishmael (the elder half-brother) and Jacob (the younger twin) and Esau (the elder twin).

The father of Peter and Andrew was Jonah ("Dove" in Hebrew)—the same name as that of Jonah, the Prophet to Nineveh, who came from the village of Gath-Hepher ("wine press"), two miles from Nazareth. Jonah, perhaps with intentional irony, was a common name for men in the fishing trade. The sons of Jonah started out in the little fishing village of Bethsaida, but as their fishing business prospered, they moved to the larger town of Capernaum, bought a big house, and formed a partnership with Zebedee and his sons, James and John (Luke 5:7, 10).

EARLY SPIRITUAL QUEST

The Eastern Orthodox Church honors Andrew with the title *protókletos*—the first-called of Jesus' disciples (John 1:40).[1] Andrew and his

---

1. This passage mentions two first-called disciples. It positively identifies one as Andrew. The other remains anonymous. However, since all the other disciples first called

business partner, John the son of Zebedee, first went to hear the message of John the Baptist in the High Holy Days of AD 29, which ran from Rosh Hashanah Eve (Monday, September 24) through the last day of the Feast of Tabernacles (Thursday, October 18). In that year, crowds of people from Jerusalem went to Bethany on the Jordan, about twenty miles east of Jerusalem, to hear the Baptist preach.

The Baptist began his ministry at the age of thirty-two in Tiberius Caesar's fifteenth year on or before Saturday, August 18, AD 29, the last day of Tiberius' fifteenth year (Luke 3:1).   John preached, "Repent, for the kingdom of heaven is at hand." Isaiah referred to John when he described a "voice of one crying in the wilderness," saying, "Make ready the way of the Lord, make his paths straight" (Matt 3:1–3). Pharisees and Sadducees from Jerusalem went to question him.

John baptized his thirty-one-year-old cousin, Jesus, around Sunday, September 2, AD 29.[2] Jesus would not have been baptized the day before, on the Sabbath, not necessarily because it would have been a problem for Jesus, but because there would have been few, if any, Jews out and about to witness the event.

After being baptized, Jesus ventured into the wilderness and fasted for forty days. The Feast of Tabernacles began on October 9, the thirty-seventh day of Jesus' fasting. On the Sabbath, October 13, Satan tempted Jesus, and on Monday, October 15, after the Sabbath, priests and Levites traveled out from Jerusalem to question John the Baptist about his identity again (John 1:19).

The next day, Tuesday, October 16, Jesus returned from his sojourn in the wilderness to the banks of the Jordan, where the Baptist first called him the Lamb of God (John 1:29). The next day, Wednesday, October 17, the Baptist proclaimed for a second time, as he saw Jesus passing by, "Behold, the Lamb of God (John 1:36). On this day, Andrew and John were present, and hearing this, they followed Jesus, who turned to them and said, "What do you seek?" They asked, "Rabbi, where are you staying?" Jesus said, "Come, and you will see." This was a very natural conversation during the Feast of Tabernacles. During this feast, God commanded the Jews to come before him (make a pilgrimage to

---

by Jesus are named at the Wedding of Cana except one, and since only John's gospel records the wedding (making John a probable eyewitness), the unnamed disciple is likely John, consistent with John's literary technique of not explicitly naming himself.

2. See "Pinpointing the Start of Jesus' Ministry" at www.thebiblehistoryguy.com. No other date works.

Jerusalem) and to construct booths, tents, or huts (tabernacles; Hebrew: *sukkot*) and live in them for a week to commemorate Israel's wandering in the Exodus. One can infer from Josephus that as many as 2.7 million Jews descended upon Jerusalem for pilgrimage feasts during the first century,[3] so there was not enough room in the city to house everyone. People stayed in the homes of relatives and friends and even strangers in the surrounding countryside. During the Passover week of AD 33, Jesus and his disciples stayed either in Bethany or on the Mount of Olives. So, during the Feast of Tabernacles in this year of AD 29, it was logical for Andrew and John to ask Jesus where he was staying. It might have been in a makeshift booth almost anywhere.

Andrew and John spent that day until about 4 p.m. in Jesus' company. Then Andrew went and found his brother Peter and told him, "We have found the Messiah" (John 1:41). Although Andrew immediately followed the Lord, Jesus had not yet chosen him as a full-time disciple. He was still a casual follower. In fact, Andrew may still have considered himself a disciple of John the Baptist and may have remained so until Jesus called him personally around May 1 of AD 30, over seven months later. The next day, Thursday, October 18, Jesus called Philip and Nathanael and started back toward Galilee in the company of these two disciples, plus Andrew, Peter, and John.

THE WEDDING AT CANA

On the third day, Sunday, October 21, 17 Tishri, there was a wedding at Cana in Galilee, and the mother of Jesus was there. Jesus also was invited to the wedding with his disciples. "On the third day" means on the third day since calling Philip and Nathanael. The day Jesus called them was the last day of the Feast of Tabernacles, so it was natural that it would be the right day to return to Galilee, as the Fall pilgrimage to Jerusalem for the High Holy Days ended.

The walk from Bethany on the Jordan to Cana, following the eastern route along the Jordan River to avoid hostile Samaria, was a journey of about eighty-two miles. In Jesus' day, people walked everywhere, every day, so unless they were very old or young, they were fit and would probably average a pace of about 3.7 miles per hour. So, this journey would take a total of about twenty-two hours. When traveling, Jesus and his disciples

---

3. Josephus, *Jewish War*, 6:9:3.

probably walked about ten hours on each non-Sabbath day. On Thursday, aware that a Sabbath was coming the next day, they probably pushed it. Sunrise was at 5:45 a.m., and sunset was at 5:06 p.m. in Israel on that day, giving about eleven daylight hours. They probably managed ten hours' walking, covering thirty-seven miles. They spent the night somewhere in the Jordan Valley, probably in some village with friends.

The next day was Friday, and so they would have wanted to start early—again around 6 a.m.—and finish early, around 3 p.m., so that they might find a house to stay in an hour before sunset to observe the Sabbath. They might have walked only nine hours on that day, about thirty-three miles. That would leave only about twelve miles to cover on the final day, Sunday, the day of the wedding. If they rose at dawn on Sunday and started walking at 6 a.m., they would reach Cana in three hours, at about 9 a.m., plenty of time to wash from their journey and prepare to join the wedding party.

Jesus' mother was already there. Mary likely had walked from Nazareth. She did not have to walk from Jerusalem like Jesus and his followers because, as a woman, she was not required to make the pilgrimages. From Nazareth to Cana was about a two-hour walk. Possibly Jesus met Mary in Nazareth and accompanied her north to Cana. Possibly Mary had already gone to Cana before the Sabbath to help prepare for the wedding. Since the end of the story says that Jesus left the wedding with his mother, his brothers, and his disciples, obviously, his brothers also attended. The word "brothers" in Greek probably means brothers and sisters since it is unlikely that Mary's daughters would have missed a family wedding. Jesus' brothers may have been in Jerusalem for the High Holy Days and may also have just arrived from Judaea, perhaps in the company of Jesus and his five new disciples. His sisters may have been in Nazareth with Mary and may have come with her directly from there. In any case, Jesus' family was all at the wedding, which suggests, along with Mary's taking command of events, that the bridegroom was a relative of Jesus. In fact, the bridegroom may have been Simon the Zealot, who would later become one of the Twelve Disciples, and who may have been the brother of James the Less, half-brother of Matthew Levi, and, like them, Jesus' cousin.[4] Nathanael Bartholomew, who was also present, was a resident of Cana.

---

4. See "Relationships in Jesus' Community" at www.thebiblehistoryguy.com.

When the wine at the feast ran out, Jesus' mother said to him, "They have no wine." Jesus said to her, "Woman, what does this have to do with me? My hour has not yet come." Jesus' reply to Mary's request was brusque—not disrespectful, but firm. He was telling Mary that his role had changed. A mere fifty-five days ago, he had left Galilee as the head of his family's household, her eldest son. Now, baptized, triumphant over Satan, and with five disciples, his agenda was God's agenda, no longer that of his earthly family.

Mary said to the servants, "Do whatever he tells you." Six stone water jars, each holding twenty or thirty gallons, were there for the Jewish rites of purification. Jesus said to the servants, "Fill the jars with water." Jesus complied with Mary's request, but he redefined the purpose of the event. Jesus would not let his earthly family run his ministry. He and the Father were one, and God was running it. Mary told the servants, perhaps with some asperity, to do whatever Jesus told them. But she yielded authority to him, where it belonged.

The servants filled the six jars to the brim. Then Jesus said to them, "Now draw some out and take it to the master of the feast." So, they took it. When the master of the feast tasted the water now become wine and did not know where it came from (though the servants who had drawn the water knew), the master of the feast called the bridegroom and said to him, "Everyone serves the good wine first, and when people have drunk freely, then the poor wine. But you have kept the good wine until now."

That the wine ran out and that Mary wanted there to be more suggests that Jesus and his family were attending a feast that was not abstemious. The six stone jars held 120 to 180 gallons of water, the equivalent of 600 to 900 of our modern 750 mL bottles of wine. This does not mean that the wedding party drank all of them in one day. The abundance of the miracle reflected the wonderful power of God. Jesus produced more than the necessary amount of food to feed the 5,000 and the 4,000, as Elijah produced more flour and oil than the widow of Zarephath could consume in one day (1 Kings 17:15), and Elisha produced more oil for the wife of one of the prophets than she could consume in one day (2 Kings 4:3–7). The Bible prohibits addictive and uncontrolled drunkenness (Prov 20:1, Gal 5:19–21, Eph 5:18), not the drinking of alcohol and enjoying the pleasure it gives in moderation (Ps 104:14–15, Eccl 9:7, 1 Tim 5:23).

Jesus said, "I am the true vine, and my Father is the gardener . . . . you are the branches" (John 15:1–5). The function of a grapevine is to turn water into wine. Jesus' miracle at Cana had great symbolic significance. Jesus transforms people. He turned fishermen into fishers of men. He turned water into wine. He turns sinners into saints.

This, the first of his signs, Jesus did at Cana in Galilee and manifested his glory. His disciples believed in him. Jesus would later do at least one other miracle at Cana—healing the official's son—but that would be on Sunday, April 28, AD 30, about five months later.

HOLIDAY ON THE SEA OF GALILEE

After the wedding, Jesus went down to Capernaum with his mother, his brothers, his sisters, and his disciples, and they stayed there for a few days. We know that Jesus had four half-brothers—James, Joses, Simon, and Judas (Matt 13:55–56, Mark 6:3). Of these, at least James and Judas would come to believe that their resurrected half-brother was the Christ. They would write the New Testament books of James and Jude. Jesus also had at least three half-sisters, whose names the Bible does not record. So, there were at least eight children in Mary's home. Mary and the seven children lived in Nazareth (Mark 6:3), where her husband, Joseph (probably now deceased), established their home after he, Mary, and Jesus returned from Egypt.

Instead of going home to Nazareth, Jesus and his family went instead to Capernaum, which was about an eight-hour walk from Cana, compared to a two-hour walk to Nazareth. Going to Capernaum to stay a few days on the shores of Lake Galilee in autumn sounds rather like a holiday. Since James and John, the sons of Zebedee, were likely Jesus' first cousins,[5] and since Zebedee was rich, he probably had a big house. So, Mary and the seven children may have stayed at her sister's home, while the disciples may have stayed in Peter's house, which was also large. This seems to have been an intimate time of relaxation at the shore for the family and friends of Jesus after the miracle in Cana. The purpose of this holiday may have been nothing but leisure, but perhaps Jesus used the time to set the tone for the next phase of his life, the mission of the promised Messiah.

Scripture makes no further mention of Jesus and the disciples until the Passover of the following year, AD 30, when Jesus first cleansed the temple. Presumably, the same disciples were obediently on pilgrimage

---

5. See "Relationships in Jesus' Community" at www.thebiblehistoryguy.com.

to Jerusalem then (John 2:13) and thus witnessed the event. At that time, Jesus instructed Nicodemus secretly in someone's house, probably that of John (John 3:2). On Sunday, April 14, following the first Sabbath after Passover, Jesus left Jerusalem and began baptizing in the Judaean countryside. Despite Jesus' growing fame, John the Baptist was free from jealousy about him (John 3:30).

THE SAMARITAN WOMAN AT THE WELL

Then John the Baptist was taken into custody by Herod, and Jesus decided to leave Judaea for Galilee. Rather than follow the Jordan route, Jesus took the unusual step of traveling straight through Samaria. Jews avoided hostile Samaria whenever possible, but John wrote that Jesus had to pass through Samaria. Why did he have to? Perhaps, after arresting John the Baptist, the authorities were looking for Jesus, too, and this may have forced him to take an unusual route. Moreover, Jesus traveled overnight, suggesting a hasty flight, and arrived at a well in the town of Sychar (Shechem) at 6 a.m.

While his disciples went into the town of Sychar for food, he met and conversed with a Samaritan woman at Jacob's well (John 4:5–7). Impressed by Jesus' wisdom, the woman brought people from the town, and all of them agreed that Jesus must be the Christ. Jesus commented that this recognition by the estranged Samaritans proved that a prophet was without honor in his hometown. He stayed for two more days over the Sabbath among these traditional antagonists of the Jews. Then he returned to Galilee, where the Galileans welcomed him. They, too, had been to Jerusalem on pilgrimage and had witnessed what he had done there (John 4:45). We do not really know which disciples traveled with Jesus for this Passover and which simply attended the feast in Jerusalem and saw him more casually. It is probable that the inner circle, Peter, Andrew, James, and John, were with him all the way.

CALLING THE FOUR FISHERMEN

Around May 1, AD 30, 242 days (nearly eight months) after his baptism, Jesus returned to the lakeshore at Capernaum. He saw the two brothers, Peter and Andrew, casting a net into the sea. He said to them, "Follow me, and I will make you fishers of men." They left their nets at once and followed him. Shortly after, they saw the business partners of Peter and Andrew, the sons of Zebedee, James and John. He called them, and immediately they left mending their nets, abandoning their father and servants in their fishing boat, and followed him (Matt 4:22). At last, Andrew, Peter, James, and John were full-time disciples. Andrew followed Jesus throughout the rest of his earthly ministry.

ANDREW'S ROLE

Andrew was a people person. He went searching for John the Baptist and found Jesus and then hastened to tell his brother Peter. At the feeding of the five thousand, in March, AD 31, Andrew was not shy, but was mingling with the crowd. He was the one who introduced the boy with loaves and fishes to Jesus. He appears to have convinced the boy to sacrifice his lunch and, considering that there were five thousand hungry people and not much food, Andrew must have been persuasive (John 6:8–9). As both Andrew and the boy were from Bethsaida, perhaps they knew each other. Perhaps they were related.

When Greeks[6] desired to meet Jesus on Palm Sunday, AD 33, they approached Philip, a disciple with a Greek name. "Sir," they said, "we wish to see Jesus." Philip told Andrew (another disciple with a Greek name), and Andrew took Philip to tell Jesus (John 12:20–22).

Andrew was present at some of Jesus' most intimate teachings. He, along with Peter, James, and John, were the only disciples present at the Sermon on the Mount. On Tuesday, March 29, AD 33, on the Mount of Olives, opposite the Temple, Peter, Andrew, James, and John privately asked the Lord about the times of the end, saying, "Tell us, when will these things be, and what will be the sign when all these things are going to be fulfilled?" Jesus told them not to be deceived by false teachers, by wars and rumors of wars, by nation rising against nation, by earthquakes, and famines, for these were all the birth pangs of the End (Mark 13:3–8).

Andrew witnessed Jesus' Ascension. He was present in the Upper Room on the evening of Resurrection Sunday with Thomas absent and was there a week later when Jesus again appeared to the Eleven with

---

6. These "Greeks" were actually Armenians. Abgar, the king of the Armenians, truly believed Jesus was the Son of God. He sent a letter to Jesus, asking Him to come to him and cure him of his pains. The bearers of the letter met Jesus at Jerusalem "but not daring to tell Jesus . . . told it to Philip and Andrew, who repeated it to their Master." Moses of Chorene, *History of Armenia*, 5.

Thomas present. Andrew was among the Eleven when his brother, Peter, led them to choose Matthias to replace Judas. Andrew witnessed the birth of the Church on Pentecost, Sunday, May 22, AD 33, and attended the Jerusalem Council in AD 49.

ANDREW'S MISSIONS

When Andrew left Jerusalem to spread the Gospel is unknown. It may have been about the same time his brother Peter went to Rome, in AD 43. The Bible fixes Andrew back in Judaea at the Jerusalem Council in AD 49, because "the apostles," presumably all of them, attended (except James, the son of Zebedee, who had died in AD 44). So, Andrew may have traveled for about six years, from AD 43–49, returned to Jerusalem, and then may have set out on missionary journeys again.

Hippolytus says that he "preached to the Scythians and Thracians."[7] Eusebius confirms his mission to Scythia.[8] The Scythians were a nomadic people who lived in what is now southern Russia, Ukraine, Romania, and Bulgaria. Thrace was a Hellenic territory in part of what is now Bulgaria and along the eastern shore of the Black Sea. So, Andrew's missionary trips, which are not recorded in Scripture, seem to describe a large arc across Central Asia, Eastern Europe, Northern Anatolia, and Greece. There would have been ample time in six years to accomplish these journeys. He may have founded churches as far north as Volga and Kyiv. Andrew is thus the patron saint of Russia and Romania.

The apocryphal *Acts of Andrew and Matthias*[9] says that Andrew saw in a dream that Matthias, the apostle who replaced Judas Iscariot, had been imprisoned in a savage land inhabited by cannibals. They blinded Matthias, but when the risen Christ sent Andrew to save him, Andrew miraculously restored his sight. Andrew triumphed over the cannibals through prayer and freed Matthias. The apocryphal *Acts of Andrew* further says that Andrew continued to Byzantium (which three hundred years later would become the Christian city of Constantinople) and founded this great See, becoming its patron saint.[10] Andrew

---

7. Hippolytus, *List of the Apostles and Disciples*.

8. Eusebius, *Church History*, 3:1:1.

9. *The Acts of Andrew and Matthias*. This is a highly fanciful account, and while it may contain a grain of truth, swallowing the entire narrative requires a liberal pinch of salt.

10. *The Acts of Andrew*. "See" derives from the Latin word *sedes* or "seat."

then continued to Greece, traveling to Thrace, Macedonia, Corinth, and finally Patras.[11]

ANDREW'S DEATH

The *Acts of Andrew* and Tertullian[12] say that in Patras, the Roman proconsul of Achaia (Greece), Aegeates, heard Andrew's preaching and demanded that he and his Christian brethren worship the Hellenic gods. Andrew refused. He said that these "gods" were demons who lured men to destruction. He carried out an extensive public debate with Aegeates, inviting him to follow Christ. Aegeates said that it was absurd and obscene for anyone to follow a man who had been executed on a cross and said that he would rather extract God's secrets from Andrew by torture than by debating him. Andrew replied that salvation came through faith, not violence, and that Jesus' death on the Cross was God's victory, not a disgrace. Aegeates threw Andrew in prison with this ultimatum: either worship the Hellenic gods or die on a cross himself.

Aegeates' wife, Maximilla, moved by Andrew's preaching, took a vow of celibacy. Aegeates was outraged. He told Maximilla that if she renounced this vow, he would forgive her and even release Andrew. If she did not, he would execute Andrew. Maximilla visited Andrew in prison and told him of her dilemma. She said she wanted to hold fast to her celibate vow. Andrew praised her and encouraged her to do so, even if it cost his life.[13]

From the entire province, an angry crowd of twenty thousand gathered and threatened to storm the prison to release Andrew and to kill Aegeates. Andrew implored them to keep the peace. The next day, Aegeates had Andrew hauled before him and asked if he were ready to pour a libation to the pagan gods. Andrew replied that up till then he had spoken kindly to Aegeates. Now he told the proconsul that he was headed for hell if he did not repent and that no threat of execution could deter Andrew from speaking plainly. Andrew added that the proconsul

---

11. Hippolytus, *List of the Apostles and Disciples*.

12. Tertullian, *Acts and Martyrdom of the Holy Apostle Andrew*.

13. The Bible condones marriage (Gen 2:18, Prov 18:22, Matt 19:6, 1 Tim 3:2) and only endorses celibacy in certain circumstances (1 Cor 7:32–33, Rev 14:4). Therefore, Andrew's advice was not that chastity was better than intimacy in any marriage, but this particular marriage was obviously problematic and probably abusive.

had no real power to punish any Christian, since to die was to enter eternal life with Christ, which was a reward.

Enraged, Aegeates ordered Andrew's execution. Calmly, Andrew took off his clothes and presented himself to be tied to a cross.[14] Sadistically, Aegeates tied Andrew to a sideways cross. This was so that, as he hung dying, he would be within reach of wild dogs, who might ravenously tear at his limbs and increase his suffering and humiliation. Aegeates also ordered his soldiers not to break any of Andrew's joints, so that he might suffer prolonged agony as he hung.[15]

Twenty thousand protesters mobbed the cross. Smiling, Andrew preached to them with eloquence and lucidity for three days and nights. Astonished at the wisdom of his words and the undimmed light of his intellect while he suffered, the crowd became furious at Aegeates' injustice and, on the fourth day, demanded that Aegeates set Andrew free. Seeing that the crowd was dangerous, Aegeates agreed. Maximilla rejoiced with the others at Andrew's liberation.

When Aegeates approached the cross to untie the apostle, however, Andrew persisted in confronting the proconsul, saying that he did not believe Aegeates was doing this because he repented, but merely from fear of the mob. Andrew prayed that God should not let an adversary of Christ free him. A bright light suffused the cross, so dazzling that the people could not look upon it. It shimmered for about half an hour, and then Andrew died. Maximilla, with no regard for her nobility, personally removed Andrew's body from the cross, anointed it with costly spices, and buried him in her own tomb.

Aegeates implored his wife to disassociate herself from these Christians. He offered to leave her all his wealth if she would agree. But she separated from him and devoted herself to a celibate life in the Christian community. Furious, Aegeates decided to lodge an official accusation with Nero Caesar against Maximilla and the rebels in Achaia. Before he could do so, however, in the dead of night he arose and, tormented by a demon, fell from a great height. He rolled into the

---

14. Usually, the Romans tied victims to a Cross. Nailing Jesus' forearms and ankles to the Cross was an act of extra cruelty.

15. Death on a cross comes from becoming too weak to expel air from the lungs and take a fresh breath; the victim dies of asphyxiation. If the joints are intact, the victim has some leverage to continue to push air from his lungs; when the joints or limbs are broken, that leverage is gone.

middle of the city marketplace and breathed his last. By tradition, he died on the last day of November.

We do not know when this all was supposed to happen, exactly, but we can make an educated guess. The emperor Claudius designated Achaia a proconsular province in AD 44. Lucius Junius Gallio, the brother of the Roman philosopher Seneca, served as proconsul in this same province of Achaia, probably from AD 51–53. Acts 18 reports that Gallio refused to punish Paul, who was in Corinth around AD 50–51, when the Jews requested that Gallio silence him. Aegeates was, therefore, probably proconsul sometime after AD 53.

After the death of Claudius, Nero became emperor in AD 54. He ruled normally at first. However, after the Great Fire of Rome in AD 64, popular rumors placed the blame for the fire on Nero. The gossip was that he had purposely torched Rome to clear ground for his new magnificent golden palace. Seeking a scapegoat, Nero began persecuting Christians on a massive scale. This tribulation probably began about August 25, AD 64, thirty-one days after the Great Fire. It lasted until June 9, AD 68, the date of Nero's suicide. Within these 1,385 days was the time when Aegeates' stance could have found favor with his boss in Rome. Nero killed Peter probably on May 5, AD 68. We do not know certainly when Andrew died, but it seems reasonable that he died after AD 64, when the Neronian persecution of Christians had begun. If so, he may have predeceased his brother Peter by as many as four years.

SCOTLAND AND ELSEWHERE

No ancient tradition confirms that Andrew ever visited Scotland, but a Christian named Saint Regulus took a few bones thought to be relics of Andrew from Greece to Scotland in the fourth or fifth century. He buried them in a town called Fife at a place he named "Saint Andrew's," and Andrew became Scotland's patron saint. The flag of Scotland displays Saint Andrew's sideways cross. When England forged a union of England, Scotland, and Protestant Ireland and called it the United Kingdom, it superimposed the vertical Cross of Saint George on a sideways Saint Andrew's Cross to create a double-cross flag, the Union Jack.

Saint Andrews, Scotland, is the place where golf was invented in the fifteenth century, without, however, any known apostolic endorsement.

The winners of tournaments at the Royal and Ancient Golf Club are listed with a Saint Andrew's Cross marking their names.

Andrew became the patron saint of several other places, which, like Scotland, he may never have visited, including Amalfi, Prussia, Sicily, and Malta. Andrew was a seeker of truth, an outgoing ambassador of the Gospel, a follower always introducing others to the Messiah, a persuasive speaker, a loyal friend, a brave and hard-working evangelist, and faithful even to death.

JAMES, SON OF THUNDER

JAMES WAS VARIOUSLY THE second or the third in the lists of the apostles. James and John were brothers, the sons of Zebedee and of Mary Salome. The fact that James' name almost always appears before John's (except in Luke 8:51, 9:28, and Acts 1:13) suggests that James was John's elder brother, but we have no firmer proof of their ages than that. James is Yaakov or Jacob ("one who laughs") in Hebrew. James in Greek became Iakovos, Jacobus in Latin, Jacques in French, Iago (Santiago— Saint James) or Jaime in Spanish, Giacomo in Italian, Jakob in German, and James in English.

Three prominent people bear the name of James in the New Testament: (1) James the Great (or Elder), the son of Zebedee and brother of the apostle John, (2) James the Less (or Younger), the son of Alphaeus, another of the original Twelve Apostles, and (3) James the Just, half-brother of Jesus, leader of the Jerusalem Church. Archaeological finds reveal many artifacts bearing the extremely common names of James, Judas, and Jesus (Joshua) in first-century Judaea. They were almost the equivalents of our "Tom, Dick, and Harry."

James and John were probably Jesus' first cousins and probably knew him from boyhood. If Salome was the wife of Zebedee and the sister of Jesus' mother, Mary, then James and John were Jesus' first cousins and probably knew him from boyhood, and James may have been partially or entirely a Levite.[1]

The sons of Zebedee were apparently well-to-do. Mark tells us that when Jesus called James and John, they left their father Zebedee in the

---

1. See "Relationships in Jesus' Community" at www.thebiblehistoryguy.com.

boat with the hired servants (Mark 1:20). If they could afford to hire servants, their fishing business must have had some substance. A further hint of the wealth of Zebedee's family is found in Matthew 27:56, which depicts Zebedee's wife counted among the many women of Galilee who were following and ministering "of their substance" to the Lord. In the first century this presumably required masculine permission, leisure, and means. James' brother, John, had connections with the High Priest in Jerusalem, evidence that the family was prominent, respected, and probably were major donors (John 18:15–16). And James, John, Peter, and Andrew were business partners (Luke 5:7, 10).

When John the Baptist revealed that his cousin, Jesus, was the Lamb of God, Andrew went and found his brother Peter and told him (John 1:41). John does not mention going to tell James about Jesus at the same time that Andrew told Peter. Perhaps James was back in Galilee, tending the family business. Perhaps he was in Jerusalem observing the Feast of Tabernacles. Did James meet Jesus and recognize him as the Messiah at this time? Did James join the others on the return trip to Galilee and attend the wedding at Cana? Scripture makes no mention of it.

In all four gospels, in the lists of the apostles, Peter, Andrew, James, and John form the first group. They are a prominent and chosen team, especially Peter, James, and John. Jesus allowed these three alone to witness the miracle of raising Jairus' daughter (Luke 8:51). Only Peter, James, and John were present at the Transfiguration (Matt 17:1–2). Only Peter, James, and John witnessed Jesus' agony in the Garden of Gethsemane—and failed him by falling asleep (Mark 14:33–41). Jesus surely knew that James would be the first apostle to die in AD 44. So, his inclusion of James in these events equipped him for a post-Resurrection ministry of only eleven years.

John never mentioned his brother James in his gospel. This is in keeping with John's humble reserve when writing about himself and his family. But humility was probably an acquired family trait. Jesus had a special nickname for James and John. "[To] James the son of Zebedee and John the brother of James . . . he gave the name Boanerges, that is, Sons of Thunder" (Mark 3:17). The Sons of Thunder argued with the other disciples, told outsiders not to cast out demons in Jesus' name, and asked Jesus if they, like Elijah, could bring fire from heaven on Samaritans who had refused Jesus hospitality. They wanted to be Jesus' "enforcers." On Jesus' last journey to Jerusalem, the Zebedee brothers asked Jesus, to give them special preferment.

James and John, the sons of Zebedee, came up to him and said to him, "Teacher, we want you to do for us whatever we ask of you." And he said to them, "What do you want me to do for you?" And they said to him, "Grant us to sit, one at your right hand and one at your left, in your glory." Jesus said to them, "You do not know what you are asking. Are you able to drink the cup that I drink, or to be baptized with the baptism with which I am baptized?" And they said to him, "We are able." And Jesus said to them, "The cup that I drink you will drink, and with the baptism with which I am baptized, you will be baptized, but to sit at my right hand or at my left is not mine to grant, but it is for those for whom it has been prepared." And when the Ten heard it, they began to be indignant at James and John. And Jesus called them to him and said to them, "You know that those who are considered rulers of the Gentiles lord it over them, and their great ones exercise authority over them. But it shall not be so among you. But whoever would be great among you must be your servant, and whoever would be first among you must be slave of all. For even the Son of Man came not to be served but to serve, and to give his life as a ransom for many" (Mark 10:35–45).

The Sons of Thunder probably still expected Jesus' kingdom to be an earthly restoration of the Maccabean monarchy.[2] James and John were (erroneously) sure they were fit to be King Jesus' chief ministers once a triumphant Judah had ejected Rome. Their request adds some weight to the argument that James and John were Jesus' first cousins; in a dynasty, family members would naturally receive royal preferment.

Thunder is a good name for them—a big noise that follows lightning but which, unlike lightning, has no power. And Jesus did not even

---

2. The Maccabees were a family of Levites (not Jews) who led a revolt against the Greek Syrian kings of the Seleucid empire. They ruled in Judaea from 140–37 BC, when Rome installed Herod the Great as King of the Jews in their place. The patriarch of the Maccabee dynasty was Mattathias, who was a High Priest and a Levite. The name Maccabee means "hammer," and it was the nickname of Judas Maccabaeus, who hammered the rulers of the Seleucid empire in battle and forged a new, independent Jewish state. The Maccabees assumed the titles of both King and High Priest. As Levites, they could legitimately claim only the latter, for the kings of Judah were all of the tribe of Judah (Jews), not Levi. Thus, they were a flawed model of the promised Messianic kingdom. Jesus fit the required profile for a new Messianic king. He was of the tribe of Judah, a descendant of David, and a charismatic leader. He was alive at exactly the right time in history—in fact, prophetically, Jesus lived in history's last window of opportunity for the Messiah to come (Dan 9:24–27). He was foreshadowed by his namesake, Joshua, who had first conquered the Promised Land with God's help. And his miracles showed that God endorsed him.

call them "thunder." He called them sons of thunder. How proud they must have been of this impressive nickname, until its ironic insignificance sunk in. Perhaps this is why John, the beloved disciple, learned to be so modest about references to himself in his gospel, in his letters, and in Revelation. His relationship with Jesus taught him humility very different from the character with which he and James were born.

As one of the Twelve, James was present in the Upper Room on Resurrection Sunday. He was in the Upper Room with Thomas present on the following Monday. He was at Jesus' Ascension. He helped to choose Matthias. And he was at the birth of the Church on the day of Pentecost in AD 33. He died, however, before the Jerusalem Council in AD 49.

JAMES' DEATH

Jesus asked James and John if they were able to drink the cup that Jesus would drink, that of martyrdom. They replied that they were able, and James died a martyr a few short years later, in the Passover week of March 30–April 7, AD 44.

Herod Agrippa I, son of Aristobulus and grandson of Herod the Great, reigned at that time over a dominion greater than that of his grandfather. The Herodian kings were Idumeans, that is, Edomites, descendants of Esau and rivals and enemies of Jacob's descendants, the Jews. They ruled at the pleasure of Rome, and Rome wanted only three things from them: (1) to keep Judaea in order, (2) to act as a buffer state against enemy Parthia, and (3) to keep the tax revenues flowing. So, Herod Agrippa I desired to placate the Jews in every way, which meant showing (if not actually having) great regard for the Law of Moses and Jewish customs. Since Christians, especially Jewish Christians offended the Jews, Herod Agrippa I inflicted ostentatious cruelties on the Jerusalem Church during the Passover of AD 44. James was Herod Agrippa's first celebrity victim.

> About that time Herod the king laid violent hands on some who belonged to the Church. He killed James the brother of John with the sword, and when he saw that it pleased the Jews, he proceeded to arrest Peter also. This was during the days of Unleavened Bread (Acts 12:1–3).

According to Eusebius, "the one who led James to the judgment seat, when he saw him bearing his testimony, was moved and confessed that he was himself also a Christian. They were both therefore . . . led away together; and on the way he begged James to forgive him. And he, after considering a little, said, 'Peace be with you,' and kissed him. And thus, they were both beheaded at the same time."[3] James' brother John may have seen his martyrdom. The word martyr is Greek for "witness."

JAMES AND SPAIN

According to tradition, James preached Christianity in Spain.[4] The Bible says that in the Jewish persecution of Christians by Paul, which began in late AD 33 and continued until Paul's conversion in April, AD 34, all believers "except the apostles" scattered throughout Judaea and Samaria (Acts 8:1). Those who scattered preached the gospel wherever they went (Acts 8:4). This scattering lasted until about June, AD 37 (Acts 11:19–22). If the apostles did not scatter in this interval when all the others scattered, one might conclude that James did not leave Jerusalem until the summer of AD 37. Since, however, Philip, Peter, and John preached outside of Jerusalem during the period of scattering, the meaning of Acts 8:1 is not necessarily that the apostles remained confined to Jerusalem but that they did not scurry away in fear. They proclaimed the gospel abroad confidently and intentionally. James could, therefore, have traveled to Spain in the spring of AD 34, the same year when Peter founded the church in Antioch. If so, he must have returned before the Fall Holy Days of AD 43 (sailing after Yom Kippur was dangerous), since this would have placed him in Jerusalem for the Passover of AD 44, where and when he died. James would thus have had plenty of time, about ten years, to bring the Gospel to Spain.

Tradition, for which there is no ancient attestation, says that the remains of James the Elder were taken to Compostela in Spain. The medieval legend is that a mystical ship with a crew of angels took his relics across the sea. While the heavenly ship is fanciful, someone may nevertheless have taken James' relics to Spain. James' presumptive burial place in Spain was a major site of pilgrimage in the Middle Ages, and the Spaniards, fighting to drive the Moors out of Iberia, adopted the battle cry, "Santiago de Compostela," meaning "Saint James of Compostela!"

---

3. Eusebius, *Church History*, 2:9:2–3.
4. O'Kane, *Little Lives of the Great Saints*, 28.

The papal bull[5] of Leo XIII in 1884 affirmed the authenticity of James' relics in Spain.

James was the first apostle to die. His brother John was the last. James was a martyr. John died a natural death.

---

5. A bull derives its name from the Latin word *bulla*, which is the seal applied to papal decrees. The English word "bulletin" derives from it. *Bulla* comes from the Latin verb *bullire*, which means "to boil," referring to the fact the material used to make a seal, whether wax, lead, or gold, had to be melted in order to stick to the document and receive a signet impression.

JOHN, THE APOSTLE OF LOVE

JAMES AND JOHN WERE brothers, the sons of Zebedee and Mary Salome. John is Yochanan in Hebrew, meaning "God is gracious." The name in Greek became Ioannis, Iohannes in Latin, Jean in French, Juan in Spanish, Giovanni in Italian, Johann in German, and John in English.

There are two prominent Johns in the New Testament: (1) John the Baptist, the son of Zacharias, a Levite, and Elizabeth, second cousin of Jesus, and (2) John the apostle, first cousin of Jesus. If Salome was the wife of Zebedee and was the sister of Jesus' mother, Mary, then James and John were first cousins of Jesus and probably knew Jesus from boyhood, and John may have been partially or entirely a Levite.[1]

JOHN'S WEALTH

The sons of Zebedee were apparently well-off. John was known to the High Priest in Jerusalem, as the following passage, suggesting wealth and respect, shows:

> Simon Peter followed Jesus, and so did another disciple. Since that disciple was known to the High Priest, he entered with Jesus into the court of the High Priest, but Peter stood outside at the door. So the other disciple, who was known to the High Priest, went out and spoke to the servant girl who kept watch at the door, and brought Peter in (John 18:15–16).

---

1. See "Relationships in Jesus' Community" at www.thebiblehistoryguy.com.

The "other disciple" is, most scholars agree, John, the author of John's gospel. John also appeared to have had a home in Jerusalem, implied in John 3, because although Jesus' nocturnal interview with Nicodemus was secret, John probably was there, as he is the only gospel writer to record it. Since Nicodemus went to Jesus, and since Jesus did not have a home (Matt 8:20, Luke 9:58), the event probably occurred in John's house.

There is another clue that John had a Jerusalem house. When Jesus on the Cross put his mother (probably John's aunt) into John's care, John took Mary into his household "from that hour" (John 19:26–27). If John's only house was in Galilee, he might not have been able to take Mary into his household "from that hour." A household in Jerusalem as well as in Galilee implies some wealth. Of course, Jesus might have been using the word "household" figuratively, meaning John took Mary into his "care." But this, together with the Nicodemus clue, is suggestive of his having a Jerusalem home.

The fact that John had the leisure to leave his business, observe the Fall Pilgrimage to Jerusalem, and to enroll as the Baptist's disciple in AD 29 further suggests that John had means. Of course, every faithful Jew should have observed the pilgrimage feasts, and each year millions did; but the Jewish population represented ten percent of the Roman Empire at that time. If all of them had come on pilgrimage to Jerusalem, their numbers would have been about 4.5 million,[2] not the 2.7 million that Josephus recorded on one Passover.[3] And if we include the Jewish population outside the Roman Empire, in Babylon, Parthia, Ethiopia, and India, the number would have been even greater. So, clearly, many Jews lacked the means or the will to observe the pilgrimages the way John did.

JOHN'S HUMILITY

In his gospel, John mentions two disciples following John the Baptist, specifying one of them, Andrew, and leaving the other unnamed (John 1:40). This literary technique of referring to himself obliquely is consistent in John's accounts, so John is almost certainly the unnamed other disciple. In a further demonstration of modesty, John did not give himself or his brother, James, any speaking part in his gospel; only the synoptic

---

2. Using ten percent of the estimated total population of the empire, "Roman Empire Population," *UNRV Roman History*.

3. Josephus, *Jewish War*, 6:9:3.

gospels record speeches by the sons of Zebedee. This humility is striking because John was prominent in the history of Jesus. He was a business partner of Peter and Andrew and was almost certainly the cousin of John the Baptist and of Jesus.[4] Even if he was not related, John probably knew most of Jesus' disciples from childhood.

Peter, Andrew, James, and John were Jesus' inmost circle, especially Peter, James, and John. These three alone were allowed to witness the miracle of raising Jairus' daughter. They alone were present at the Transfiguration. They witnessed Jesus' agony in the Garden of Gethsemane and failed him by falling asleep. Jesus sent only John and Peter into Jerusalem to prepare the Last Supper (Luke 22:8). At the Last Supper, the place of John, the disciple Jesus loved, was next to Jesus. John was probably also that "other disciple" who with Peter followed Christ after his arrest into the palace of the High Priest (John 18:15–16). Modest as he was, perhaps John's referring to himself as the disciple that Jesus loved was a bit of veiled self-praise.

The world-shaking phenomena of Christ's ministry were arising out of John's small family and business circle. He had connections to brag about. Yet he and all the other apostles made no attempt (after the Resurrection) to establish a "Jesus elite" with themselves as celebrities. They never claimed Jesus' legacy as a family dynasty, as the leaders of other prominent families, like that of the High Priest Ananias (Annas), promoted their legacies. Daniel foretold four worldly empires that a fifth eternal empire would succeed (Dan 2:44, 7:27). This was the Kingdom of God that Jesus said was at hand (Matt 4:17, Mark 1:15) and which the apostles labored to serve. The apostles grasped the divine meaning of Christ's work. They served, suffered, and died, not to aggrandize themselves, but to bring the Word to the world.

AT THE CROSS

John alone remained near his Master at the foot of the Cross with the mother of Jesus (his aunt) and the other women from Galilee, including John's mother, Mary Salome (Matt 27:56, Mark 15:40, John 19:25). Peter had denied Jesus and had run away. All the other disciples, including John's brother, James, had also abandoned him (Matt 26:56, Mark 14:50). Jesus' Roman executioners gambled for his clothes, physically

---

4. See "Relationships in Jesus' Community" at www.thebiblehistoryguy.com.

tormented him, and jeered as he hung in indescribable agony for hours. Yet when Jesus looked down from the Cross, he could take comfort in the sight of one man courageous and affectionate enough to be there, "the disciple that Jesus loved."

No wonder Peter felt so troubled when Jesus asked him three times after the Resurrection if Peter loved him. Only one man and four named women had braved the wrath of Rome and the High Priest to kneel in devotion at the Cross. No wonder Jesus said to his grieving mother, "Woman, behold your son!" and then to John, "Behold your mother" (John 19:26–27). In Mary's household were at least seven other children, four boys and (at least) three unnamed girls (Matt 13:55–56, Mark 6:3). Two of the boys, James and Judas, would become prominent disciples of their half-brother Jesus, the Messiah. They would each write a book in the New Testament (James and Jude). But it was to the faithful and beloved John that Jesus consigned his precious mother. From that hour, John took this helpless, shattered widow into his household (John 19:27).

Jesus' choice for Mary's protector was logical since John was probably Mary's nephew, was probably Jesus' cousin, probably had a household in Jerusalem, was probably wealthy, and was destined to outlive all the other apostles except Simon the Zealot. There are two traditions: (1) John took Mary with him to Ephesus when he became bishop there, and she died in Ephesus, and (2) Mary lived in John's household in Jerusalem until her death there. Since neither tradition is certain, two locations, one at Ephesus and one at Jerusalem, are venerated today as the place of Mary's death.

AFTER THE RESURRECTION

John, with Peter, was the first of the disciples to hasten to Jesus' tomb and to believe that Christ truly had risen.

> Now on the first day of the week Mary Magdalene came to the tomb early, while it was still dark, and saw that the stone had been taken away from the tomb. So she ran and went to Simon Peter and the other disciple, the one whom Jesus loved, and said to them, "They have taken the Lord out of the tomb, and we do not know where they have laid him." So Peter went out with the other disciple, and they were going toward the tomb. Both of them were running together, but the other disciple outran Peter and reached the tomb first. And stooping to look in, he saw the

> linen cloths lying there, but he did not go in. Then Simon Peter came, following him, and went into the tomb. He saw the linen cloths lying there, and the face cloth, which had been on Jesus' head, not lying with the linen cloths but folded up in a place by itself. Then the other disciple, who had reached the tomb first, also went in, and he saw and believed (John 20:1–8).

John reveals an amusing competitiveness by reporting that he beat Peter to the tomb. This recalls his asking, along with his brother James, to sit at Jesus' right and left hand when Christ should come into his kingdom. But John's recording of Peter's courage to enter the tomb first, while John held back, shows that this Son of Thunder had learned some humility. Nevertheless, John stated that he believed at once, perhaps suggesting that Peter did not yet believe the evidence of his eyes. When later Christ appeared at the Sea of Galilee, John was the first of the seven disciples to recognize the Master he loved standing on the shore.

> After this Jesus revealed himself again to the disciples by the Sea of Tiberias, and he revealed himself in this way. Simon Peter, Thomas (called the Twin), Nathanael of Cana in Galilee, the sons of Zebedee, and two others of his disciples were together. Simon Peter said to them, "I am going fishing." They said to him, "We will go with you." They went out and got into the boat, but that night they caught nothing. Just as day was breaking, Jesus stood on the shore; yet the disciples did not know that it was Jesus. Jesus said to them, "Children, do you have any fish?" They answered him, "No." He said to them, "Cast the net on the right side of the boat, and you will find some." So they cast it, and now they were not able to haul it in, because of the quantity of fish. That disciple whom Jesus loved therefore said to Peter, "It is the Lord!" When Simon Peter heard that it was the Lord, he put on his outer garment, for he was stripped for work, and threw himself into the sea. The other disciples came in the boat, dragging the net full of fish, for they were not far from the land, but about a hundred yards off. When they got out on land, they saw a charcoal fire in place, with fish laid out on it and bread. Jesus said to them, "Bring some of the fish that you have just caught." So Simon Peter went aboard and hauled the net ashore, full of large fish, 153 of them. And although there were so many, the net was not torn. Jesus said to them, "Come and have breakfast." Now none of the disciples dared ask him, "Who are you?" They knew it was the Lord. Jesus came and took the bread and gave it to them, and so with the fish. This

was now the third time that Jesus was revealed to the disciples after he was raised from the dead (John 21:1–14).

John showed how close his relationship was to his Lord and Master by the title with which he was accustomed to indicating himself: "the disciple whom Jesus loved." John the Apostle and Lazarus were probably Jesus' best friends during his earthly ministry (John 11:11, 33, 35, 13:23, 20:2, 21:7, 20).

JOHN'S LEADERSHIP

John was, with Andrew, the first of the disciples to follow Jesus (John 1:35–37). He was present in the Upper Room on Resurrection Sunday, was in the Upper Room with Thomas present on the following Monday, was at Jesus' Ascension, was at the choosing of Matthias, was at the birth of the Church on the day of Pentecost in AD 33, helped Peter evangelize Samaria, was, with Peter and James (Jesus' half-brother) in Jerusalem to give Paul the right hand of fellowship in AD 47, and was at the Jerusalem Council in AD 49.

ARREST

After Christ's Ascension and the descent of the Holy Spirit on Pentecost, John, together with Peter, took a prominent role in leading the Church. He was there when Peter healed the lame beggar at the Beautiful Gate (Acts 3:1–10). The Sadducees threw Peter and John into prison for "teaching the people and proclaiming in Jesus the Resurrection from the dead" (Acts 4:2). John, with Peter, defied them and continued to preach with authority and courage.

> Now when they saw the boldness of Peter and John, and perceived that they were uneducated, common men, they were astonished. And they recognized that they had been with Jesus. But seeing the man who was healed standing beside them, they had nothing to say in opposition. But when they had commanded them to leave the council, they conferred with one another, saying, "What shall we do with these men? For that a notable sign has been performed through them is evident to all the inhabitants of Jerusalem, and we cannot deny it. But in order that it may spread no further among the people, let us

warn them to speak no more to anyone in this name." So they called them and charged them not to speak or teach at all in the name of Jesus. But Peter and John answered them, "Whether it is right in the sight of God to listen to you rather than to God, you must judge, for we cannot but speak of what we have seen and heard." And when they had further threatened them, they let them go, finding no way to punish them, because of the people, for all were praising God for what had happened. For the man on whom this sign of healing was performed was more than forty years old. When they were released, they went to their friends and reported what the Chief Priests and the elders had said to them (Acts 4:13–23).

SAMARIA

The apostles sent John with Peter to investigate Philip's astonishing conversion of the reviled Samaritans to Christ.

> Now when the apostles at Jerusalem heard that Samaria had received the word of God, they sent to them Peter and John, who came down and prayed for them that they might receive the Holy Spirit, for he had not yet fallen on any of them, but they had only been baptized in the name of the Lord Jesus. Then they laid their hands on them and they received the Holy Spirit (Acts 8:14–17).

This was ironic, since James and John, the Sons of Thunder, had asked Jesus to let them call fire from heaven down upon the Samaritan villages that rejected Jesus (Luke 9:54).

IN THE JERUSALEM CHURCH

We have no positive information about how long after the Resurrection John remained in Judaea. He was in Jerusalem in AD 47, when Paul met him there and called him, along with Peter and James (the half-brother of Jesus) pillars of the church (Gal 2:7–10). John agreed with Paul at this time that the Greek Christian, Titus, did not need to be circumcised. He also agreed that Paul was a true apostle, and he gave him the right hand of fellowship. John was almost certainly at the Jerusalem Council, AD 49, because Scripture tells us that the apostles and elders presided, and the term "apostles" probably included all Eleven, minus John's deceased brother, James (Acts 15:4).

THE GREAT COMMISSION

John doubtless obeyed Jesus' Great Commission (Matt 28:19), and therefore he probably left Judaea and evangelized somewhere. Eventually John ended up as the leader of the church in Ephesus.[5] Since Paul planted the first seeds of the Ephesian church in AD 51 (Acts 18:19) and last met with the Ephesian leaders in AD 54 (Acts 20:17), and since Scripture makes no mention of John's presence there while Paul was there, John probably went to Ephesus after AD 54. That leaves at least five years of John's life, from the Jerusalem Council in AD 49 until AD 54, unaccounted for. He probably went somewhere to evangelize. His three epistles and Revelation suggest that John was well acquainted with conditions in the various Christian communities around Ephesus, and Eusebius says he governed churches all across that region.[6] From Ephesus, later in life, John probably went to Rome, because Jerome says the emperor Domitian banished him to the island of Patmos in AD 94, which suggests he was exiled there from Rome.[7]

DOMITIAN'S PERSECUTION OF JOHN

The apocryphal *Acts of John*[8] says that the Roman emperor Domitian (the younger son of Vespasian), who reigned from AD 81–96, persecuted the Jews. The Jews wrote a letter to Domitian, complaining of the Christians, and, accordingly, Domitian persecuted them. Eusebius wrote that Tertullian confirmed the cruel, general persecution of Christians under Domitian.[9] Hearing of John's teaching in Ephesus, the emperor summoned John to Rome. On his voyage to Italy, John's ascetic habits impressed his captors.

When John appeared before Domitian, the emperor commanded him to drink poison. John drank some of it. It had no effect on him.

---

5. Eusebius, *Church History*, 3:1:1, 20:11, 23:4, 6.
6. Eusebius, *Church History*, 3:23:1
7. Jerome, *On Illustrious Men*.
8. *The Acts of John*.
9. Eusebius, *Church History*, 3:17.

Jesus had said that when his followers would "drink any deadly poison, it [would] not hurt them" (Mark 16:18). Suspecting that the drink did not contain enough poison, Domitian experimentally forced a criminal to drink the rest of the cup. The criminal died, but John revived him. This is why the early Church used the symbol of a chalice with a snake slithering from it as John's emblem. The snake represented the Satanic power of poison leaking from the cup. After this, John also raised a Roman girl to life who had been slain by an unclean spirit.

Domitian then tried to kill John by immersing him in boiling oil. The Church of *San Giovanni in Olio* (Saint John in Oil) in Rome commemorates the event. The apostle survived lengthy immersion in the boiling oil without being burned, preaching all the while to his would-be executioners. Domitian concluded that he was dealing with some powerful magician and so he banished John to the island of Patmos, not far from John's hometown of Ephesus.[10] Tertullian, the third-century Church Father, wrote, "The apostle John was first plunged, unhurt, into boiling oil, and thence remitted to his island exile."[11] Jerome claims that John's exile was in AD 94.[12]

SHIPWRECK

After Domitian's death, his successor, the emperor Nerva, freed John from Patmos.[13] On his homeward journey, John was shipwrecked. He survived by floating on a piece of cork. He made landfall at Miletus[14] and then returned to Ephesus.[15]

CERINTHUS

Polycarp, John's disciple and successor as bishop of Ephesus, recorded that John once entered a public bath, where he learned that a notorious glutton, sexual pervert, and pagan, Cerinthus, was within.

---

10. *The Golden Legend*, "Chapter 9: On St. John the Apostle and Evangelist."
11. Tertullian, *Prescription Against Heresies*, Chapter 36.
12. Jerome, *On Illustrious Men*.
13. Eusebius, *Church History*, 3:20:9–10
14. *The Acts of John*.
15. Orosius, *Histories Against the Pagans*, 7:11

John sprang from the place and rushed out of the door, for he could not bear to remain under the same roof with him. And he advised those that were with him to do the same, saying, "Let us flee, lest the bath fall; for Cerinthus, the enemy of the truth, is within."[16]

JOHN'S LAST DAYS

Jerome recorded that John, as an old man, had to be carried to church in Ephesus by the elders. At these meetings, he used to say nothing more than, "Little children, love each other." After a while, the disciples were tired of always hearing the same words and asked, "Master, why do you always say this?" John replied, "It is the Lord's command. And if this alone be done, it is enough."[17]

JOHN'S DEATH

Jerome wrote that in Ephesus John continued to found and build churches across Asia Minor, until, worn out by old age, he died in AD 98.[18] He must have been in his nineties. Jesus had foretold that John would live a long life and die a natural death (John 21:22–23). He lived into the reign of the emperor Trajan (AD 98–117).[19] Hippolytus wrote that Simon the Zealot died at the age of 120 years.[20] If so, he, and not John, was the longest-lived apostle.

THE GOSPEL OF JOHN

It is said that Matthew wrote his gospel to the Jews, Luke to the Gentiles, and John to the world. Eusebius wrote:

16. Eusebius, *Church History*, 3:28:6.
17. Jerome, *Commentary on Galatians*, 6.
18. Jerome, *On Illustrious Men*. Jerome calculates this date, assuming that it was sixty-eight years after Jesus' Crucifixion. Jerome consistently makes the erroneous assumption that the Crucifixion was in AD 30. It was definitely in AD 33 because in all the years from AD 29–33, Passover fell on a Friday only in AD 33, and Jesus was crucified on Passover Friday. Correcting for Jerome's error yields the date of AD 98.
19. Eusebius, *Church History*, 3:23:3.
20. Hippolytus, *List of the Apostles and Disciples*.

> When Mark and Luke had already published their gospels, they say that John, who had employed all his time in proclaiming the Gospel orally, finally proceeded to write for the following reason. The three gospels already mentioned having come into the hands of all and into his own too, they say that he accepted them and bore witness to their truthfulness; but that there was lacking in them an account of the deeds done by Christ at the beginning of his ministry . . . John, accordingly, in his gospel, records the deeds of Christ which were performed before the Baptist was cast into prison, but the other three evangelists mention the events which happened after that time.[21]

According to the third-century Christian writer Gaius, John's fellow disciples and bishops entreated him to write his gospel. John replied, "Fast with me for three days. What may be revealed to any of us, let us reveal it to each other." That same night, Andrew had a revelation that John was to write an account of Christ under his own name, and so he did.[22] If this is correct, and if Andrew died in the Neronian persecution of AD 64, this event occurred no later than that year. Mark wrote his gospel in AD 43, the year Peter founded the church in Rome. Matthew wrote his gospel around AD 49. Luke composed his gospel between AD 49–59. John may have composed his gospel between AD 59–64, a mere twenty-six to thirty-one years after the Resurrection. Certainly, John composed it before AD 70, since it, like Revelation, makes no mention of Rome destroying the Temple.

This would explain why John's gospel contains different material than the others and takes a different point of view and tone. For this reason, the gospels of Matthew, Mark, and Luke are called synoptic, that is, "seeing with a single eye," while the fourth gospel looks at Jesus' ministry through another lens. For example, only John records Jesus' first miracle, turning water into wine at the wedding in Cana (John 2:11), Jesus' first cleansing of the Temple (John 2:15), and the story of Nicodemus' secret, nocturnal interview with Jesus (John 3:1–2), which probably occurred in John's house. This is the sort of material to which the other gospel writers could not have been eyewitnesses and which John would have wanted to hand down.

John's gospel is also rich in time markers regarding Jesus' early ministry. This suggests a book written soon after the events because it

---

21. Eusebius, *Church History*, 3:24:7–12.
22. *Muratorian Canon*, Fragment III.

would have been difficult to recall all the dates and make no mistakes many years later.

THE PERICOPE OF ADULTERY

Only John's gospel narrates the story of the adulterous woman whom the Jewish leaders dragged before Jesus for stoning (John 7:53–8:11). This passage is known as the "Pericope of Adultery" or the passage on adultery. The story also fits well with events in John's gospel that surround it. It occurred at the end of the Feast of Tabernacles in AD 31. On the last day of the Feast, many people believed in Jesus, wondering aloud, "When the Christ appears, will he do more signs than this man has done?" (John 7:31). The Temple officers reported to the Pharisees that they had tried but were unable to seize Jesus. Jesus proclaimed in the Temple that he was the source of living water. Nicodemus defended Jesus. The other Pharisees rebuked Nicodemus, stating that no prophet comes from Galilee.[23] The scribes and Pharisees were frustrated and angry and itching to find a way to trap Jesus once and for all.

Everyone went to their homes, but Jesus went to the Mount of Olives (John 8:1). Jesus returned to the Temple early the next morning to teach. The scribes and Pharisees had apparently been conspiring all night and had managed to capture a woman in the act of adultery (John 8:3). Perhaps one of their number had committed that act. They dragged her before Jesus bright and early to accuse her and ensnare him. Jesus heard their accusations without comment. He bent down and wrote something in the dust with his finger. As they persisted in accusing the woman, Jesus rose and said, "Let him who is without sin among you be the first to throw a stone at her." Then he bent down again and continued to write on the ground. When they heard this, the woman's accusers melted away, one by one, leaving Jesus and the woman alone. "Has no one condemned you?" asked Jesus. "No one, Lord," she replied. "Neither do I condemn you," said Jesus. "From now on sin no more." There are many fanciful conjectures about what Jesus wrote in the dust, but the Bible simply does not say.

The earliest surviving Greek manuscripts do not contain the Pericope, causing some scholars to consider it inauthentic. However, in 1941

---

23. In this the Pharisees displayed their faulty knowledge of Scripture, for Jonah came from Gath-hepher, two miles from Nazareth, and Nahum may have given his name to Capernaum, "Town of Nahum."

a large collection of the writings of Didymus the Blind (ca. AD 313–398) was discovered in Egypt. These refer to the Pericope's being found in several copies of John's gospel. Thus, the Pericope was present in its usual place in some Greek manuscripts known in Alexandria and elsewhere from the fourth century onwards. The fourth-century Codex Vaticanus, written in Egypt, marks the end of John chapter 7 with an umlaut (¨), indicating that an alternative reading was known at this point. Jerome reported that the Pericope was to be found in its usual place in "many Greek and Latin manuscripts" in Rome and the Latin West in the late Fourth Century. He included it in his Vulgate (Latin) translation of the Bible, which the Council of Trent pronounced authentic. Some Latin Fathers of the fourth and fifth Centuries, including Ambrose and Augustine, confirmed this view. Augustine claimed that the passage may have been wrongly excluded from some manuscripts to avoid the impression that Jesus sanctioned adultery.

> Certain persons of little faith, or rather enemies of the true faith, fearing, I suppose, lest their wives should be given impunity in sinning, removed from their manuscripts the Lord's act of forgiveness toward the adulteress, as if he who had said, "Sin no more," had granted permission to sin.[24]

Several early Church Fathers quoted parts of this passage, apparently considering it genuine. C.S. Lewis also noted that the detail of Jesus writing in the dust has the distinct feeling of an eyewitness account.

So, the argument against the authenticity of this passage is that it is not in the earliest and most reliable manuscripts. The arguments for the authenticity of the passage are (1) it is in some early manuscripts, (2) early Church Fathers quoted verses from this passage as genuine, (3) some respected Church Fathers defended the whole passage as genuine, (4) the passage contains no contradiction of the rest of Scripture, (5) the passage is consistent with the character of Jesus, his critics, and with those whom he touched with love, (6) the passage fits neatly into the surrounding narrative in John's gospel, and (7) the passage seems stylistically genuine. The arguments for the authenticity of the Pericope therefore outweigh the arguments against.

It may be that the Pericope was part of John's original sermon notes. He may have preached the story often. He may have excluded it from the first edition of his published gospel, thinking the story a bit too racy.

---

24. Augustine, *De Adulterinis Conjugiis* 2:6–7.

Others may have reassured him of the story's theological value and persuaded him to add it back in.

THE HARMONY OF THE FOUR GOSPELS

Although the gospels of Matthew, Mark, and Luke are synoptic, "seeing with agreeing eyes" or "having the same point of view," this does not mean that John's gospel contradicts them. The four gospels contain no contradictions. They offer supplementary details. For example, Matthew recorded one angel at Jesus' tomb (Matt 28:2). Luke recorded two, of which only one spoke (Luke 24:4–7).[25] This is not a contradiction, but an additional supporting detail. If two angels were there, of course, there had to be one. Additive and non-contradictory details strengthen the gospels' credibility. If all four gospels were identical, they would simply be copies. Since the gospels contain differences, but no contradictions, they act as independent, corroborating witnesses. While the whole Bible is provably true, we have only one witness of the Torah, Moses, whereas we have multiple witnesses of Jesus' life: Matthew, Mark, Luke, and John, not to mention the contents of Acts and the epistles.

If the evangelists had decided to invent the story of Jesus and devise clever lies about his miracles, it would have been difficult to keep all their accounts in perfect accord. In today's electronic media, different reports of current events not only disagree on many facts but also often miss the basic truth. This happens both accidentally and on account of deliberate bias. It is also true about non-inspired books from the ancient world. The miraculous integrity of Scripture is one of the reasons that we can know the Bible is divine, rather than only human, in origin. Its reliability is more than remarkable; it is unique in the record of human achievement. Billions of written words throughout history prove amply that human authors simply cannot achieve a comparably harmonious testimony, however hard they try.

Ancient writers, especially Hebrew writers, sometimes wrote chronologically and sometimes topically out of chronological order. An example is the anthology of parables in Matthew 13. Did Jesus tell all these parables in one sitting? Maybe. But Jesus probably repeated them over several years to help his disciples remember them. The literary style

---

25. It is true that the manuscript says of the angels that "they said" εἶπαν πρὸς, *eipan pros*, to the women, but it is absurd to imagine that the two angels spoke the same words at the same time like the chorus in a Greek play.

of Matthew 13 feels like the author decided to collect many parables with complementary meanings in one place.

One example of an apparent conflict between the gospels is the telling of Jesus ejecting the money changers from the Temple. John places this event early in Jesus' ministry, while Matthew and Luke place it on Jesus' triumphal entry to Jerusalem, and Mark places it on the Monday after Palm Sunday. This is not a contradiction. Jesus cleansed the Temple three times, first during the first Passover of Jesus' ministry, Thursday, April 4, AD 30 (John 2:15), second on Palm Sunday, March 27, AD 33 (Matt 21:12, Luke 19:45), and third on the Monday following Palm Sunday, March 28, AD 33 (Mark 11:15). No wonder the Jewish leaders were upset with him! The Temple money-changing business was largely in the hands of the family of Ananias (Annas), the defrocked High Priest, and Joseph Caiaphas, the High Priest, who was Ananias' son-in-law. Jesus repeatedly wrecked their affairs and further inflamed their desire to get Pilate to kill Jesus.

The synoptic evangelists included time markers in their gospels but to a lesser extent than John. Today, we can use computer programs to compare the biblical time markers to Jewish festival dates, astronomical events, and the Roman calendar of the first century. It is nothing short of miraculous when one considers that the gospel writers achieved perfect accuracy with none of our sophisticated computer tools. They had memory, honesty, and the inspiration of the Holy Spirit, and they never, not even once, got a date wrong. If we can rely on John's precision with respect to ordinary events, we can rely on his reporting of Jesus' supernatural works, like the raising of Lazarus from the dead.[26]

THE APOSTLE OF LOVE AND THE NEW COMMANDMENT

John has earned the title "the Apostle of Love" because so much of his writing emphasizes God's love (John 3:16, 14:21, 23, 15:9, 12, 21:17, 1 John 4:7, 11, 12, 18, 19, 20, 5:2). In the gospel of John, Jesus said "A new commandment I give to you, that you love one another. Just as I have loved you, you also are to love one another. By this all people will know that you are my disciples if you have love for one another" (John

---

26. Jesus raised three people from the dead: Jairus' daughter (Matt 9:25, Mark 5:42, Luke 8:55), a widow's son (Luke 7:15), and Lazarus (John 11:44).

13:34–35). John also recorded this statement by Jesus: "Greater love has no one than this, that someone lay down his life for his friends" (John 15:13). Finally, John took the concept of love to its apotheosis when he wrote, "God is love" (1 John 4:16).

REVELATION: AUTHORSHIP

Some controversy exists about whether John wrote Revelation (also called the Apocalypse or the "Unveiling"). One reason for doubting that John was its author is the uneven style of the Greek writing compared to the smooth simplicity of John's gospel and epistles. Revelation seems grammatically loose, whereas the other writings of John are polished. One German scholar, Ludwig Radermacher, wrote that Revelation is "the most uncultured literary production that has come down to us from antiquity." Of course, if we consider book sales, John's "uncultured" work has swamped the demand for Radermacher's *Neuetestamentliche Grammatik*, which is now out of print.[27] Most modern critics did not grow up from childhood speaking, reading, and writing Greek, whereas most of the writers of the apostolic and patristic eras did. If those Greek speakers did not find the style of Revelation and of John's other writings too different to have come from the same pen, the sensibilities of modern scholars may be too delicate. Nevertheless, the Greek in Revelation and even its style in English strain common literary form. The fourth gospel and John's epistles display a simple poise very different from Revelation's breathless, reckless style. But this is not a conclusive argument for authorship other than John's. John may not have been a very good Greek writer. His first language may have been Aramaic, not Greek. He may have used a scribe to take down and edit his gospel and letters, while perhaps no such help was available to him when he composed Revelation. Or perhaps the wild intensity of the visions in Revelation caused John to create a veritable grammar of his own.

Moreover, Revelation's author identifies himself simply as "John" (Rev 1:1, 4, 9, 22:1). Who else, in the early days of the Church, could expect everyone to recognize him simply by calling himself "John?" The early Church Fathers, Justin Martyr, Irenaeus, Clement of Alexandria, and Tertullian unanimously identified the author of Revelation as John, the son of Zebedee, the apostle. And the only books in the New Testament

---

27. In 2016, Gideon's alone sold an estimated 100 Bibles per minute, *WordsRated*.

that refer to Jesus as the Word and the Lamb of God are the Gospel of John and Revelation, further evidence of singular authorship.

THE DATE OF REVELATION

The two main theories about when John wrote Revelation are that John wrote it when he was exiled to Patmos during the reign of the emperor Domitian, around AD 96,[28] or that he wrote it during Nero's persecution of Christians, from AD 64–68.[29] If the first theory is true, John wrote Revelation after the fall of the Second Temple in AD 70. If the second theory is true, John wrote Revelation before the Temple's fall.

John stated that he saw the Revelation in the following circumstances:

> I, John, your brother and partner in the tribulation and the kingdom and the patient endurance that are in Jesus, was on the island called Patmos on account of the word of God and the testimony of Jesus. I was in the Spirit on the Lord's Day, and I heard behind me a loud voice like a trumpet (Rev 1:9–10).

John clearly saw the Revelation on Patmos, but did he see it earlier than his exile there (before the Temple's fall) or during his exile there by Domitian (after the Temple's fall)?

A significant clue is offered by Irenaeus, a Greek bishop who grew up in Turkey and moved to Lyon, France, in the second century. He wrote about John and the composition of Revelation in his book *Against Heresies*, 5:30:3.[30] The original passage from Irenaeus does not survive, but Eusebius, the fourth-century church historian (died AD 339), quoted it in Greek:

> [The Roman Emperor] Domitian, having shown great cruelty toward many, and having unjustly put to death no small number of well-born and notable men at Rome, and having without cause exiled and confiscated the property of a great many other illustrious men, finally became a successor of Nero in his hatred and enmity toward God. He was, in fact, the second that stirred up a persecution against us, although his father Vespasian had undertaken nothing prejudicial to us. It is said that in this persecution the apostle and evangelist John, who was

---

28. Schnabel, et al., *Revelation*, 17.
29. Schnabel, et al., *Revelation*, 14.
30. Schnabel, et al., *Revelation*, 13.

still alive, was condemned to dwell on the island of Patmos in consequence of his testimony to the divine word. Irenaeus, in the fifth book of his work *Against Heresies,* where he discusses the number of the name of Antichrist, which is given in the so-called Apocalypse of John,[31] speaks as follows concerning him: if it were necessary for his name to be proclaimed openly at the present time, it would have been declared by him who saw the Revelation. For it was seen not long ago, but almost in our own generation, at the end of the reign of Domitian. To such a degree, indeed, did the teaching of our faith flourish at that time that even those writers who were far from our religion did not hesitate to mention in their histories the persecution and the martyrdoms which took place during it. And they, indeed, accurately indicated the time. For they recorded that in the fifteenth year of Domitian Flavia Domitilla, daughter of a sister of Flavius Clement, who at that time was one of the consuls of Rome, was exiled with many others to the island of Pontia in consequence of testimony borne to Christ.[32]

Eusebius quotes Irenaeus elsewhere about Revelation, as follows:

He speaks as follows concerning the Apocalypse of John and the number of the name of Antichrist:[33] as these things are so, and this number is found in all the approved and ancient copies, and those who saw John face to face confirm it, and reason teaches us that the number of the name of the beast, according to the mode of calculation among the Greeks, appears in its letters....we are not bold enough to speak confidently of the name of Antichrist. For if it were necessary that his name should be declared clearly at the present time, it would have been announced by him who saw the revelation. For it was seen not long ago, but almost in our generation, toward the end of the reign of Domitian.[34]

---

31. Eusebius says that Irenaeus "discusses the number of the name of Antichrist, which is given in the so-called Apocalypse of John." Possibly Irenaeus did discuss this, but John did not declare in Revelation who the Antichrist was because John never mentioned any Antichrist in Revelation. The number 666 (Rev 13:18) pertained to the name of a man who was symbolically portrayed as a beast. That may qualify him to fit John's definition of an antichrist (1 John 2:18, 22, 4:3, 2 John 1:7), but John neither said so in Revelation nor did he ever teach that there was only one Antichrist. While he said that there was an antichrist coming, he said that there were already many antichrists and that they were not future persons but were then currently in the world (1 John 2:18).

32. Eusebius, *Church History,* 3:17–18.

33. Again, Revelation makes no mention of The Antichrist or any antichrist.

34. Eusebius, *Church History,* 5:8:5–6.

These passages tell us the following things: (1) Emperor Domitian persecuted John, (2) he exiled John to Patmos, (3) "it" was seen not long ago, at the end of the reign of Domitian (AD 81–96), (4) in Irenaeus' day there were ancient copies of the book of Revelation extant.

The key question is: what was the "it" seen not long ago, the Revelation or John? The phrase "it was seen" in English is a single word in Greek: ἑωράθη, *eorathi*. The referent of this verb (the thing noun refers back to) can be "he, she, or it." Thus, Irenaeus may mean that the Revelation was seen at the end of Domitian's reign, or he may mean that John was seen at the end of Domitian's reign.

In Italy, Domitian tried to kill John by poison. When that failed, he tried to kill him by immersing him in boiling oil. When that failed, he sent him into exile on Patmos (see above). However, John said he saw the Revelation on Patmos but did not say when he saw it there. He did, however, say why he was there when he saw it. It was "on account of the word of God and the testimony of Jesus." He did not say at the time of writing Revelation that he was in exile or imprisoned on Patmos.

Patmos is an island in the Aegean Sea, a mere 120 miles from John's home church of Ephesus, less than one day's sailing away.[35] It is easy to imagine that over the many times John must have sailed to and from Ephesus on missionary journeys, the ships on which he hitched a ride put into Skala, Patmos' main port, to transfer cargo and passengers. Spreading the word of God and testifying about Jesus was John's vocation as an apostle. He did not need to be exiled to Patmos to evangelize the island. If John did live into the reign of the emperor Domitian, who was assassinated in AD 96, John had perhaps sixty-three years from the Year of the Cross, AD 33, till Domitian's death to visit Patmos. John, therefore, could have been on Patmos earlier than AD 96 and could have seen the Revelation then. His exile to Patmos, which occurred at a later date, may have been long after he wrote Revelation.[36] Irenaeus' phrase is, at best, ambiguous and cannot be used to prove conclusively that John saw the Revelation in the reign of Domitian.

A phrase that leaps out in Irenaeus is "those who saw John face to face." This tends to support the interpretation of the first quotation from Irenaeus, above, that what "was seen" not long ago "in the reign of Domitian" was John, not John's vision, the Revelation.

---

35. "Orbis," *The Stanford Geospatial Model of the Roman World*.
36. Elwell, *Encountering the New Testament*, 358.

Irenaeus also mentioned ancient copies of Revelation extant in his day. Irenaeus lived from about AD 130–202. If he were writing at the midpoint of his life, around AD 170, and were referring to "ancient" copies of Revelation composed toward the end of the reign of Domitian, AD 96, his definition of "ancient" would have meant copies only seventy-four years old, within living memory. In the same passage, Irenaeus says that the end of the reign of Domitian was "not long ago." How could a copy of Revelation be ancient if it were composed "not long ago?" If, by contrast, John wrote Revelation in AD 68, its oldest copies would have been about 102 years old if Irenaeus wrote this in AD 170. Any copy older than a century is better described as "ancient" than a copy that is less than a century old. Therefore, the phrase "it was seen not long ago" probably means "John was seen not long ago," not that "the Revelation was seen not long ago." John did not, therefore, necessarily write Revelation in the reign of Domitian.

There is another reason why it is likely that John wrote Revelation before AD 70, the date when the Roman general Titus destroyed Jerusalem and the Second Temple. This is the same overriding reason why probably every New Testament book was written before this event. The destruction of the Temple was not only a cataclysm for all Jews, but it was also an event specifically prophesied by Jesus.

> And as he came out of the temple, one of his disciples said to him, "Look, Teacher, what wonderful stones and what wonderful buildings!" And Jesus said to him, "Do you see these great buildings? There will not be left here one stone upon another that will not be thrown down" (Mark 13:1–2).

False witnesses at Jesus' trial used this prophecy (although twisting it) as a charge against him.

> Now the chief priests and the whole Council were seeking false testimony against Jesus that they might put him to death, but they found none, though many false witnesses came forward. At last, two came forward and said, "This man said, 'I am able to destroy the temple of God and to rebuild it in three days.'" And the high priest stood up and said, "Have you no answer to make? What is it that these men testify against you?" (Matt 26:59–62).

Onlookers at the Cross mocked Jesus about this prophecy. "Those who passed by derided him, wagging their heads, and saying, 'You who would destroy the temple and rebuild it in three days, save yourself! If you are the Son of God, come down from the cross.'" (Matt 27:40).

If any inspired Christian author had written any of the New Testament books after Jesus' prophecy was fulfilled in AD 70, surely that author would have pointed out that Jesus' prophecy had come true. They would have seized upon this fact as powerful proof of Christ's authority. And failing to mention the destruction of Jerusalem and the Temple in any book about Judaea after AD 70 would be like writing a history of World War II without mentioning Pearl Harbor or writing a history of New York City without mentioning 9/11.

The thesis of the earlier date for Revelation. John called himself "your brother and partner in the tribulation" (Rev 1:9). If by tribulation he meant the suffering the Jews inflicted on Christians, he was a brother in it indeed, for Herod Agrippa I killed his brother James in AD 44. From AD 64–68, John knew that many Christians were dying at the hands of Nero simply for their faith. He was also a partaker of the tribulation if that tribulation meant the Neronian persecution.

To be caught with a Christian text in the years when Christianity was illegal was a mortal risk. The only way Christians in Nero's Rome could safely communicate their faith was in code. Revelation is rich in symbols that those who knew the Old Testament could interpret but that pagan Roman officers, untutored in Jewish lore, could not. This is especially true of the code name 666. Of it, John wrote, "This calls for wisdom: let the one who has understanding calculate the number of the Beast, for it is the number of a man, and his number is 666" (Rev 13:18). The number of the Beast equals the name of a man. The man is Nero Caesar, Emperor of Rome.

In ancient languages, including Hebrew, Greek, and Latin, letters of the alphabet have numerical equivalents. This number-letter equivalency is called Gematria. If, for example, we assign letters to the English alphabet as follows: A=1, B=2, C=3, etc., then my name, JIM, would have these numerical equivalents: J=10, I=9, M=13. My Gematria code name may be rendered 10+9+13 = 32.

John wrote Revelation in Greek, but he spoke Aramaic and probably Hebrew, too. The Greek version of Nero Caesar transliterates into Hebrew as *Nron Qsr*, נרון קסר, and yields a numerical value of 666, as shown (read right to left):

Sum	Resh (ר)	Samekh (ס)	Qoph (ק)	Nun (נ)	Vav (ו)	Resh (ר)	Nun (נ)
666	200	60	100	50	6	200	50

Some ancient manuscripts of Revelation say, "His number is 616." This is probably a scribal error, but even such an error proves the identity of Nero because Nero's name in Latin is transliterated into Hebrew by dropping the second Nun (נ), so it becomes *Nro Qsr*, נרו קסר. In Gematria, this yields 616, as follows (reading right to left):

Sum	Resh (ר)	Samekh (ס)	Qoph (ק)	Vav (ו)	Resh (ר)	Nun (נ)
616	200	60	100	6	200	50

Evidently, some earlier copyists, assuming the Latin name of the Roman Emperor was preferable to his name in Greek, used 616 instead of 666, but they were still aware that the man in view was Nero. John warned his readers that decoding the name would call for wisdom, by which he apparently meant knowing Hebrew, the language of the wise Torah. John encoded Nero's name and wrote Revelation in a symbolic, apocalyptic style to protect Christians who would read and be blessed by the book's message of hope in tribulational times. If Roman officials could not understand Revelation's full meaning, they would have had a harder time prosecuting those who possessed it. Since Nero committed suicide on June 9, AD 68, John may have written Revelation between AD 64, the start of Nero's persecution, and mid AD 68. The preponderance of evidence thus seems to favor AD 64–68 as the date of Revelation's composition, but whether the date was AD 68 or 96 must remain open to debate because there is no absolute proof either way.

ANTICHRISTS

John never mentions an Antichrist or, indeed, any antichrist in Revelation. The only mention of antichrists anywhere in Scripture is in John's first and second epistles, in which he writes that it is the last hour, and that although his readers had heard that antichrist was coming, many antichrists had already come. By that fact, they should know that it was indeed the last hour. The last hour of what? The world? Probably of the Old Covenant, for the destruction of the Temple in AD 70 would render the observance of Mosaic Law with its many mandatory sacrifices impossible.

John also wrote that these antichrists were originally part of the Church, but they left, making it plain that they were not sincere Christians. He wrote that anyone who denies the Father and the Son is the antichrist (1 John 2:22). He further warned his readers to test every spirit to see if they are from God because many false prophets had gone out into the world. Every spirit that confesses that Jesus Christ has come in the flesh, he taught, comes from God, and every spirit that does not do so is not from God and is the spirit of antichrist, which his readers heard was not only coming into the world but was in the world already.

He encouraged his readers, saying, "Little children, you are from God and have overcome them [the antichrists], for he who is in you is greater than he who is in the world" (1 John 4:4). He further wrote that "many deceivers have gone out into the world, those who do not confess the coming of Jesus Christ in the flesh. Such a one is the deceiver and the antichrist. Watch yourselves, so that you may not lose what we have worked for but may win a full reward" (2 John 1:7–8).

PHILIP, APOSTLE TO ETHIOPIA

PHILIP WAS THE FIFTH disciple whom Jesus called, and that is the order in which he always appears in the lists of the Twelve. Philip's name is classically Greek. It means "lover of horses:" *philos* (friend) and *hippos* (horse). The most famous Philip of ancient times was Philip II, king of Macedon and father of Alexander the Great. No Hebrew or Aramaic name is recorded for this apostle, which does not necessarily mean that he was only part Jewish. Andrew, Peter's brother, is known only by his Greek name, and he was all Jewish. Philip was a Jew, but with a name like Philip, he may have had a Greek father or mother who may have converted to Judaism. Or it is possible that Philip was his Greek-equivalent name, as Paul was the Greek name that Saul used among the Gentiles.

John the Baptist introduced Andrew and John to Jesus. Andrew called Simon Peter, and then Jesus found Philip at the end of the Feast of Tabernacles in AD 29.

> The next day, [Jesus] purposed to go into Galilee, and he found Philip. And Jesus said to him, "Follow me." Now Philip was from Bethsaida, of the city of Andrew and Peter. Philip found Nathanael and said to him, "We have found him of whom Moses in the Law and also the Prophets wrote—Jesus of Nazareth, the son of Joseph" (John 1:43–45).

Like Peter and Andrew, Philip was born in Bethsaida on the northern shore of Lake Galilee, so Philip probably knew Peter and Andrew from boyhood, and since Capernaum is not far from Bethsaida, it is easy to imagine that he also knew James and John from an early age. Since after recognizing Jesus as the Messiah Philip immediately called Nathanael (of Cana), these two were friends perhaps also from childhood.

Apart from the lists of disciples, all gospel references to Philip are in the book of John. Mark and Luke did not belong to this group of childhood friends and families, and Matthew's career as a tax collector put him outside the pale until Jesus called him. John's accounts of Philip, therefore, may be another hint that Philip was a long-time friend of John, and therefore of James, Peter, and Andrew. Moreover, since James and John may have been first cousins of Jesus and since John the Baptist was a second cousin of Jesus,[1] it is reasonable to imagine that all these boys may have known Jesus and traveled with him every year to Jerusalem on the four pilgrimage feasts, which were like grand family outings. Of course, we cannot know for sure that Jesus' apostles were his childhood friends. But it is difficult to imagine, in so small a place as Galilee, in a family-centric Middle Eastern culture, that Jewish clans would fail to gather often, marking births, celebrating weddings, mourning deaths, and worshiping God.

FOLLOW ME

Philip was the fifth apostle to whom Jesus spoke the momentous words, whose power and love echo down the corridor of time, "Follow me." The Bible was not written to us but for us. Jesus said, "Follow me," to Philip and others, and through them, he also invited every human being to follow him. How do we know? He told them, "This is My blood of the covenant, which is poured out for many" (Mark 14:24), and John wrote, "As many as received him, to them he gave the right to become children of God, even to those who believe in his name" (John 1:12). Every human being on earth is called. Yet only a minority is bound for heaven. God's call, his grace, is conditional upon each individual accepting the free gift of salvation. Without acceptance, forgiveness is an incomplete transaction, a one-sided handshake.

---

1. See "Relationships in Jesus' Community" at www.thebiblehistoryguy.com.

FEEDING THE FIVE THOUSAND

John recorded three episodes in his gospel about Philip, which occurred during Jesus' earthly ministry. At the first, the feeding of the five thousand, Jesus tested Philip.

> Jesus went up on the mountain, and there he sat down with his disciples. Now, the Passover, the feast of the Jews, was at hand. Lifting up his eyes, then, and seeing that a large crowd was coming toward him, Jesus said to Philip, "Where are we to buy bread so that these people may eat?" He said this to test him, for he himself knew what he would do. Philip answered him, "Two hundred *denarii* would not buy enough bread for each of them to get a little." One of his disciples, Andrew, Simon Peter's brother, said to him, "There is a boy here who has five barley loaves and two fish, but what are they for so many?" Jesus said, "Have the people sit down." Now, there was much grass in the place. So the men sat down, about five thousand in number. Jesus then took the loaves, and when he had given thanks, he distributed them to those who were seated. So also the fish, as much as they wanted. And when they had eaten their fill, he told his disciples, "Gather up the leftover fragments, that nothing may be lost." So they gathered them up and filled twelve baskets with fragments from the five barley loaves left by those who had eaten. When the people saw the sign that he had done, they said, "This is indeed the Prophet who is to come into the world" (John 6:3–14).

The passage refers to five thousand men and does not take into account the women and children present. Even so, there were probably not so many more than five thousand present because the feeding occurred on a grassy knoll east of Bethsaida, along the north coast of the Sea of Galilee. It was not a great population center, and the crowds who were following Jesus in boats to that place and who sailed the next day back across the lake to the western shore were probably mostly men. It would be unlikely that men, women, and children in equal numbers would have braved the rigors of these lake crossings in pursuit of the Nazarene rabbi. After all, that very night, the disciples nearly perished in a storm on the lake. They were saved only by Jesus walking out on the water.

When Jesus asked Philip where they were to buy bread to feed so many people, Philip skipped over the question of where they might obtain the bread and pointed out an even greater problem: even if they were near a market, they would need two hundred *denarii* to feed this many people even for one day.

The buying power of the Roman *denarius* cannot be translated exactly into the buying power of precious metal today. Two hundred *denarii* are equal to 95.2 troy ounces of silver, which is worth about $2,392 in 2024 US dollars. But a *denarius* was also an average day's wages. In the United States, the average wages for a day are about $228. So, Philip's cost estimate might be something more like $45,680 in modern terms. This makes sense because if one were feeding fish tacos to five thousand people, assuming that one would pay $1.19 per taco, that would buy 38,387 tacos or about 7.7 tacos per person.

Philip flunked Jesus' test because Jesus asked, "Where can we buy bread?" and Philip, failing to realize that Jesus was the bread of life, the new manna, instead calculated the cost. The bread motif in Jesus' ministry recurred to illustrate what the real source of our sustenance is. Jesus was, after all, born in Bethlehem, which means "House of Bread." Key verses speaking of bread is this:

> And the tempter came and said to him, "If you are the Son of God, command these stones to become loaves of bread." But he answered, "It is written, "Man shall not live by bread alone, but by every word that comes from the mouth of God" (Matt 4:3–4).
>
> Give us this day our daily bread (Matt 6:11).
>
> Jesus then said to them, "Truly, truly, I say to you, it was not Moses who gave you the bread from heaven, but my Father gives you the true bread from heaven. For the bread of God is he who comes down from heaven and gives life to the world." They said to him, "Sir, give us this bread always." Jesus said to them, "I am the bread of life; whoever comes to me shall not hunger, and whoever believes in me shall never thirst" (John 6:32–35).
>
> Now, they had forgotten to bring bread, and they had only one loaf with them in the boat. And he cautioned them, saying, "Watch out; beware of the leaven of the Pharisees and the leaven of Herod." And they began discussing with one another the fact that they had no bread. And Jesus, aware of this, said to them, "Why are you discussing the fact that you have no bread? Do you not yet perceive or understand? Are your hearts hardened? Having eyes, do you not see, and having ears, do you not hear? And do you not remember? When I broke the five loaves for the five thousand, how many baskets full of broken pieces did you

take up?" They said to him, "Twelve." "And the seven for the four thousand, how many baskets full of broken pieces did you take up?" And they said to him, "Seven." And he said to them, "Do you not yet understand" (Mark 8:14–21).

Now as they were eating, Jesus took bread, and after blessing it broke it and gave it to the disciples, and said, "Take, eat; this is my body" (Matt 26:26).

When he was at table with them, he took the bread and blessed and broke it and gave it to them. And their eyes were opened, and they recognized him. And he vanished from their sight (Luke 24:30–31).

Jesus wanted to convey to Philip the priceless value of the bread of heaven, not the cost of bread.

JESUS AND THE GREEKS

The next episode that John recorded about Philip was the request of certain Greeks to meet Jesus. This occurred on Monday, March 28, AD 33, five days before the Crucifixion.

Now, among those who went up to worship at the feast were some Greeks. So, these came to Philip, who was from Bethsaida in Galilee, and asked him, "Sir, we wish to see Jesus." Philip went and told Andrew; Andrew and Philip went and told Jesus. And Jesus answered them, "The hour has come for the Son of Man to be glorified. Truly, truly, I say to you, unless a grain of wheat falls into the earth and dies, it remains alone, but if it dies, it bears much fruit. Whoever loves his life loses it, and whoever hates his life in this world will keep it for eternal life. If anyone serves me, he must follow me, and where I am, there will my servant be also. If anyone serves me, the Father will honor him" (John 12:20–26).

The Greeks seeking to meet Jesus seemed to gravitate toward the disciple who had a Greek name. Yet Philip did not take the Greeks straight to Jesus. First, he consulted Andrew, the disciple who loved to introduce people to Jesus (and who also had a Greek name). Andrew took the Greeks to the Master.

These "Greeks" were actually Armenians. Abgar, the king of the Armenians, truly believed Jesus was the Son of God. He sent a letter to

Jesus, asking Him to come to him and cure him of his pains. The bearers of the letter met Jesus at Jerusalem "but not daring to tell Jesus . . . told it to Philip and Andrew, who repeated it to their Master."[2] Jesus told them these things: (1) the hour of his glorification had come, (2) through death, a seed bears fruit, (3) this life is worthless without eternal life, and (4) following Jesus is the pathway to God. In these brief statements, Jesus imparted the whole Gospel to the Greeks by saying, in paraphrase, "Observe what is about to happen in the next few days. You will see me killed, raised, and exalted. Understand and follow me to life eternal."

If these Greeks remained in Jerusalem till Friday, they would have witnessed Jesus' Crucifixion. If they remained till Sunday, they would have witnessed his Resurrection. Since John wrote his gospel to the world, this is a meaningful foreshadowing of how the apostles, notably Peter and Paul, would carry the Good News to the Gentiles. But the first to do this was Philip, who, after the Resurrection, preached in estranged, half-pagan Samaria and proselytized a eunuch from Ethiopia. Possibly observing Jesus' witness to the Greeks helped equip Philip for these opportunities.

SEEING THE FATHER

In the final gospel reference to Philip, at the Last Supper, he seemed to struggle with Jesus' teaching and asked to see the Father so that he might believe Jesus' extraordinary claims. Jesus marveled at Philip's failure, after witnessing so many miracles, to grasp that Jesus was God incarnate.

> "If you had known me, you would have known my Father also. From now on, you do know him and have seen him." Philip said to him, "Lord, show us the Father, and it is enough for us." Jesus said to him, "Have I been with you so long, and you still do not know me, Philip? Whoever has seen me has seen the Father. How can you say, 'Show us the Father'? Do you not believe that I am in the Father and the Father is in me? The words that I say to you I do not speak on my own authority, but the Father who dwells in me does his works. Believe me that I am in the Father, and the Father is in me, or else believe on account of the works themselves. Truly, truly, I say to you, whoever believes in me will also do the works that I do, and greater works than these will he

---

2. Moses of Chorene, *History of Armenia*, 5. Also, see "Armenia's Apostolic Heritage," below.

do because I am going to the Father. Whatever you ask in my name, this I will do, that the Father may be glorified in the Son. If you ask me anything in my name, I will do it. 'If you love me, you will keep my commandments" (John 14:7–15).

As one of the Twelve, Philip was present in the Upper Room on Resurrection Sunday, in the Upper Room with Thomas present on the following Monday, at Jesus' Ascension, at the meeting to choose Matthias to replace Judas, at the birth of the Church on the day of Pentecost in AD 33, and at the Jerusalem Council in AD 49.

THE HISTORY OF SAMARIA

The next Bible reference to Philip, in Acts, shows him preaching among the Samaritans. Samaria was the remnant of Ephraim, the ancient Northern Kingdom of Israel. Israel was originally one kingdom under King Saul. As Saul's power waned, two tribes of Israel's twelve tribes, Judah and Benjamin, gave their allegiance to King David. When Saul died, the ten other tribes also went over to David. When David died, his son Solomon became king and held all twelve tribes together for most of his reign. As Solomon strayed away from God, however, Jeroboam, the son of Nabat of the tribe of Ephraim, conspired to become king. When Solomon discovered the plot, Jeroboam fled to Egypt for the protection of Pharaoh Shishak.

When Solomon died, Jeroboam returned from exile. Solomon's son, Rehoboam, tried to hold the kingdom together, but he attempted it through cruel dictatorship. The northern Ten Tribes resented such treatment. In 931 BC, Jeroboam successfully made himself king of the Ten Tribes, which became a separate Northern Kingdom. It went under the nicknames of Ephraim, Samaria, and Israel. Ephraim referred to the son of Joseph, who had ruled in Egypt, and this was Jeroboam's tribe. Samaria referred to the region's capital city. Omri, the father of King Ahab, had bought a hill site from someone named Shemer for two talents of silver and named the place Samaria ("Shomron" in Hebrew) after Shemer.

The Southern Kingdom, commonly called Judah, consisted of two tribes, Judah and Benjamin (and some Levites, who served in the Temple). When the single Kingdom of Israel split, Judah remained loyal to David's grandson, Rehoboam. Jerusalem was the capital of Judah, and so Solomon's Temple was under Judah's control. To ensure that his subjects did not drift back into allegiance with Rehoboam, Jeroboam established a rival place of worship on Mount Gerizim in Samaria. Eventually, both kingdoms turned away from God and followed pagan practices.

The prophets Elijah, Elisha, Hosea, and Amos warned the Northern Kingdom of God's wrath, but all nineteen of the Northern kings persisted in evil. From 722–718 BC, God used Assyria to destroy the Northern Kingdom (and engulf the rest of the Middle East) while miraculously sparing a tiny oasis of freedom, Judah. Assyria deported and scattered the Ten Tribes into what became known as the Diaspora (Greek for dispersion). The Ten Tribes were then mostly lost to history, hence, "the lost tribes of Israel." The Assyrians populated the Northern Kingdom with Aramaic-speaking settlers, who brought pagan religious practices into the territory. Yet there was always some remnant of the original Hebrews, and these intermarried with the settlers, mixing the worship of Yahweh with Assyrian cults, thus creating a syncretistic religion.[3]

The prophets Isaiah, Jeremiah, Joel, Micah, Habakkuk, and Zephaniah warned the Southern Kingdom of God's wrath, but only eight of their nineteen rulers did good in the eyes of God. King Josiah brought about godly reforms in Jerusalem in the early days of Jeremiah, Daniel, and Ezekiel, but the last four kings of Judah were evil, and in 586 BC, God used Nebuchadnezzar, King of Babylon, to destroy Judah, Jerusalem, and Solomon's Temple. God preserved a Jewish remnant, as Nebuchadnezzar deported about 14,000–18,000 Jews to Babylon in exile.[4] Jeremiah prophesied, with amazing accuracy, that the captivity would last seventy years (Jer 25:12). When Cyrus the Great conquered Babylon and added it to his Persian empire in 539 BC, he permitted the Jews to return to Judah. Under Zerubbabel (an ancestor of Jesus) and Jeshua (the High Priest), and encouraged by the prophets Zechariah and Haggai, the Jews rebuilt the Temple by 515 BC. After Esther and Mordecai saved the Jews from Persian genocide in 475 BC, Ezra led a second return of Jewish survivors to Jerusalem, followed by Nehemiah, who governed Judah and rebuilt Jerusalem's walls. The prophet Malachi ministered in their time.

---

3. The Samaritans still survive as a small community in Israel today, and they regard themselves as the guardians of pure Yahwism.

4. Gottheil, et al., "Babylonian Captivity," *Jewish Encyclopedia*.

PHILIP'S FIRST MISSIONARY JOURNEY

So, because of all this history, the Jews despised the Samaritans as half-breeds. The Messiah, however, had come to save not just the Jews but everyone, including Samaritans, not because any particular nation or race deserved salvation but because God so loved the world. In the tale of the Good Samaritan, the Samaritan showed more charity to a wounded Jew than did a priest or a Levite (Luke 10:33). The narrative of Jesus' encounter with the Samaritan woman at the well (John 4:7–42) shows that (1) the Samaritans yearned for God and the Messiah, (2) the Jews despised the Samaritans, and (3) Jesus had come to save them. The Samaritan woman quickly recognized the Messiah, while even Jesus' half-brothers and the learned Pharisees and scribes in Jerusalem failed to do so. Not only that, when she told the town of Sychar (Shechem) about Jesus, they all recognized him as the Messiah, and he spent two days with them, over the Sabbath.

In AD 33, Saul (Paul) began ferociously to persecute Christians, which may have prompted Philip to evangelize outside Jerusalem. Paul's persecution probably did not drive Philip out of Jerusalem because the Bible says that Saul's persecution scattered all except the apostles (Acts 8:1). It also says that those who had been scattered preached the Gospel wherever they went (Acts 8:4). Therefore, Philip's evangelistic work was simply obedience to Jesus' statement that the disciples would be his witnesses in Jerusalem, Judaea, Samaria, and to the ends of the earth (Acts 1:8). Nevertheless, the evangelistic outreach of Philip to Samaria, Gaza, and Caesarea, right after the stoning of Stephen must have seemed like an epidemic of Christianity to Paul. So, like a general seeking to outflank his enemy, he applied for priestly permission to head the Christian heretics off at Damascus, north of Samaria. Philip's zig-zag ministry evaded Paul, and Paul met with unexpected results, becoming a convert to Christ on the Damascus Road.

Meanwhile, Philip reached the city of Samaria (today's Nablus) and proclaimed Christ. He performed miracles, casting out demons and healing the paralyzed and the lame. The citizens of Samaria were overjoyed, and they listened attentively to Philip's preaching. Philip was the first apostle to bring the Gospel to the non-Jewish world. The age-old strife between Samaria and Judah was resolved forever in Jesus Christ. Jesus was the fulfillment of all the types and shadows of the Old

Covenant and the eternal replacement of the Temple that the Romans would finally demolish in AD 70.

There was, however, a man in Samaria named Simon Magus or Simon the Magician. He impressed the Samaritans with his magic and made himself out to be someone great. The Samaritans thought Simon wielded the power of God. But when they heard Philip's message about the kingdom of God and Jesus Christ, they were baptized, both men and women. When Simon saw Philip's miracles, he was amazed. He believed, got baptized, and began following Philip.

When the apostles in Jerusalem heard that Samaria had received the Gospel, they sent Peter and John to investigate. When they saw that the reports were true, they prayed for the Samaritans, laid hands on them, and the Samaritans received the Holy Spirit. When Simon Magus saw this, he said, "Give me this power also, so that anyone on whom I lay my hands may receive the Holy Spirit." But Peter said to him, "May your silver perish with you because you thought you could obtain the gift of God with money! You have neither part nor lot in this matter, for your heart is not right before God. Repent, therefore, of this wickedness of yours, and pray to the Lord that, if possible, the intent of your heart may be forgiven you. For I see that you are in the gall of bitterness and in the bond of iniquity." Simon answered, "Pray for me to the Lord, that nothing of what you have said may come upon me."

This sounds like Simon was truly a seeker, but in reality, his heart was not right with God. He went to Rome and resumed his practice of magic arts there. Invoking the power of demons, he claimed to be a god. He won many followers and so impressed the emperor Claudius that he erected a statue in Simon's honor on the island in the Tiber River.[5] Peter pursued Simon to Rome and defeated his chicanery once and for all.

Peter and John then preached the word of the Lord in many Samaritan villages. This was ironic because John and his brother James had once asked Jesus if he would permit them to call down fire from heaven on the Samaritan villages that had refused him hospitality. After ministering in Samaria, Peter, John, and Philip returned to Jerusalem.

---

5. Justin Martyr, *First Apology*, 26, *Dialogue with Trypho*, 120.

PHILIP'S SECOND MISSIONARY JOURNEY

Back in Jerusalem, an angel of the Lord came to Philip and told him to take the road south to Gaza. As he walked along the desert road, he met an Ethiopian eunuch, a court official of Candace, queen of the Ethiopians. The eunuch was in charge of all her treasure. He had come to Jerusalem to worship and was returning home, riding in a chariot and reading the book of Isaiah. Since he was riding and reading, there must have been a charioteer with the eunuch, and so the chariot must have been like a coach. The Holy Spirit spoke to Philip, saying, "Go over and join this chariot." So, Philip ran to him and heard him reading aloud. He asked, "Do you understand what you are reading?" The Ethiopian said, "How can I unless someone guides me?" And he invited Philip to come up and sit with him.

The passage of Scripture that the eunuch was reading was this: "Like a sheep, he was led to the slaughter and like a lamb before its shearer is silent, so he opens not his mouth. In his humiliation, justice was denied him. Who can describe his generation? For his life is taken away from the earth" (Acts 8:32–33, Isa 53:7–8). The eunuch asked Philip whether the prophet was speaking of himself or someone else. Using the Messianic passages of Isaiah 53, Philip told the eunuch the whole Gospel. As they traveled, they came to a place with water, and the eunuch asked, "What prevents me from being baptized?" He commanded the chariot to stop, and both he and Philip went down to the water, where Philip baptized him. When they came out of the water, the Spirit of the Lord carried Philip away. The eunuch saw him no more, but he went along his way, rejoicing. This perhaps means that the Holy Spirit carried Philip away miraculously. It may also simply mean that inspired by God, Philip departed for Azotus and that he and the eunuch never met again.

ETHIOPIA

Why had an Ethiopian come to Jerusalem to worship? Why, of all people, the treasurer of Queen Candace? There was an ancient community of Jews in Ethiopia. There was also an early community of Christians. According to the *Kebre Negast*, an Ethiopian holy book, Menelik I, an Ethiopian ruler who was supposedly the son of King Solomon and the Queen of Sheba, took the Ark of the Covenant to Ethiopia. From AD 1320 to 1620, Ethiopian Jews and Christians waged war until the

Christians conquered the Jews. The Christians placed what they claim was the original Ark of the Covenant in the Church of Saint Mary of Zion in the mountain city of Axum. To this day, they jealously guard the ark, and only their patriarch may view it once a year.

This tradition is questionable. Jeremiah mentioned the ark (Jer 3:16) in a way suggestive of its presence in the Temple in his day (three centuries after Solomon). When Nebuchadnezzar looted the Temple in 586 BC, he took all the cups and plates to Babylon, the very plates that Belshazzar would insultingly use to drink toasts to Babylonian gods on the night when God's finger wrote his doom on a wall (2 Kings 24:13, 2 Chron 36:7, 18, Dan 5:2). Nebuchadnezzar may have taken the ark with him. Or the ark may have perished when Nebuchadnezzar burned the Temple down (2 Kings 25:9, Jer 52:13).

Whatever the truth, the existence of an ancient community of Jews and Christians in Ethiopia is certain. And the Old Testament shows that Ethiopia was part of God's plan, as David said: "Nobles shall come from Egypt; Cush [Ethiopia] shall hasten to stretch out her hands to God" (Ps 68:31). In describing a time when God would reject unbelieving Israel and accept the worship of other people, the prophet Zephaniah, fifty years before Nebuchadnezzar's destruction of Jerusalem, wrote:

> "For at that time I will change the speech of the peoples to a pure speech, that all of them may call upon the name of the Lord and serve him with one accord. From beyond the rivers of Cush [Ethiopia], my worshipers, the daughter of my dispersed ones, shall bring my offering. On that day, you shall not be put to shame because of the deeds by which you have rebelled against me; for then I will remove from your midst your proudly exultant ones, and you shall no longer be haughty in my holy mountain" (Zeph 3:9–11).

Isaiah also prophesied this event.

> Ah, land of whirring wings that is beyond the rivers of Cush, which sends ambassadors by the sea, in vessels of papyrus on the waters! Go, you swift messengers, to a nation tall and smooth, to a people feared near and far, a nation mighty and conquering, whose land the rivers divide . . . At that time, tribute will be brought to the LORD of hosts from a people tall and smooth, from a people feared near and far, a nation mighty and conquering, whose land the rivers divide, to Mount Zion, the place of the name of the LORD of hosts (Isa 18:1–7).

The land of whirring wings is evocative of the fact that locust hordes in the Middle East often arise out of Ethiopia. The vessels of papyrus refer to the boats on which the Ethiopians plied the many rivers that divided their land, especially the Blue Nile, whose source is in Lake Tana. The phrase "a people tall and smooth" aptly describes the typical physique of Ethiopians, whose bodies are tall, slender, and not very hairy, compared to Middle Easterners.

The Ethiopians were a formidable military nation in antiquity. The Twenty-Fifth Dynasty of Egypt (747–656 BC) was ruled by Ethiopian pharaohs. Isaiah prophesied that Ethiopia would bring tribute to Jerusalem, which is exactly what the eunuch was doing, and that God's people should send swift messengers to Ethiopia, which is what the evangelistic mission Philip was fulfilling.

In the context of these passages, here is what was going on at the time when Philip met the Ethiopian. The Pharisees and scribes had rejected the Messiah and felt no shame about it. Other people—Greeks, Armenians, Romans, and Samaritans—were accepting Christ and joining the community of God. The treasurer of the queen of Ethiopia was returning from a journey of worship and offerings to Jerusalem, searching the Messianic passages in Isaiah 53 for the truth. In thirty-seven years, Rome would destroy the Second Temple and end the rule of the proud Jewish leaders upon the holy mountain of Zion. So, the eunuch and Philip were meeting at a crossroads in history prophesied by David one thousand years before, by Isaiah about 775 years before, and by Zephaniah about 670 years before.

CONCLUSION OF PHILIP'S SECOND MISSIONARY JOURNEY

After arriving in Azotus (Ashdod), Philip went north to the seaport of Caesarea, preaching the Gospel in all the towns along the way. Altogether, Philip's travels in AD 33 were as follows: (1) from Jerusalem to Samaria, forty-five miles or a fifteen-hour walk to the north, (2) back to Jerusalem, (3) from Jerusalem to Gaza, eighty-five miles or a seventeen-hour walk to the southwest, (4) from Gaza to Azotus, twenty-five miles or an eight-hour walk north along the Mediterranean coast, and (5) from Azotus to Caesarea, sixty-two miles north or a twenty-hour walk along the coastal road, a total of 262 miles.

PHILIP THE APOSTLE AND PHILIP THE DEACON

Some traditions confuse Philip the Apostle with Philip the Evangelist, who was one of the Seven chosen to serve the widows of the Church. A clear reading of the text precludes this.

> Now, in these days, when the disciples were increasing in number, a complaint by the Hellenists arose against the Hebrews because their widows were being neglected in the daily distribution. And the twelve summoned the full number of the disciples and said, "It is not right that we should give up preaching the word of God to serve tables. Therefore, brothers, pick out from among you seven men of good repute, full of the Spirit and of wisdom, whom we will appoint to this duty. But we will devote ourselves to prayer and to the ministry of the word." And what they said pleased the whole gathering, and they chose Stephen, a man full of faith and of the Holy Spirit, and Philip, and Prochorus, and Nicanor, and Timon, and Parmenas, and Nicolaus, a proselyte of Antioch. These they set before the apostles, and they prayed and laid their hands on them" (Acts 6:1–6).

Since these seven men, including Philip, were brought before the Twelve Apostles, including Philip the apostle, the two Philips must have been two different men. If the Twelve appointed seven to do work unsuitable for the Twelve, the Philip of the Seven cannot have been the Philip of the Twelve. The deacon Philip, one of the Seven, appeared again in Acts.

"On the next day we departed and came to Caesarea, and we entered the house of Philip the evangelist, who was one of the seven and stayed with him. He had four unmarried daughters, who prophesied" (Acts 21:8–9). Eusebius seems to have confused the two Philips,[6] demonstrating that the early Church Fathers, while valuable as sources, are sometimes wrong. The canon of Scripture never is.[7]

FRANCE

There is a tradition in France that Philip evangelized Gaul (ancient France). Philip appears in French art as an especially revered saint. There may be a grain of truth in this. Galatia was a province of Turkey invaded and settled

---

6. Eusebius, *Church History*, 3:31:4.

7. Canon, by the way, comes from the Greek word *kanon*, "measuring stick," so the Bible is the standard against which all other texts are measured.

by Gauls (ancient inhabitants of France) during the reign of Alexander the Great (the late fourth century BC). They displaced the native Hittites and called the region they conquered Galatia, Gallia of the East, or, if we were to make it sound more modern, "Asian France." That Philip, like Paul on his second missionary journey, should have preached in Galatia seems credible. If he preached among the Gauls of Galatia, it is easy to see how tradition might stretch the point to say that Philip preached among the Gauls, the French. Of course, it is also possible that preaching among the Gauls of Galatia inspired Philip to carry the Gospel to their brethren in France. Or Galatian converts may have carried Philip's message from Galatia home to France. All of this is simply unknown. In any case, Philip is the only apostle anciently associated with France.

PHILIP'S DEATH

Hippolytus wrote: "Philip preached in Phrygia and was crucified in Hierapolis (modern Pamukkale, Turkey, near Colossae, Laodicea, and Galatia) with his head downward in the time of Domitian (AD 81–96) and was buried there.[8] If this is so, he shared the same form of crucifixion that Peter suffered back in AD 68. Perhaps Philip agreed with Peter that he was unworthy to die in the same manner as that of his Lord. Eusebius quoted Polycrates of Ephesus as also affirming that Philip died in Hierapolis, although this is the same dubious passage in Eusebius that erroneously confuses Philip the Apostle with Philip of the Seven Servants.[9]

In Hierapolis, a spring of chemical-rich, lukewarm water sparkles over a giant, crystallized waterfall. In ancient times, invalids from afar visited this famous spa, making it an ideal crossroads where Philip could meet travelers and spread the Gospel. Since John and Philip were friends, apparently from childhood, they may have enjoyed ministering in provinces that were fairly near to each other, Ephesus and Hierapolis.

The apocryphal *Acts of Philip*[10] gives an account of Philip's martyrdom. In this story, Philip, Bartholomew, and Philip's sister, Mariamne, were ministering in Hierapolis when Philip miraculously healed and converted the wife of the city's proconsul. The proconsul was enraged at this challenge to his pagan cult. He tortured Philip, Bartholomew, and

---

8. Hippolytus, *List of the Apostles and Disciples.*
9. Eusebius, *Church History*, 3:31:4.
10. *Acts of Philip.*

Mariamne. Then he crucified Philip and Bartholomew upside down. The dying Philip preached from his cross. As a result of Philip's preaching, the crowd released Bartholomew from his cross, but Philip suffered a martyr's death. This book is unreliable, so its account of Philip's death may have a grain of truth or may be pure fable.

Pope John III (AD 560–572) moved the remains of Philip from Hierapolis to the Church of the Holy Apostles of Saint Philip and Saint James in Rome. Today visitors can see a large marble sarcophagus said to contain the bones of Philip and James.

PHILIP'S NATURE

Philip eagerly responded to Christ's call, willingly asked and answered questions in his search for truth, even at the risk of getting it wrong, and boldly took the Good News to the world. The brief sketch of him in Acts suggests that his missionary work was daring, joyful, untiring, and especially blessed by miraculous acts of the Holy Spirit.

NATHANAEL BARTHOLOMEW, APOSTLE TO ARMENIA

Nathanael Bartholomew was the sixth in the lists of the apostles. Matthew, Mark, and Luke mentioned Bartholomew but never Nathanael, whereas John mentioned Nathanael but never Bartholomew. Since all four evangelists recorded only twelve main disciples, the conclusion that Bartholomew and Nathanael were the same man is inescapable. Nathanael means "gift of God," and Bartholomew means Bar Tolmai or "son of Tolmai."

The most extensive record of Nathanael is in the Gospel of John, whose author may have been a long-time friend. Nathanael clearly was a friend of Philip, who led him to Jesus during the Feast of Tabernacles in AD 29.

> Now Philip was from Bethsaida, the city of Andrew and Peter. Philip found Nathanael and said to him, "We have found him of whom Moses in the Law and also the prophets wrote, Jesus of Nazareth, the son of Joseph." Nathanael said to him, "Can anything good come out of Nazareth?" Philip said to him, "Come and see." Jesus saw Nathanael coming toward him and said of him, "Behold, an Israelite indeed, in whom there is no deceit!" Nathanael said to him, "How do you know me?" Jesus answered him, "Before Philip called you, when you were under the fig tree, I saw you." Nathanael answered him, "Rabbi, you are the Son of God! You are the King of Israel!" Jesus answered him, "Because I said to you, 'I saw you under the fig tree,' do you believe? You will see greater things than these." And he said to him, "Truly, truly, I say to you, you will see heaven

opened, and the angels of God ascending and descending on the Son of Man" (John 1:44–51).

This promised vision of heaven opening was consciously reminiscent of Jacob's ladder. At Bethel, Jacob had a dream about a "ladder set up on the earth, and the top of it reached heaven. And the angels of God were ascending and descending on it. And the LORD stood above it" and blessed the Promised Land for Jacob (Gen 28:12–14). This image is of a bridge between God and man, and, of course, Jesus was that ultimate bridge.

Jesus' promised vision could not have referred to the Transfiguration on Mount Hermon when Jesus appeared with Moses and Elijah. This occurred around April 29 of AD 31, 559 days or little more than eighteen months later, and Nathanael was not one of the three disciples Jesus invited to the top of the mountain. He brought only Peter, James, and John. Nathanael was one of the other nine disciples at the foot of Mount Hermon, trying unsuccessfully to exorcise a demon that could only come out with prayer and fasting. But Nathanael did witness Jesus' Ascension from the Bethany side (east side) of the Mount of Olives. Two angels spoke to the apostles then (Acts 1:10–11), and Nathanael saw them with the rest. This occurred on Friday, Sabbath Eve, May 13, AD 33, the forty-first day after Resurrection Sunday (the feast of First Fruits). It was about forty-three months or more than three and a half years after Nathanael's first conversation with Jesus at Bethany beyond the Jordan. The Ascension may have been what Jesus prophesied that Nathanael would see. Of course, Jesus may just have been speaking figuratively, meaning that Nathanael would witness many miraculous things, allowing him to peer into the kingdom of heaven.

Nathanael was a Galilean from Cana (John 21:2). If he was startled at his first encounter with Jesus when Jesus saw him under a fig tree from afar, he must have been further amazed to learn that Jesus was heading to a wedding in Cana, the very place he called home. When Nathanael asked if anything good could come from Nazareth, he probably did not especially despise the town. Since Nahum and Jonah both likely came from Galilee, he must have understood that good things could come from there. But since he, along with the priests of Jerusalem, expected the Messiah to come from Bethlehem, what he may have meant was that "the great good" Israel was anticipating at this time (according to the prophecy of Dan 9:24–27) would come not from Nazareth in Galilee but from Bethlehem in Judaea (Mic 5:2). It is also possible that Nathanael was speaking in a humble sense, basically astonished that the Messiah would come from his neighborhood. He may essentially have been saying, "Is he really one of us?"

Nathanael was quick to identify Jesus with the Son of God, a remarkable insight in so short a time. This supports the idea that all of Israel was in the grip of great Messianic expectations in the first century. Old Testament prophesies, especially Genesis 49:10 and Daniel 9:24–27, fixed the time for the Messiah's appearance in a tight window around the time of Jesus. Nathanael was on a hair trigger.

Nathanael attended the wedding at Cana, witnessed Jesus turning water into wine, and afterward joined Jesus' family and four other disciples on a trip to Capernaum.

The Bible says no more of Nathanael Bartholomew except that he was one of the Twelve. It is evident that, with them, he was present in the Upper Room on Resurrection Sunday, was in the Upper Room with Thomas present on the following Monday, saw Jesus' Ascension, helped choose Matthias to replace Judas, witnessed the birth of the Church on the day of Pentecost in AD 33, and attended the Jerusalem Council in AD 49.

NATHANAEL BARTHOLOMEW'S MISSIONARY JOURNEYS

The apocryphal *Acts of Philip* holds that Nathanael Bartholomew traveled to Hierapolis in Turkey with Philip. The two preached the Gospel and healed and converted the wife of a Roman proconsul. The proconsul ordered the execution of the two apostles. Philip was crucified. Nathanael Bartholomew was crucified but was released. Hippolytus wrote: "Bartholomew, again, preached to the Indians, to whom he also gave the Gospel according to Matthew, and was crucified with his head downward, and was buried in Allanum [or Albanum], a town of great Armenia."[1] So, the story is that Nathanael preached in India and then came back west to Armenia, carrying a copy of Matthew's gospel. He arrived in Armenia about AD 66[2] and converted many Armenians.

---

1. Hippolytus, *List of the Apostles and Disciples*.
2. "Saints Thaddaeus and Bartholomew," *The Armenian Prelacy*.

NATHANAEL BARTHOLOMEW'S DEATH

The Armenian King Astyages, angry that Bartholomew converted his brother and that he refused to worship pagan gods, had the apostle skinned alive. He then beheaded him or crucified him, or perhaps both, in the city of Albanopolis (Derbent) on the western shore of the Caspian Sea, in what is now Russia but in ancient times was known as Greater Armenia. Michelangelo portrayed Bartholomew in the *Last Judgment* in the Sistine Chapel with his skin hanging over his arm. He became the patron saint of tanners.

Bartholomew's tomb is in the part of Iran that once was Greater Armenia. He, along with Judas Thaddaeus, is a patron saint of Armenia. Bartholomew's relics were allegedly transported to Lipari, near Sicily, in the seventh century, to Benevento, Italy, in AD 809, and to Rome in AD 983. Today they repose in the *Basilica di San Bartolomeo all'Isola* on the island in the River Tiber. Fragments of Bartholomew's skull were supposedly transferred to Frankfurt, Germany, while one of his arms is venerated in Canterbury Cathedral in England today.

THOMAS THE TWIN

THOMAS IS THE SEVENTH in the list of the disciples. Although the Bible records little of Thomas, John's depiction of him in the fourth gospel delineates his character vividly. His name in Aramaic, Tauma, means twin, which is Didymos in Greek. Scripture never says who his twin was. Later apocryphal writings, in which Thomas figures prominently, say that Jesus was Thomas' twin, which is, of course, impossible.

The fourth-century Church historian Eusebius refers to this apostle as Judas Thomas,[1] so his full name was Judas Thomas Didymus. There were five men named Judas among Jesus' disciples: (1) Judas Thomas Didymus (the Twin), (2) Judas Thaddaeus Lebbaeus, son of James, (3) Simon Judas, the Zealot, (4) Judas Iscariot, son of Simon, and (5) Jesus' half-brother Judas, who wrote the biblical book of Jude. Since there were five prominent contemporary men named Judas, this is probably why Thomas was called by a distinguishing nickname, "the Twin."

DEVOTED TO JESUS

Matthew, Mark, and Luke named Thomas as one of the Twelve, but only John recorded Thomas' role in the account of Lazarus, which occurred a mere three months before the Crucifixion.

> Now Jesus loved Martha and her sister and Lazarus. So, when he heard that Lazarus was ill, he stayed two days longer in the place where he was. Then, after this, he said to the disciples, "Let us go to Judaea again." The disciples said to him, "Rabbi, the Jews were

---

1. Eusebius, *Church History*, 1:13:10

just now seeking to stone you, and are you going there again?" Jesus answered, "Are there not twelve hours in the day? If anyone walks in the day, he does not stumble because he sees the light of this world. But if anyone walks in the night, he stumbles because the light is not in him." After saying these things, he said to them, "Our friend Lazarus has fallen asleep, but I go to awaken him." The disciples said to him, "Lord if he has fallen asleep, he will recover." Now Jesus had spoken of his death, but they thought that he meant taking rest in sleep. Then Jesus told them plainly, "Lazarus has died, and for your sake, I am glad that I was not there, so that you may believe. But let us go to him." So, Thomas, called the Twin, said to his fellow disciples, 'Let us also go, that we may die with him'" (John 11:5–16).

Was Thomas a fatalist? A pessimist? Or was he so zealous for Jesus that he would rather have died with the Master than to have lived without him? The ensuing passages show that Thomas was passionately devoted to his Lord. This dialogue occurred at the Last Supper:

> [Jesus said], "Let not your hearts be troubled. Believe in God; believe also in me. In my Father's house are many rooms. If it were not so, would I have told you that I go to prepare a place for you? And if I go and prepare a place for you, I will come again and will take you to myself, that where I am you may be also. And you know the way to where I am going." Thomas said to him, "Lord, we do not know where you are going. How can we know the way?' Jesus said to him, 'I am the way, and the truth, and the life. No one comes to the Father except through me. If you had known me, you would have known my Father also. From now on, you do know him and have seen him" (John 14:1–7).

Thomas was ready to ask Jesus the bluntest of questions. But just as three months before Thomas was prepared to follow Jesus to Judaea and probable death, here again Thomas implied that he wanted to know where Jesus was going so that he could follow him at any cost. Jesus' response to Thomas is one of the Lord's most quoted and beautiful sayings: Jesus is the way, the truth, and the life, and no one comes to the Father but through him.

JESUS' POST-RESURRECTION APPEARANCE TO PETER

After his appearance to the women at the tomb, the next person Jesus appeared to after his Resurrection was Peter (Mark 16:7, Luke 24:34, 1 Cor 15:5). Mark, Luke, and Paul all recorded that Jesus appeared singularly to Peter, but they gave no details of the encounter. Perhaps Peter kept the details private. Possibly, this was because it was an emotional encounter, following Peter's triple denial of Jesus, Jesus' rebuking Peter silently with a piercing glance, and Peter's bitter weeping over his failure, all only two days before.

JESUS ON THE EMMAUS ROAD

Jesus next appeared to two followers, one named Cleophas, probably Jesus' uncle,[2] on the road to Emmaus, seven miles northwest of Jerusalem, in the late afternoon of Resurrection Sunday. As Cleophas and his companion broke bread with Jesus at sunset, they suddenly recognized him, and he vanished from their presence. They hurried back to Jerusalem to meet the disciples, only to find them in a state of great excitement, for the risen Lord had already appeared to Peter.

JESUS' FIRST APPEARANCE IN THE UPPER ROOM

As they were speaking, Jesus appeared to the Ten Disciples, to Cleophas and his companion, and to others assembled in the Upper Room that Resurrection Sunday evening. Thomas must have just left the room after the arrival of Cleophas and his companion but before the appearance of Jesus because Luke recorded that (1) Cleophas and his companion met the Eleven, including Thomas (Luke 24:33) and others assembled with them in the Upper Room, and John recorded that (2) when Jesus appeared, Thomas was absent, and there were only the Ten (John 20:24). Why did Thomas leave the Upper Room after hearing Jesus had appeared to Peter but before Jesus arrived? Reading between the lines, it sounds like Thomas was overcome with emotion and either needed time alone or went to look for Jesus. Here are the passages of Scripture describing this momentous post-Resurrection appearance of Jesus.

---

2. See "Relationships in Jesus' Community" at www.thebiblehistoryguy.com.

> On the evening of that day, the first day of the week, the doors being locked where the disciples were for fear of the Jews, Jesus came and stood among them and said to them, "Peace be with you." When he had said this, he showed them his hands and his side. Then, the disciples were glad when they saw the Lord (John 20:19–20).
>
> As they were talking about these things, Jesus himself stood among them and said to them, "Peace to you!" But they were startled and frightened and thought they saw a spirit. And he said to them, "Why are you troubled, and why do doubts arise in your hearts? See my hands and my feet, that it is I myself. Touch me and see. For a spirit does not have flesh and bones as you see that I have." And when he had said this, he showed them his hands and his feet. And while they still disbelieved for joy and were marveling, he said to them, "Have you anything here to eat?" They gave him a piece of broiled fish, and he took it and ate before them (Luke 24:36–43).

Notice that, just like Thomas, the ten disciples doubted. Only after Jesus showed them his hands and his side were they glad to see the Lord. Yet even then, they disbelieved until Jesus proved his physical reality by eating a piece of broiled fish.

JESUS' SECOND APPEARANCE IN THE UPPER ROOM

The following Monday, Jesus appeared again to the Eleven Disciples in the Upper Room with Thomas present (John 20:26). It occurred eight days after Resurrection Sunday, on Monday, April 11, AD 33, in the Upper Room. The most famous account of Thomas is this, which earned him the nickname "Doubting Thomas."

> Now Thomas, one of the Twelve, called the Twin, was not with them when Jesus came. So the other disciples told him, "We have seen the Lord." But he said to them, "Unless I see in his hands the mark of the nails and place my finger into the mark of the nails, and place my hand into his side, I will never believe." Eight days later, his disciples were inside again, and Thomas was with them. Although the doors were locked, Jesus came and stood among them and said, "Peace be with you." Then he said to Thomas, "Put your finger here and see my hands, and put out your hand and place it in my side. Do not disbelieve but believe." Thomas answered him, "My Lord

and my God!" Jesus said to him, "Have you believed because you have seen me? Blessed are those who have not seen and yet have believed." (John 20:24–29).

Although this account has earned Thomas the reputation of a skeptic, the passage really affirms that Thomas was a profound believer. The other disciples were glad only after Jesus showed them his hands and his side. Thomas' request to see these proofs of Jesus' Resurrection was no different than the proofs the other disciples had required. They were just as doubtful as Thomas was. Also, Thomas, the man of passionate impulse, made the greatest possible theological statement in response to these proofs. He cried, "My Lord and my God!" Thomas grasped the miraculous fact that Jesus was both the Messiah and *theanthropos*, the God-Man.

Jesus not only accepted the title of Lord and God but also commended Thomas for believing and commended even more those who believed in Jesus' deity without seeing physical proof of it. Jesus could only have accepted worship as God if he were God; if he were not, accepting honor due to God alone would make Jesus a blasphemer or insane. In other passages of Scripture, we see that God-fearing men and angels never accepted worship due only to their Creator.

> When Peter entered, Cornelius met him and fell down at his feet and worshiped him. But Peter lifted him up, saying, "Stand up; I too am a man" (Acts 10:25–26).

> Then I fell down at his feet to worship him, but he said to me, "You must not do that! I am a fellow servant with you and your brothers who hold to the testimony of Jesus. Worship God (Rev 19:10).

> I, John, am the one who heard and saw these things. And when I heard and saw them, I fell down to worship at the feet of the angel who showed them to me, but he said to me, 'You must not do that! I am a fellow servant with you and your brothers, the prophets, and with those who keep the words of this book. Worship God (Rev 22:8–9).

FINAL APPEARANCES IN SCRIPTURE

John mentions Thomas one more time in the fourth gospel when Jesus meets seven of the Twelve on the shore of the Sea of Galilee after his Resurrection.

> After this, Jesus revealed himself again to the disciples by the Sea of Tiberias, and he revealed himself in this way. Simon Peter, Thomas (called the Twin), Nathanael of Cana in Galilee, the sons of Zebedee, and two others of his disciples were together. Simon Peter said to them, "I am going fishing." They said to him, "We will go with you." They went out and got into the boat, but that night, they caught nothing. Just as day was breaking, Jesus stood on the shore, yet the disciples did not know that it was Jesus. Jesus said to them, "Children, do you have any fish?" They answered him, "No." He said to them, "Cast the net on the right side of the boat, and you will find some." So, they cast it, and now they were not able to haul it in because of the quantity of fish (John 21:1–6).

The final direct biblical reference to Thomas, by Luke, depicts him present once again in the Upper Room at Jerusalem, with the surviving Eleven of the Twelve, along with Mary, the mother of Jesus, as well as with Jesus' brothers (probably James and Judas and possibly the two unnamed others). This was the day of the Ascension, Sunday, May 13, AD 33.

> Then they returned to Jerusalem from the mount called Olivet, which is near Jerusalem, a Sabbath day's journey away. And when they had entered, they went up to the Upper Room, where they were staying, Peter and John and James and Andrew, Philip and Thomas, Bartholomew and Matthew, James the son of Alphaeus and Simon the Zealot and Judas, the son of James. All these, with one accord, were devoting themselves to prayer, together with the women and Mary, the mother of Jesus, and his brothers (Acts 1:12–14).

Scripture tells us no more of Thomas directly. But, as one of the original Twelve, he was at the meeting to choose Matthias as a replacement for Judas. He witnessed the birth of the Church on the day of Pentecost in AD 33, and he participated in the Jerusalem Council in AD 49.

GNOSTICS

There is a body of apocryphal literature about Thomas. The Gnostics wrote much of it. The Gnostics were people who believed that, in order to free oneself from the material world, one needed *gnosis* or special knowledge. The Gnostics fraudulently used Thomas' name as the supposed author of books that handed down secret teachings, allowing only the elect to know the truths of God. What worse representative could the Gnostics possibly have chosen? Thomas was the man who was ready to let the Jews stone him with Jesus; he wanted to follow Jesus wherever he was going, wanted physical proof that Jesus was alive after seeing him die, and confidently proclaimed that Jesus was Lord and God. Thomas, like Peter, was one of the most outspoken, blunt apostles. In fact, none of the apostles was especially secretive or esoteric. They were not Gnostics.

GNOSTICS, AGNOSTICS, ATHEISTS, AND THE PROOF OF GOD

What is the difference between Gnostics, agnostics, and atheists? An atheist says that God does not exist. He is sure about that. An agnostic says that he has insufficient knowledge to tell whether God exists or not. He not only thinks that he does not know, but he also thinks nobody can know. If either theism or atheism is true, that is, if it is possible to know whether God does or does not exist, then agnosticism cannot be true.

Agnostics try to challenge atheists by asking them to prove the non-existence of God. They know that proving the non-existence of anything is philosophically impossible. There is no such thing as nothing, for nothing, to be something, would need to exist and therefore could not be nothing. It is, however, possible to solve the atheistic and agnostic puzzles by proving the existence of God on the basis of pure logic.

GOD IS A FACT

The existence of God can be proven by considering four cosmological theses. Of the origin of the universe, only four things can be true: (1) it does not really exist. It is an illusion, (2) it always existed from eternity past, (3) it created itself, or (4) it was created.

If the universe is an illusion, then you do not exist since you are part of the universe. But if you are thinking that you do not exist, you are thinking. Since to think you must exist, you exist. René Descartes summarized this by saying, "*Cogito ergo sum*—I think, therefore I am."

Isaac Newton's Second Law of Thermodynamics and all scientific observations tell us that the universe is "winding down." If the universe existed from eternity past, it would have gone extinct an eternity ago.

To create itself, the universe would have to exist before it existed to bring itself into existence. Nothing comes from nothing, as Parmenides observed.[3]

The only remaining possibility is that the universe was created, and if it was created, it necessarily had a Creator.

The Creator, like the universe, cannot: (1) be an illusion, since an illusion cannot create a reality; (2) be created, because then the Creator would need a Creator, who would then need a Creator, who would then need a Creator, *ad infinitum*, posing the problem of infinite regression; or (3) have created itself, because nothing comes from nothing. Therefore, the Creator must be eternally self-existent and uncreated.

The Creator is the unmoved Prime Mover, the uncaused First Cause. All effects have causes, but not all causes are the effects of some other cause. The First Cause (the Creator) has no cause. All effects emanate from him. The First Cause is God, the Necessary Being: if anything exists, God must exist. Since this is logically demonstrable, it is possible to know this, so agnosticism is invalid.

Since this logically proves the necessary existence of God, atheism is also invalid. Since all that is required to know this is logic, not some secret knowledge, Gnosticism is invalid. Since logic alone produces this conclusion, neither faith nor Scripture is needed to prove that God is a fact.

THOMAS' MARTYRDOM IN INDIA

While Gnostic books, like the *Gospel of Thomas* and the *Acts of Thomas*, are obviously late forgeries (one has only to read a few pages to see how weak they are compared to the majestic style of the Bible), they may contain germs of truth: one or two germs, but not an epidemic. According

---

3. Parmenides of Elea was a fifth-century BC, pre-Socratic Greek philosopher. This dictum later became famous in Latin, articulated by Lucretius in *De Rerum Natura*: "*Ex nihilo nihil fit.*"

to the *Acts of Thomas*, a book possibly written in Edessa, Syria, around AD 200, the apostles divided the world between them so that each might evangelize a region. India fell to Thomas.

According to this story, after AD 49 (the Council of Jerusalem), an Indian envoy named Abban took Thomas to the wedding feast of a king named Gundafor, who reigned in India at that time. Gundafor supposedly entrusted money to Thomas to build a palace, but the apostle spent it on the poor instead. Gundafor imprisoned Thomas, but he escaped by a miracle (reminiscent of Peter's and Paul's escapes from jail), which inspired Gundafor to become a Christian.

Thomas then preached throughout the Subcontinent until he came to the city of a certain King Mazdai. He converted Mazdai's Queen, Tertia, and their son, Vazan. Tertia took a vow of celibacy, which infuriated her husband. Mazdai condemned Thomas to death. Four of the king's soldiers led him to a hill outside the city, where they pierced him with spears. They buried Thomas in the tomb of their kings, but later, his remains were moved to the West.

Another tradition, still believed in India today, says that Thomas made missionary journeys as far south as Mylapore, near Madras, and suffered martyrdom there. Hippolytus wrote: "Thomas preached to the Parthians, Medes, Persians, Hyrcanians, Bactrians, and Margians, and was thrust through the four members of his body with a pine spear at Calamene, the city of India, and was buried there."[4]

The story behind the story may simply be that Thomas preached in Persia and India and, being an apostle, did what apostles did: converted many, healed the sick and lame, raised the dead, and suffered martyrdom for his politically incorrect testimony. If so, he traveled an astonishing four thousand miles. When Portuguese explorers first discovered the Malabar Coast of India in the 1500s, they were convinced that it harbored communities of Christians.

THOMAS' RELICS

Thomas's relics purportedly reached Edessa (modern Turkey) in the fourth century. As the Muslim Turks conquered more and more of the Byzantine Empire, Thomas' bones were taken to the Greek island of

---

4. Hippolytus, *List of the Apostles and Disciples*.

Chios in AD 1258 and finally to Ortona, in Italy, where they allegedly rest today.

This fourth-century hymn by Saint Ephraim[5] of Syria celebrated the mission of Thomas in India.

HYMN TO THOMAS

> To a distant land of spiritual night
> He went and, clothed in baptismal white,
> Wedded India to God's only Son,
> And banished darkness through a sacred dawn.
> As a merchant king by treasure is blessed,
> So holy Edessa in grace possessed
> The relics from the apostle's field,
> The most precious pearl that the East could yield.[6]

Keeping the tradition alive, a 1972 an Indian postage stamp commemorated Thomas' mission to India.

---

5. Saint Ephraim was born around AD 306 in Syria. When his home came under Persian rule in AD 363, Ephraim and many Christians moved to Edessa in Asia Minor (Greater Armenia). Ephraim died there in AD 373 while ministering to plague victims. He wrote over one thousand poems. His descriptions of heaven and hell may have inspired Dante.

6. This author's paraphrase of a translation is intended to make the verses scan, rhyme, and convey the spirit of the original poem.

MATTHEW LEVI, THE TAX COLLECTOR

Matthew is the eighth in the list of the apostles. Matthew means "Gift of God" in Hebrew. Levi and Matthew are the same man, a tax collector. Jesus may have conferred the affectionate nickname of Matthew, "gift of God," on Levi because even though he was a despised tax collector, he would leave all to follow the Lord and would write an inspired and beautiful gospel. This may explain why Mark and Luke called him Levi, his real name, while Matthew enjoyed referring to himself by the nickname that Jesus probably gave him.

Matthew was a tax collector at Capernaum under Herod Antipas, tetrarch over Galilee and Peraea. This king was the second husband of Herodias and was the stepfather of Salome, who demanded the head of John the Baptist on a platter. Since Matthew lived in Capernaum, he probably was Galilean. He was a Levite, but the Pharisees despised him, as they despised all tax collectors. Matthew's friends were reprobates like himself, as indicated by the guests he invited to the party after being called by Jesus. If Jesus had been running for public office, he could hardly have done worse than to consort with the people he so often did: Gentiles, adulterous women, lepers, paralytics, and tax collectors.

The accounts of Matthew's calling in Matthew, Mark, and Luke are similar and harmonize as follows.

CALLING MATTHEW

After casting demons into the swine in Gadara, on the eastern shore of the Sea of Galilee, Jesus entered a boat and crossed back over to his own city, Capernaum. After healing a paralytic, he went to Peter's house. When he next left the house, he passed by the tax booth and saw the tax collector, Matthew Levi, the son of Alphaeus. Jesus said to him, "Follow me." Leaving everything, Matthew rose and followed him. Jesus called Matthew after calling the Four Fisherman, sometime between June and July AD 30, 288 days or more than nine months after his baptism in the Jordan.

MATTHEW'S FEAST

Levi hosted a great feast for Jesus at his house. There was a large company of tax collectors, sinners, and others reclining at table with Jesus and his disciples. The Pharisees and their scribes grumbled at Jesus' disciples, saying, "Why do you eat and drink with tax collectors and sinners?" Jesus answered them, "Those who are well have no need of a physician, but those who are sick. I have not come to call the righteous but sinners to repentance" (Mark 2:17, Matt 9:12–13, Luke 5:31–32). Apparently, the scribes and the Pharisees were not sufficiently offended to refrain from attending Matthew's sumptuous feast; they simply complained that tax collectors and sinners were also invited.

MATTHEW'S RELATIONSHIPS

Since Matthew and James the Less were both sons of a man named Alphaeus, Matthew may have been the half-brother of James the Less and thus may have been Jesus' cousin. Also, Simon the Zealot may have been Jesus' cousin, the half-brother of Matthew Levi, the full brother of James the Less, and the bridegroom of the wedding at Cana.

The names Alphaeus and Cleophas (Clopas) referred to the same man. He was the brother of Joseph, the stepfather of Jesus. Cleophas' wife, Mary, had two husbands, and she was the mother of James the Bishop (probably James the Less), Simon (probably the Zealot), and two other sons named Thaddaeus (probably not Judas Thaddaeus Lebbaeus, the apostle) and Joseph. If Alphaeus was Joseph's brother, he was of the tribe of Judah, and so their sons, James the Less and Simon the Zealot would have been Jews. If Mary's first husband was a Levite and by him she gave birth to Matthew, that would explain why Matthew was called Levi. If, after the death of Mary's first husband, Alphaeus married Mary and adopted Matthew, that would explain his also being called the son of Alphaeus. Thus, James the Less and Simon the Zealot were probably full brothers to each other and half-brothers to Matthew Levi, which helps to explain why Matthew became an outcast tax collector.[1]

Matthew's black sheep status might make Matthew's prompt response to Jesus' call more understandable. He may have been inwardly grieving for some time about his sinful life. He was a Levite serving Rome rather than the Temple of God. He may have yearned to be reconciled with his family. If Simon the Zealot were the bridegroom at the Wedding of Cana and Matthew's half-brother, it must have hurt for him to be uninvited. Even so, in so small a community as Galilee, he must have heard of the miracle of Jesus turning water into wine.

ROMAN TAXES

Rome's method of collecting taxes was to engage locals who knew which people had money and where they kept it. Rome divided each province into tax districts. Local entrepreneurs bid for the office of tax collector. The winner made a contract to collect a certain sum of money for Rome, and whatever he collected above and beyond was his to keep. Rome did not care how much it was. A chief tax collector, like Zacchaeus in Luke 19, owned the contract for his region, Jericho. He employed others, like Matthew, to collect taxes in the villages. Matthew was not a chief tax collector, so in his district, Galilee, he would have been subordinate to someone like Zacchaeus.

Rome exacted three kinds of tax: a land tax, a head tax, and a customs tax of two to five percent on the value of goods imported to or exported from a province. Tax collectors set up booths at city gates to assess merchandise coming to market. Fishermen like Peter, Andrew, James, and John would pay a customs tax on exports of dried fish from the Sea of Galilee to Syria, which was an important local revenue stream. In fact, they likely paid such taxes directly to Matthew, who was a collector in their tax district. Matthew had probably wrenched money

---

1. Eusebius, *Church History*, 3:11:2. Papias of Hierapolis, "Fragment X." Papias lived from about AD 70–163, very near to the events in the New Testament.

from them unjustly for years. So, they may have known and disliked Matthew personally. While following Jesus the disciples might often have reminisced about those bad, old days.

The people hated tax collectors as they hated thieves. Under Roman law, a subject of the empire was guilty until proven innocent. All a tax collector had to do was report a person for tax fraud to Herod or Rome, and the police state would allow or even help the tax collectors to take almost anything they liked by extortion. They could molest wives or daughters, sell children into slavery, and seize property or money. From a distance of twenty centuries, we tend to romanticize ancient Rome. Even the word "romanticize," a word that comes from the name Rome, reveals how we gild Rome's lily. A romance is "a Roman story." But in Jesus' day, Rome was a giant, heartless mafia. If Caesar Augustus decided that all the world should be taxed, he could not care less if it meant uprooting a simple carpenter and his pregnant wife and forcing them to journey three days to Bethlehem to be registered and pay up. Jesus reflected on the popular loathing of tax collectors when he said:

> "If your brother sins against you, go and tell him his fault, between you and him alone. If he listens to you, you have gained your brother. But if he does not listen, take one or two others along with you, that every charge may be established by the evidence of two or three witnesses. If he refuses to listen to them, tell it to the Church. And if he refuses to listen even to the Church, let him be to you as a Gentile and a tax collector" (Matt 18:15–17).

Matthew, the tax collector, in an act of faithful humility, recorded this teaching of Jesus. He might have omitted it if he had been more defensive and less humble. The Pharisees thought uncleanness was conveyed by touch or association. To enter the houses of tax collectors, sinners, and Gentiles was, therefore, taboo. "Now the tax collectors and sinners were all drawing near to hear him. And the Pharisees and the scribes grumbled, saying, 'This man receives sinners and eats with them'" (Luke 15:1–2). We can learn something about Matthew's profession through Luke's account of the tax collector Zacchaeus.

> He entered Jericho and was passing through. And there was a man named Zacchaeus. He was a chief tax collector and was rich. And he was seeking to see who Jesus was, but on account of the crowd he could not, because he was small of stature. So, he ran on ahead and climbed up into a sycamore tree to see him,

for he was about to pass that way. And when Jesus came to the place, he looked up and said to him, "Zacchaeus, hurry and come down, for I must stay at your house today." So he hurried and came down and received him joyfully. And when they saw it, they all grumbled, "he has gone in to be the guest of a man who is a sinner." And Zacchaeus stood and said to the Lord, "Behold, Lord, the half of my goods I give to the poor. And if I have defrauded anyone of anything, I restore it fourfold." And Jesus said to him, "Today salvation has come to this house since he also is a son of Abraham. For the Son of Man came to seek and to save the lost" (Luke 19:1–10).

Note that Zacchaeus said, "If I have defrauded anyone of anything, I will give him back four times as much." Jesus must have smiled. There really can have been no "if" about it, or Zacchaeus would not have said this. Zacchaeus had defrauded many of much. And since Jesus pronounced that Zacchaeus was saved, it is likely that Zacchaeus, a man of numbers, was using an exact formula.

The legal restitution for theft under Mosaic Law was to pay back double. "If a man gives to his neighbor money or goods to keep safe, and it is stolen from the man's house, then, if the thief is found, he shall pay double" (Exod 22:7). So, we may deduce that Zacchaeus, as a tax collector, was particularly rapacious. If Zacchaeus realized that to repent properly of his theft, he would have to pay back four times what he had stolen, that means his customary practice must have been to seize twice as much as he should have. For example, if a taxpayer owed Rome $100, and it would have been normal for the tax collector to exact $150, keeping $50 for himself, what Zacchaeus is implying is that his practice was to collect twice over the customary commission of $50, that is, an extra $50. So, Zacchaeus' tax burden on the taxpayer would have been $200. Rome would have received $100, and Zacchaeus would have kept $100 for himself. Now, if Zacchaeus was offering to pay back fourfold what he had stolen, he was offering to pay back 4 x $50 = $200. Zacchaeus was actually offering to go $100 "in the hole." Paying back fourfold meant that Zacchaeus was sincere in his desire to gain the approval and forgiveness of Jesus. No wonder Jesus said that salvation had come that day to Zacchaeus' house. Zacchaeus was not counting on earthly treasure but was laying up treasure in heaven. He was ready to stop serving two masters, God and Mammon, and to begin serving God alone. Jesus' approval, of course, was based on Zacchaeus' heart and the free gift of grace, not on a legalistic formula, but Zacchaeus could not have comprehended that yet.

MATTHEW'S MINISTRY

So, Matthew was probably a rank below Zacchaeus and spent his days in a tax booth in Capernaum, near Peter's big house, waiting to collect a toll on any goods transported past him as they entered or left the region ruled by Herod Antipas. Jesus' words, "Follow me!" must have pierced Matthew's soul, for he chose to leave wealth for poverty in an instant. This must have been complicated. His boss, the chief tax collector of the district, must have been apoplectic. From Luke's words, it sounds as though he left his booth, records, and cash without a backward glance.

Without his official role as a tax collector, Matthew had no protection but that of Jesus. He could no longer appeal to Rome's or Herod's henchmen to shield him from the hatred of the populace. There must have been many neighbors and relatives who would have loved to settle scores with Matthew in a dark alley. Jesus' protection would prove eternally effective, but how could Matthew have known that in an instant? Yet, such was the power of Jesus' call.

When Matthew invited Jesus to a great feast, he invited Pharisees and scribes, as well as his tax collector friends. He wanted reconciliation. And he was evangelizing already. The religious leaders went. The food and wine were free and probably good. But they grumbled about the sinful company to the disciples, who apparently did not know what to say.

At this stage, the only disciples Jesus had called to full-time ministry were Peter, Andrew, James, and John. Probably, they felt awkward and embarrassed about the inclusion of Matthew. Even though James and John may have been cousins of Mathew, as men in the fishing business, they doubtless knew and had hated Matthew as the obnoxious collector of customs duties in the past. But Jesus was perfectly comfortable. He replied on behalf of the disciples to the Pharisees in his usual, incontrovertible way, saying, "Those who are well have no need of a physician, but those who are sick. I have not come to call the righteous but sinners to repentance" (Mark 2:17, Matt 9:12–13, Luke 5:31–32). Jesus' elegant answer rebuked the Pharisees while at the same time embracing the sinners. He did not care about a person's reputation. He had come to save the outcast and the unloved. This is what the Pharisees and scribes should have done.

Matthew must have felt proud but also chagrined. By inviting Jesus to his house, he had exposed the Lord to the criticism of the Pharisees and scribes. He had shamed a guest, something deeply wounding to any host in the Middle East. The disciples must gradually have felt drawn to Matthew as they saw the Master eat with him, laugh with him, and treat him kindly.

THE TEMPLE TAX

Matthew, keenly interested in taxes and finance, is the only gospel writer to record this unusual account:

> When they came to Capernaum, the collectors of the two-drachma tax went up to Peter and said, "Does your teacher not pay the tax?" He said, "Yes." And when he came into the house, Jesus spoke to him first, saying, "What do you think, Simon? From whom do kings of the earth take toll or tax? From their sons or from others?" And when he said, "From others," Jesus said to him, "Then the sons are free. However, not to give offense to them, go to the sea and cast a hook and take the first fish that comes up, and when you open its mouth, you will find a shekel. Take that and give it to them for me and for yourself" (Matt 17:24–27).

Matthew followed Jesus throughout his earthly ministry, witnessing the Crucifixion and the Resurrection. He was in prayer in the Upper Room on the evening of Resurrection Sunday, on April 3, AD 33.

> Then they returned to Jerusalem from the mount called Olivet, which is near Jerusalem, a Sabbath day's journey away. And when they had entered, they went up to the Upper Room, where they were staying, Peter and John and James and Andrew, Philip and Thomas, Bartholomew and Matthew, James the son of Alphaeus and Simon the Zealot and Judas, the son of James. All these, with one accord, were devoting themselves to prayer, together with the women and Mary, the mother of Jesus, and his brothers (Acts 1:12–14).

As one of the Twelve, Matthew was in the Upper Room with Thomas present on the Monday after Resurrection Sunday; he helped choose

Matthias, witnessed Jesus' Ascension, and saw the birth of the Church on the day of Pentecost in AD 33.

Irenaeus states that Matthew preached the Gospel among the Jews. Clement of Alexandria claims he did this for fifteen years after the Resurrection, or until AD 48. Matthew, with the surviving eleven apostles, was at the Council of Jerusalem in AD 49. After the Council, Matthew would heed the call of the Great Commission and go to evangelize other nations, which Eusebius says he did, but not before giving his gospel in Hebrew to the Jews, thus compensating "those whom he was obliged to leave for the loss of his presence."[2] Thus, Matthew probably composed his gospel before or in AD 49.

MATTHEW'S DEATH

Matthew may have evangelized an area south of the Caspian Sea called Ethiopia (not Ethiopia in Africa). Some writers claim that he evangelized in Syria, Macedonia, and Parthia (Persia). Ancient tradition suggests that Matthew died a martyr; however, there is disagreement as to whether he was burned, stoned, or beheaded. Hippolytus says he died in Hierees, in Parthia, near the Caspian Sea.[3]

MATTHEW'S GOSPEL

The gospel of Matthew is inspired, that is, written through the Holy Spirit. Jerome says that he wrote it in Hebrew for the benefit of the Jews in Judaea and that afterward, it was translated into Greek. He also says that up to Jerome's day a copy of Matthew was preserved in the library of Caesarea. He cites, as evidence of its composition in Hebrew, that whenever Matthew quotes the Old Testament, he follows the Hebrew Bible, not the Septuagint, which was the popular Greek translation of the Bible in Matthew's day.[4] Matthew quoted the Old Testament ninety-nine times, more than the other three gospels put together. This fits with his identity as a Levite.

Matthew opened his gospel with a genealogy of Jesus, meaning to prove that Jesus is the Christ. Luke's gospel contains a different genealogy

---

2. Eusebius, *Church History*, 3:24:6.
3. Hippolytus, *List of the Apostles and Disciples*.
4. Jerome, *On Illustrious Men*.

of Jesus. Critics often contend that this represents a contradiction in Scripture and proves that the Bible contains errors. This is untrue. The two genealogies are both legitimate and accurate ancestries of Jesus. There is no contradiction whatever.

Skeptics claim that Matthew's genealogy is incomplete. In fact, his genealogy deliberately omits certain people for both biblical and symbolic reasons. Another critique is that Jesus cannot be King of the Jews because Matthew wrote that Jesus was descended from King Jeconiah, whom God had cursed. In fact, Jesus was not descended from King Jeconiah but from another Jeconiah, the eldest son of King Josiah, and that Jeconiah was not cursed. One last challenge is that Jesus cannot be both king and priest since the kings of Judah were always of the tribe of Judah, and priests were always of the tribe of Levi. However, as the legal son of Joseph, son of David (Matt 1:20), Jesus was also a son of David. The sons of David were not only kings, but they were also priests (2 Sam 8:18). Since Mary was related to Zechariah and Elizabeth, who were both Levites (Luke 1:5), Jesus also descended from Levi on his mother's side. (Both Mary's parents or only one may have been of Levi.) Therefore, Jesus was qualified to be both king (Matt 2:2, Rev 19:16) and priest, on the order of Melchizedek (Heb 7:17).[5]

If one had to spend the rest of one's life on a desert island and could choose only one book to take along, the gospel of Matthew would be a wonderful choice. Matthew's words adorn God's message with inspired beauty in many passages. One of the loveliest, surely, is this: "Go therefore and make disciples of all nations, baptizing them in the name of the Father and of the Son and of the Holy Spirit, teaching them to observe all that I have commanded you. And behold, I am with you always, to the end of the age (Matt 28:19–20).

---

5. For a full explanation, see "The Genealogies of Matthew and Luke" at www.thebiblehistoryguy.com.

JAMES, SON OF ALPHAEUS, "THE LESS"

JAMES WAS THE NINTH in the lists of the apostles. There are three prominent men named James in the New Testament: (1) James, the son of Zebedee, known as James the Great or Elder, possibly the father of Judas Thaddaeus Lebbaeus; (2) James, the son of Alphaeus, the Less or the Younger, of the original Twelve, possibly the brother of Matthew Levi, and (3) James, the half-brother of Jesus, named "James the Just," leader of the Jerusalem Church after Christ's Resurrection and author of the New Testament book of James.

No one really knows why James was called "the Less." Perhaps he was (1) younger than James, the son of Zebedee, (2) shorter than James, the son of Zebedee, or (3) less famous than James, the son of Zebedee. An extra-biblical tradition holds that James the Less resembled Jesus and that for this reason, Judas Iscariot promised to kiss Jesus to identify him in the Garden of Gethsemane so the Temple soldiers would be sure to arrest the right man. If Jesus and James the Less were cousins, there may well have been a family resemblance. Anyway, Jesus' entire group, apart possibly from Judas Iscariot, was composed of young Galileans of similar age, accents, customs, and appearance. This, and the dark of night, in an age before the invention of eyeglasses, make it easy to see why Judas would need to help the soldiers to recognize Jesus.

RELATIONSHIPS

Since Matthew and James the Less were both sons of a man named Alphaeus, Matthew may have been the half-brother of James the Less and thus may have been Jesus' cousin. Also, Simon the Zealot may have been Jesus' cousin, the half-brother of Matthew Levi, the full brother of James the Less, and the bridegroom at the wedding at Cana.[1]

JAMES' MISSION

As one of the Twelve, James the Less was present in the Upper Room on Resurrection Sunday evening and in the Upper Room with Thomas present on the following Monday; he witnessed Jesus' Ascension; he was at the meeting to choose Matthias as a replacement for Judas; he saw the birth of the Church on the day of Pentecost in AD 33; and he attended the Jerusalem Council in AD 49. Nothing else is known for certain about his life and ministry. Tradition holds that he brought the Gospel to Judaea, Armenia, Greece, and Egypt.

THE DEATH OF JAMES THE LESS

Reportedly, James died a martyr in Ostrakine, on the north coast of the Sinai Peninsula in Egypt, where he was preaching. His symbol is a carpenter's saw because his body was supposedly sawed to pieces after his crucifixion. Alternatively, Hippolytus wrote: "James the son of Alphaeus, when preaching in Jerusalem, was stoned to death by the Jews and was buried there beside the Temple."[2]

---

1. See "Matthew's Relationships" above.
2. Hippolytus, *List of the Apostles and Disciples*.

JUDAS THADDAEUS LEBBAEUS, "DEAR HEART"

JUDAS THADDAEUS LEBBAEUS IS variously the tenth or the eleventh in the lists of the disciples. Four apostles bear the name of Judas (1) Judas Thaddaeus Lebbaeus (Saint Jude), (2) Judas Thomas Didymus, (3) Judas Iscariot, and (4) Simon Judas the Zealot (according to Hippolytus). In addition, the half-brother of Jesus was also named Judas. He wrote the biblical book of Jude. Since no Christian writer would wish to confuse Judas, the betrayer of Jesus, with a faithful apostle, it is not surprising that the other two Judases were better known by their nicknames, Thaddaeus and Thomas. Thaddaeus and Lebbaeus both mean "beloved" or "near to the heart"—"dear heart"—in Greek and Aramaic, respectively.

Luke identified Judas Thaddaeus as Judas of James (Luke 6:16), so he was possibly the son of James, the son of Zebedee, and thus perhaps Jesus' second cousin.[1] Apart from the lists of disciples, John's is the only gospel to give an account of Judas Thaddaeus in Scripture:

> [Jesus said], "Whoever has my commandments and keeps them, he it is who loves me. And he who loves me will be loved by my Father, and I will love him and manifest myself to him." Judas (not Iscariot) said to him, "Lord, how is it that you will manifest yourself to us and not to the world?" Jesus answered him, "If anyone loves me, he will keep my word, and my Father will love him, and we will come to him and make our home with him. Whoever does not love me does not keep my words. And the word that you hear is not mine but the Father's who sent me.

---

1. See "Relationships in Jesus' Community" at www.thebiblehistoryguy.com.

These things I have spoken to you while I am still with you. But the Helper, the Holy Spirit, whom the Father will send in my name, he will teach you all things and bring to your remembrance all that I have said to you" (John 14:21–26).

This is the only speaking part in Scripture ascribed to Thaddaeus, and it is the last question any disciple asked Jesus before his arrest in Gethsemane. As one of the eleven surviving apostles, Thaddaeus was present in the Upper Room on Resurrection Sunday, was in the Upper Room with Thomas present on the following Monday, witnessed Jesus' Ascension, helped choose Matthias as a replacement for Judas, saw the birth of the Church on the day of Pentecost in AD 33, and attended the Jerusalem Council in AD 49. Tradition holds that he brought the Gospel to Armenia in AD 43.[2] Eusebius, the fourth-century Church historian, describes his Armenian mission as follows.[3]

JESUS' LETTER AND THADDAEUS' MISSION TO EDESSA

The miracles and divinity of Christ were reported in countries far away from Judaea. King Abgarus, who ruled Greater Armenia beyond the Euphrates, was afflicted with a terrible disease that no physician could cure. He sent a message to Jesus, begging him to come heal him. Eusebius, who claimed that the letter was preserved in the archives of Edessa, the capital of Greater Armenia, down to his day, cites the entire letter, translated from the Syriac language.

> Abgarus, ruler of Edessa, to Jesus the excellent Savior who has appeared in the country of Jerusalem, greeting. I have heard the reports of you and of your cures as performed by you without medicines or herbs. For it is said that you make the blind to see and the lame to walk, that you cleanse lepers and cast out impure spirits and demons, and that you heal those afflicted with lingering disease and raise the dead. And having heard all these things concerning you, I have concluded that one of two things must be true: either you are God and having come down from heaven, you do these things, or else you, who does these things, are the Son of God. I have therefore written to you to ask you if you would take the trouble to come to me and heal the

2. "Saints Thaddaeus and Bartholomew," *The Armenian Prelacy*.
3. Eusebius, *Church History*, 1:13:1–20.

disease which I have. For I have heard that the Jews are murmuring against you and are plotting to injure you. But I have a very small yet noble city, which is great enough for us both." The answer of Jesus to the ruler Abgarus by the courier Ananias: "Blessed are you who have believed in me without having seen me. For it is written concerning me, that they who have seen me will not believe in me, and that they who have not seen me will believe and be saved. But in regard to what you have written me, that I should come to you, it is necessary for me to fulfill all things here for which I have been sent, and after I have fulfilled them thus to be taken up again to him that sent me. But after I have been taken up, I will send to you one of my disciples, that he may heal your disease and give life to you and yours."

MISSION TO ARMENIA

After the Resurrection and Ascension, Thomas urged Thaddaeus to go to Edessa. There Thaddaeus began, in the power of God, to heal every disease and infirmity, causing all to wonder. When Abgarus heard of this, he suspected that this was the disciple Jesus had promised him. Abgarus summoned Thaddaeus, and as soon as he appeared before the king, Abgarus saw a vision and prostrated himself before the apostle. Everyone at court was astonished because they could not see the vision, which appeared to Abgarus alone. The king asked Thomas, "Are you, in truth, a disciple of Jesus, the Son of God?" Thaddaeus replied, "Because you believed in him who sent me, the petitions of your heart shall be granted." Abgarus said, "I believed in him so much that I wanted to take my army and destroy those Jews who crucified him. I was deterred only by the power of the Romans." Thaddaeus said, "Our Lord has fulfilled his Father's will and has been taken up to his Father." Abgarus said, "I, too, believe in him and his Father." With that, Thaddaeus placed his hand upon the king, and immediately, Abgarus was cured of his disease. Then, a certain Abdus, afflicted with gout, came and fell at Thaddaeus' feet. Thaddaeus laid hands on him, blessed him, and he, too, was healed. And so Thaddaeus cured many other citizens of Edessa, worked signs and wonders, and preached the word of God.

King Abgarus thanked Thaddaeus for the healing, but he wanted more. He wanted to know all about Jesus, how he was born and of the marvelous deeds he did. Thaddaeus asked the king to assemble all the citizens of Edessa the next day. Then Thaddaeus publicly declared how

Jesus was born, the details of his mission, the reason he was sent by the Father, the power of his works, the mysteries he proclaimed in the world, the humiliation of his death, his Resurrection, and his Ascension to the Father. Hearing this, the king offered Thaddaeus gold and silver, but the apostle refused it, saying that since he had forsaken his own possessions to follow Christ, it would not be right for him to take the possessions of another. These things were all done in the three hundred and fortieth year of the founding of Edessa or AD 33.[4]

THE CHURCH OF SAINT THADDAEUS THE APOSTLE

This author's wife, Madlene, was baptized at the age of thirteen at the Church of Saint Thaddaeus the Apostle in Dedmashen, near Tabriz, in the West Azerbaijan Province of Iran, which was once part of Greater Armenia. She says:

"The church is one of the oldest in the world. It is typical of ancient Armenian church architecture. It stands on a hill overlooking a wide valley through which the Tigris River flows. Beyond the rim of the valley, the snowclad peaks of Mount Ararat and Massis arise. Every year, many Christians make a pilgrimage to this shrine. First, they arrive at Tabriz and spend the night. Then, they drive out to the church in the morning. They do not drive there by night because there are bandits on the rural roads. Since the church is really in the middle of nowhere, the local Armenian diocese pitches hundreds of tents on the hillside around the church, where the pilgrims stay for the night before the ceremony.

The next morning, the *Catholicos*, or head of the Armenian church in the Iranian prelacy, conducts a mass and performs many baptisms. There are so many pilgrims that the church is open for two or three days. On my day, I was the last person in a long line. The priest made the sign of the cross on my forehead with myrrh-infused oil and then baptized me. Since the church is in a desert place and since there are so many pilgrims, there is not enough water for immersion, so they baptize by sprinkling."

---

4. This date refers to the 340th year of the Kingdom of Edessa, whose founding was in the Third Year of the 117th Olympiad, 308 BC. From 308 BC to AD 33, the Year of the Cross was, in fact, 341 years, but just as a child is only one year old after the first twelve months of life, so with a kingdom. Thus, in 307 BC, the Edessene Kingdom was one year old, and in AD 33, it was 340 years old.

THADDAEUS' DEATH

According to tradition, after preaching in Armenia and Mesopotamia, Thaddaeus suffered martyrdom in Berytus (modern Beirut, Lebanon) around AD 65. If so, he died three years before the presumed date of Peter's and Paul's execution in Rome. Thaddaeus supposedly was killed with a halberd (a long-handled war axe).

His relics were preserved in the Church of Saint Thaddaeus in Armenia (now in Iran) until Mongol invasions caused them to be moved for safekeeping to Saint Peter's Basilica in Rome. The Armenian Apostolic Church honors Thaddaeus and Bartholomew as its patron saints.

SIMON THE ZEALOT

SIMON IS VARIOUSLY THE tenth or the eleventh in the lists of the disciples. There are nine Simons in the New Testament: (1) Simon Peter, (2) Simon Judas the Zealot, (3) Simon the half-brother of Jesus (Matt 6:), (4) Simon the Leper (Matt 14:), (5) Simon the Pharisee (Luke 7:4), (6) Simon the father of Judas Iscariot (John 6:7), (7) Simon of Cyrene (Luke 23:2), (8) Simon Magus or the Magician (Acts 8:), and (9) Simon the Tanner (Acts 9:4). According to Hippolytus, the full name of the eleventh apostle was Simon Judas,[1] making him the fourth disciple to bear the name of Judas, along with (1) Judas Thomas Didymus, the Twin, (2) Judas Thaddaeus Lebbaeus, and (3) Judas Iscariot. Jesus' half-brother, who wrote the book of Jude, was also named Judas.

Scripture calls Simon "the Zealot" or "the Cananean" to distinguish him from the other Simon in the Twelve, Simon Peter. Simon the Cananean and Simon the Zealot are the same person, "zealot" being a translation into Greek (*zelotes*) of the Aramaic word for "zealous" or "jealous" (*ganana*) represented by the English transliteration "Cananean." Simon means "he who hears."

ZEALOTS

Josephus identifies four main first-century Jewish sects: (1) the Pharisees, (2) the Sadducees, (3) the Essenes, and (4) the Zealots.[2] The Zealots objected to Roman emperor worship and taxation. They wanted a

---

1. Hippolytus, *List of the Apostles and Disciples*.
2. Josephus, *The Jewish War*, 2:8:2–14, 7:8:1, *Antiquities of the Jews*, 13:5:9, 18:1:2.

Jewish king descended from David. As a Zealot, probably Simon's first interest in Jesus' ministry was that he saw Jesus as a leader like Moses who could expel Rome by force.

RELATIONSHIPS

Simon may have been Jesus' cousin, the half-brother of Matthew Levi and full brother of James the Less. He may have been the bridegroom at the wedding in Cana. Given Mary's dominant role in the wedding at Cana, she may have been Simon's aunt.[3]

SIMON'S MINISTRY

In the lists of disciples, Simon always comes before Judas Iscariot, perhaps because they may have shared Zealot politics. Because of their being listed as "team-mates," Simon and Judas Iscariot possibly went together when Jesus sent the disciples out in pairs (Matt 10:4). In this case, Simon may have been the performer of miracles empowered by the Holy Spirit if Judas Iscariot was never a true believer. On the other hand, if Judas was a believer at that time, he may have performed miracles together with Simon and may have lost his faith and power of the Holy Spirit later.

Unlike Judas Iscariot, Simon the Zealot came to understand and embrace Jesus' teaching. He abandoned Zealot politics and accepted Christ's Great Commission. As one of eleven survivors of the original Twelve Apostles, Simon was present in the Upper Room on Resurrection Sunday, was in the Upper Room with Thomas present on the following Monday, saw Jesus' Ascension, helped choose Matthias as the replacement for Judas Iscariot, witnessed the birth of the Church on the day of Pentecost in AD 33, and attended the Jerusalem Council of AD 49.

THE DEATH OF SIMON THE ZEALOT

The Golden Legend says that under the emperor Hadrian, Simon died by crucifixion in Jerusalem.[4] Hippolytus wrote that Simon the Zealot became bishop of Jerusalem after James the Just and that he died at the

---

3. See "Matthew's Relationships" above.
4. *The Golden Legend*, "159: Saints Simon and Jude."

age of 120.⁵ If so, he, and not John the son of Zebedee, was probably the longest-lived apostle. If one assumes that Simon was about thirty years old, like Jesus, at the Wedding of Cana, he would thus have died around AD 123.

---

5. Hippolytus, *List of the Apostles and Disciples*.

JUDAS ISCARIOT, THE TRAITOR

JUDAS IS THE TWELFTH in the list of the disciples. Judas in Greek is Ioudas, and in Hebrew is Judah, meaning "praised." In his gospel, John called him "son of Simon Iscariot" (John 6:71, 13:2, 26). Four apostles bear the name of Judas (1) Judas Thaddaeus Lebbaeus (Saint Jude), (2) Judas Thomas Didymus, the Twin, (3) Judas Iscariot, and (4) Simon Judas the Zealot. In addition, the half-brother of Jesus was also named Judas. He wrote the biblical book of Jude. Since no Christian writer would wish to confuse Judas, the betrayer of Jesus, with a faithful apostle, it is not surprising that the other two Judases were better known by their alternate names, Thaddaeus and Thomas. The traitorous disciple was known as Judas Iscariot. Iscariot means "from Kerioth," a city in Judaea.

Jesus called Judas to discipleship along with the other Twelve. He was the only one of the Twelve possibly not from Galilee, although perhaps his father, Simon, moved from Kerioth to Galilee and raised Judas there. Judas probably walked with Jesus during his entire earthly ministry, from the baptism of John to the Crucifixion. This is logical since those were the credentials Peter wanted Judas' replacement to have. Anyway, Judas certainly followed Jesus for most of his ministry. Yet Scripture never mentions him without some reference to his betrayal.

Objective contemporary observers of Judas would have considered him a role model. They might have wished to be just like him, a loyal and specially chosen servant of Jesus. The reality was that Satan indwelled Judas. Jesus knew all along that Judas would betray him. In March AD 31, two years before Judas' betrayal, Jesus said, "'Did I not choose you, the Twelve? And yet one of you is a devil.' He spoke of

Judas, the son of Simon Iscariot, for he, one of the Twelve, was going to betray him" (John 6:70–71).

AT THE HOME OF MARY OF BETHANY

John reported that Judas acted as treasurer for the disciples, though he was always a thief (John 12:6). He revealed this in the context of the account of Mary of Bethany, who poured expensive perfume on Jesus' feet on Friday, March 25, AD 33, one week before the Crucifixion.

> Six days before the Passover, Jesus therefore came to Bethany, where Lazarus was, whom Jesus had raised from the dead. So, they gave a dinner for him there. Martha served, and Lazarus was one of those reclining with him at table. Mary, therefore, took a pound of expensive ointment made from pure nard and anointed the feet of Jesus and wiped his feet with her hair. The house was filled with the fragrance of the perfume. But Judas Iscariot, one of his disciples (he who was about to betray him), said, "Why was this ointment not sold for three hundred *denarii* and given to the poor?" He said this not because he cared about the poor, but because he was a thief, and having charge of the moneybag, he used to help himself to what was put into it. Jesus said, 'Leave her alone so that she may keep it for the day of my burial. For the poor you always have with you, but you do not always have me'" (John 12:1–8).

Three hundred *denarii* were about three hundred days' wages in the first century. The silver value in 2024 would be US $3,588, but the purchasing power of money then was far greater than it is today. Using the average daily wage in the US of $228 in 2024, the current equivalent purchasing power of three hundred *denarii* would be about $68,400.

Of course, if Jesus said that he knew that Judas would betray him a year before it happened, Jesus obviously also knew that Judas was a thief and a liar at this supper in Bethany, which was just six days before the Last Supper. Ironically, Jesus gave Judas, the dishonest disciple, the job of treasurer. Jesus had no difficulty in producing money out of nowhere; he told Peter to find a shekel in the mouth of a fish. Jesus put Judas in a position where he might confront and overcome his most personal temptation if he were willing.

SATAN ENTERS JUDAS

Scripture states that Satan entered into Judas on Wednesday of the Passion Week.

> Then Satan entered into Judas called Iscariot, who was of the number of the twelve. He went away and conferred with the Chief Priests and officers how he might betray him to them. And they were glad and agreed to give him money. So, he consented and sought an opportunity to betray him to them in the absence of a crowd (Luke 22:3–6).

Judas was not seduced into betraying Jesus. Judas took the initiative and carried out his betrayal with premeditated conviction.

THIRTY PIECES OF SILVER

Only Matthew, the accountable tax collector, recorded the amount of money Judas took in his bargain to betray Christ.

> Then one of the twelve, whose name was Judas Iscariot, went to the Chief Priests and said, "What will you give me if I deliver him over to you?" And they paid him thirty pieces of silver. And from that moment he sought an opportunity to betray him (Matt 26:14–16).

Thirty pieces of silver are the equivalent of only about $359 in silver in 2024, but again, the relative purchasing power in the first century probably was the equivalent of $6,840 in 2024 US dollars—not much considering that Mary of Bethany had just squandered ointment worth ten times that amount. Exodus established thirty shekels of silver as the price of a slave (Exod 21:32). So, the Chief Priests put a deliberately insulting price on Jesus' head, equating Jesus to a slave. Yet through Jesus' grace, there is neither Jew nor Greek, slave nor free, male nor female, for all are one in Jesus Christ (Gal 3:28).

BETRAYAL AT THE LAST SUPPER

Splicing together these passages from the four gospels paints a complete picture of the Last Supper and the arrest in Gethsemane (Matt 26:20–27:10, Mark 14:17–50, Luke 22:14–53, John 13:1–30, 18:1–11).

Before the Feast of the Passover, when Jesus knew that his hour had come to depart from this world and it was evening and the hour came, he reclined at table, and the twelve apostles were with him. The devil had already put it into the heart of Judas Iscariot, Simon's son, to betray him. Jesus, knowing that the Father had given all things into his hands and that he had come from God and was going back to God, rose from the supper. He laid aside his outer garments and, taking a towel, tied it around his waist. Then he poured water into a basin and began to wash the disciples' feet and to wipe them with the towel that was wrapped around him. He came to Simon Peter, who said to him, "Lord, do you wash my feet?" Jesus answered him, "What I am doing, you do not understand now, but afterward, you will understand." Peter said to him, "You shall never wash my feet." Jesus answered him, "If I do not wash you, you have no share with me." Simon Peter said to him, "Lord, not my feet only but also my hands and my head!" Jesus said to him, "The one who has bathed does not need to wash, except for his feet, but is completely clean. And you are clean, but not every one of you." For he knew who was to betray him; that was why he said, "Not all of you are clean."

And he said to them, "I have earnestly desired to eat this Passover with you before I suffer. For I tell you, I will not eat it until it is fulfilled in the kingdom of God." And he took a cup, and when he had given thanks, he said, "Take this and divide it among yourselves. For I tell you that from now on, I will not drink of the fruit of the vine until the kingdom of God comes."

And he took bread, and when he had given thanks, he broke it and gave it to them, saying, "This is my body, which is given for you. Do this in remembrance of me."

And likewise, the cup after they had eaten, saying, "This cup that is poured out for you is the new covenant in my blood, which is poured out for many for the forgiveness of sins. But behold, the hand of him who betrays me is with me on the table. For the Son of Man goes as it has been determined, but woe to that man by whom he is betrayed!" And they began to question one another, which of them it could be who was going to do this (Matt 26:22, Mark 14:19, Luke 22:23, John 13:22).

Then, a dispute also arose among them as to which of them was to be regarded as the greatest. Jesus said to them, "The kings of the Gentiles exercise lordship over them, and those in authority over them are called benefactors—but not so with you. Rather, let the greatest among you become as the least and the leader as one who serves. For who is the greater, one who reclines at table or one who serves? Is it not the one who reclines at table? But I am among you as the one who serves.

"You are those who have stayed with me in my trials, and I assign to you, as my Father assigned to me, a kingdom that you may eat and drink at my table in my kingdom and sit on thrones judging the twelve tribes of Israel. Simon, Simon, behold, Satan demanded to have you, that he might sift you like wheat, but I have prayed for you that your faith may not fail. And when you have turned again, strengthen your brothers."

Peter said to him, "Lord, I am ready to go with you both to prison and to death." Jesus said, "I tell you, Peter, the rooster will not crow this day until you deny three times that you know me."

After saying these things, Jesus was troubled in his spirit and testified, "Truly, truly, I say to you, one of you will betray me." The disciples looked at one another, uncertain of whom he spoke. And they were very sorrowful and began to say to him one after another, "Is it I, Lord?" Jesus said, he who has dipped his hand in the dish with me will betray me."

Although there may have been more followers of Jesus in the Upper Room for the Last Supper, Jesus was reclining at table with only the Twelve (Matt 26:20, Luke 22:14). This means that all of them would have dipped their hand in the dish of bitter herbs with him, as a required part of the Passover ceremony. Consequently, Jesus' answer at this point left the disciples still in the dark. Then Judas, who would betray him, said, "Is it I, Rabbi?" He said to him, "You have said so." Now this made the answer to the question clear to Jesus and Judas, but the others were still uncertain.

One of his disciples, whom Jesus loved (John), was reclining at table close to Jesus, so Simon Peter motioned to him to ask Jesus of whom he was speaking. So that disciple, leaning back against Jesus, said to him, "Lord, who is it?" Jesus answered, "It is he to whom I will give this morsel of bread when I have dipped it. The Son of Man goes as it is written of him, but woe to that man by whom the Son of Man is betrayed! It would have been better for that man if he had not been born."

So when he had dipped the morsel, he gave it to Judas, the son of Simon Iscariot. Then, after Judas had taken the morsel, Satan entered into him. Jesus said to him, "What you are going to do, do quickly."

This should have made the situation clear, but none of the disciples at the table knew why Jesus said this to Judas. This shows how incredible it was to the disciples that one of them would betray the Christ. Some thought that because Judas had the moneybag, Jesus was telling him,

"Buy what we need for the feast," or that he should give something to the poor. So, after receiving the morsel of bread, Judas immediately went out into the night.

Jesus said to them, "When I sent you out with no moneybag or knapsack or sandals, did you lack anything?" They said, "Nothing." He said to them, "But now let the one who has a moneybag take it, and likewise a knapsack. And let the one who has no sword sell his cloak and buy one. For I tell you that this Scripture must be fulfilled in me: 'And he was numbered with the transgressors.' For what is written about me has its fulfillment." They said, "Look, Lord, here are two swords." And he said to them, "It is enough."

IN GETHSEMANE

When they had sung a hymn, he came out and went, as was his custom, to the Mount of Olives. The disciples followed him. They went to a place called Gethsemane. And when he came to the place, he said to them, "Pray that you may not enter into temptation."

Jesus said to them, "You will all fall away, for it is written, 'I will strike the shepherd, and the sheep will be scattered.' But after I am raised up, I will go before you to Galilee." Peter said to him, "Even though they all fall away, I will not." And Jesus said to him, "Truly, I tell you, this very night, before the rooster crows twice, you will deny me three times." But he said emphatically, "If I must die with you, I will not deny you." And they all said the same.

He said to his disciples, "Sit here while I pray." He took with him only Peter, James, and John and began to be greatly distressed and troubled. He said to them, "My soul is very sorrowful, even to death. Remain here and watch." And going a little farther, about a stone's throw, he fell to the ground and prayed that, if possible, the hour might pass from him. He said, "Abba, Father, all things are possible for you. Father, if you are willing, remove this cup from me. Nevertheless, not my will, but yours, be done."

And he came and found them sleeping, and he said to Peter, "Simon, are you asleep? Could you not watch with me one hour? Watch and pray that you may not enter into temptation. The spirit indeed is willing, but the flesh is weak."

And again, he went away and prayed, saying the same words. And there appeared to him an angel from heaven, strengthening him. Being in agony, he prayed more earnestly, and his sweat became like great drops of blood falling down to the ground. When he rose from prayer, he came to the disciples and found them sleeping for sorrow, for their eyes were very heavy. He said to them, "Why are you sleeping? Rise and pray that you may not enter into temptation." And they did not know how to answer him.

Leaving them again, he went and prayed a third time and a third time, he came back and said to them, "Are you still sleeping and taking your rest? Sleep and take your rest later on. It is enough; see, the hour has come and is at hand. The Son of Man is betrayed into the hands of sinners . . . rise, let us be going; see, my betrayer is at hand."

JESUS' ARREST

Now Judas, who betrayed him, also knew the garden where Jesus was, for Jesus often met there with his disciples. Judas came with a great crowd with swords and clubs from the Chief Priests and the elders of the people. The betrayer had given them a sign, saying, "The one I will kiss is the man; seize him." Since all of Jesus' disciples were young men from Galilee, they would be difficult to distinguish from one another in the dark and in an age before the invention of eyeglasses. Judas came up to Jesus at once and said, "Greetings, Rabbi!" And he kissed him. Jesus said to him, "Friend, do what you came to do."

Jesus, knowing what would happen to him, came forward and said to them, "Whom do you seek?" They answered him, "Jesus of Nazareth." Jesus said to them, "I am he." Judas, who betrayed him, was standing with them. When Jesus said to them, "I am he," they drew back and fell to the ground. So he asked them again, "Whom do you seek?" And they said, "Jesus of Nazareth." Jesus answered, "I told you that I am he. So, if you seek me, let these men go." This was to fulfill the word that he had spoken: "Of those whom you gave me, I have lost not one."

Then Simon Peter, having a sword, drew it, struck the High Priest's servant, and cut off his right ear. The servant's name was Malchus. Jesus said to Peter, "Put your sword into its sheath; shall I not drink the cup that the Father has given me?"

JUDAS' SUICIDE

Later, when Judas, his betrayer, saw that Jesus was condemned, he changed his mind and brought back the thirty pieces of silver to the Chief Priests and the elders, saying, "I have sinned by betraying innocent blood." They said, "What is that to us? See to it yourself." And throwing down the pieces of silver into the Temple, he went and hanged himself.

The Chief Priests, taking the pieces of silver, said, "It is not lawful to put them into the treasury since it is blood money." So they took counsel and bought with them the potter's field as a burial place for strangers. Therefore, that field has been called the Field of Blood to this day. Then was fulfilled what had been spoken by the prophet Jeremiah, saying, "And they took the thirty pieces of silver, the price of him on whom some of the sons of Israel had set a price, and they gave them for the potter's field, as the Lord directed me" (Matt 27:9–10).

Judas acquired the field as a reward for his wickedness. Falling headlong, he burst open in the middle, and all his bowels gushed out. This became known to all the inhabitants of Jerusalem, so the field was called Akeldama, that is, Field of Blood, in their own language.[1]

WHO BOUGHT THE FIELD OF BLOOD?

Matthew wrote that the Chief Priests and elders bought the Potter's Field (Matt 27:9–10). Luke wrote in Acts that Judas bought this field, which the inhabitants of Jerusalem called the Field of Blood (Acts 1:18–19). This is not a contradiction. The Chief Priests bought the field in the name of Judas. They used the silver belonging to Judas because it was cursed, and they did not wish to spend it in their own names. Therefore, they said, "he bought it," although they executed the purchase on his behalf.

DID MATTHEW AND LUKE CONTRADICT EACH OTHER?

Is there a contradiction in Scripture between the account of Judas' death in Matthew and Acts? Matthew wrote that Judas hanged himself (Matt 27:5). Luke wrote in Acts that "he burst open in the middle and all his

---

1. See the section "Did Matthew Misquote Scripture" at www.thebiblehistoryguy.com.

bowels gushed out" (Acts 1:18). These accounts are not mutually exclusive. If Judas hung himself from a tree over the edge of a cliff or gully, and if his body then fell onto jagged rocks below, then his entrails would gush out just as Luke vividly described.

Judas hanged himself on Friday, April 1, AD 33, the eve of both Passover and the Sabbath. No righteous Jew would defile himself and the holy day by cutting down a corpse during the feast of Unleavened Bread, which lasted until Friday, April 8, because "whoever touches the dead body of any person shall be unclean for seven days" (Num 19:11). But April 8 was also a Sabbath Eve so that no one would have cut Judas down until the end of Passover, Sunday, April 10. Judas, therefore, hung, unattended, for ten days, decomposing and finally falling and bursting open.

Luke adds accurate detail to Matthew's account, without introducing a contradiction. His account fits the calendar of that year with precision. The day after Judas' cadaver burst, Monday, April 11, the resurrected Jesus again appeared to the disciples in the Upper Room, this time with Thomas present. What Judas missed!

WERE THE BETRAYALS OF JUDAS AND PETER DIFFERENT?

If both Judas and Peter felt remorse about betraying Jesus, why was Peter forgiven and Judas condemned? All who earnestly seek God find him, "For whoever would draw near to God must believe that he exists and that he rewards those who seek him" (Heb 11:6). In fact, God "is patient toward you, not wishing that any should perish, but that all should reach repentance" (2 Peter 3:9).

However, those who seek God on their own terms will not be saved since he "saved us, not because of works done by us in righteousness, but according to his own mercy, by the washing of regeneration and renewal of the Holy Spirit" (Titus 3:5). The Bible says, "There is a way which seems right to a man, but its end is the way to death" (Prov 14:12). Further, there are those who seek too late, namely, after they die, for "it is appointed for man to die once, and after that comes judgment" (Heb 9:27).[2]

All who come to God in this life in penitence, falling upon his mercy, receive his gracious gift of salvation. Judas felt remorse but not repentance. This is evident because Judas did not seek forgiveness from God but

---

2. See also the rich man and Lazarus in Luke 16:19–31.

from his co-conspirators, the Jewish elite. He wanted them to take back the money and remove his guilt. But only God could remove his guilt. Had Judas freely repented, God would have granted him grace. Judas regretted his sin (Matt 27:4) but did not repent. Peter regretted his sin and repented. Hence, Judas was lost (John 17:12), and Peter was saved.

DID GOD FORCE JUDAS TO BETRAY JESUS?

If God foreknew that Judas would betray Jesus, was Judas to blame? If Judas had to fulfill this prophecy because God had predestined him to do so, should it not have been God's fault? If Judas could have chosen freely not to fulfill the prophecy, could he have falsified the prophecy and proven God wrong?

This misconception of predestination arises when we try to understand time from a human, rather than a divine, perspective. The human mind is trapped in time, just as a word is trapped on a page. The word on a page cannot see what is on the page before, the page after, the end of the chapter, or the beginning of the chapter, much less the front and back cover of the book. But just as a reader can do all those things and even put the whole book on a shelf and choose to read a different book, God can contemplate, pick up, and set aside time.

God is a super-temporal (eternal) Being. Time is a created thing. The Creator created time. The Creator is greater than the Creation. Thus, the Creator is not subject to time. Time is subject to the Creator. The Creator transcends time. It is, therefore, incorrect to speak of God as knowing "in advance." If God is above and beyond time, then he knows everything at once, in one "eternal now." He does not really foreknow; he simply knows.

God can know for sure what will happen freely. But just because God is certain about a future event does not mean that it will not freely occur. The same event can be necessary from the vantage point of God and free from the standpoint of human choice. For example, if we see a child running on a wet pool deck, we may say, "That child is going to trip and fall." That does not mean we caused the child to trip and fall; we simply predicted it. God, in his omniscience, sees the future with the same certainty with which he sees the past. He knew that Judas would betray Christ. That does not mean Judas was coerced. God knew certainly that Judas would freely betray Christ.

You may say, "This is nonsense. It is impossible for something to be both mandatory and just probable." But why? Possibility and impossibility are also God's creations. God is not subject to universal laws within which he has to operate. God created all universal laws. The creator of anything is always greater than his creation. When we say something is impossible, it is only because God chose to make it impossible. Had he wished to design the universe otherwise, with, for example, square circles, it would have been possible with him because, with God, all things are possible (Matt 19:26).

A good example of this relates back to time. "With the Lord, one day is as a thousand years, and a thousand years as one day" (2 Peter 3:8). Is it possible for a day and one thousand days to pass in the same interval? On earth, it is impossible. But Einstein's Theory of Relativity says that the faster an object travels through space, the slower it travels through time. An object that travels through space at the speed of light will experience time that is very nearly at a standstill, as almost all its motion through time has been converted into its motion through space. So, in the instant of Creation, a million years at the stationary epicenter of a cosmic Big Bang might transpire in one day for an object speeding through space at the rapidly expanding edge of the universe. The apostle Peter articulated this complex concept perfectly.

DID JUDAS LOSE HIS SALVATION?

Judas' case raises the question of eternal security: Is a believer forever saved? Sincere Christians have various views about eternal security, but the Bible promises that once we are saved, we are forever saved. Jesus said we need to be born again, not born again and again and again. The Bible does not teach believers to live in eternal insecurity. But the question is: can a believer choose to become a non-believer?

Some say that if one is truly born again, one can no more become un-born again than one can undo his physical birth. But this is not a persuasive analogy because one can, of course, commit suicide. Suicide does not undo one's physical birth, but it terminates physical life. How about spiritual suicide? What about the person who once was saved but who then consciously chooses to reject an ongoing relationship with God? Is there eternal security for a former believer? Will God override the unbeliever's free choice and force him into salvation?

Paul wrote, "I am sure that neither death nor life, nor angels nor rulers, nor things present nor things to come, nor powers, nor height nor depth, nor anything else in all creation, will be able to separate us from the love of God in Christ Jesus our Lord" (Rom 8:38–39). So, these are ten things that cannot separate us from Christ: (1) death, (2) life, (3) angles, (4) rulers, (5) things present, (6) things to come, (7) powers, (8) height, (9) depth, or (10) anything else in creation. All these things cannot separate us, but Paul does not include one thing: our own choice. We can separate ourselves.

John 10:27–29 says that the Lord's sheep know his voice, he knows them, they follow him, they receive eternal life, and no one can snatch them from his hand. True, no one else can snatch them from the Lord's hand. But what if a former believer chooses to stop listening to the Lord's voice and elects to stop following him? Has he not jumped out of the Lord's hand? The sheep has himself chosen to become a goat.

The simple biblical reality is that one has the choice to be a sheep or a goat. If one chooses to be a goat or makes no choice, he will be a goat. But if one chooses to be a sheep, he becomes a new creature in Christ (2 Cor 5:17, Eph 4:24, Col 3:10). One can go back to living with the goats if he wants, but most people, having experienced life as a goat and as a sheep, will want to stick with the sheep.

WAS JUDAS EVER SAVED?

Jesus sent Judas out with the Twelve (Matt 10:1–4, Luke 9:1–2) and the Seventy-Two (Luke 10:1). If he was never saved, did Judas, like the others, preach the Good News, heal the lame, give sight to the blind, and perform the same miracles to the glory of God that the other Disciples did? The Bible says that Jesus gave authority to the Twelve, not to the Eleven. This must have, therefore, included Judas.

Perhaps Judas received the offer of this authority but never accepted it, just as God offers salvation to all as a free gift, but not all accept it. If so, Judas may not have performed signs and wonders; he may merely have witnessed his companion (probably Simon the Zealot) do so when Jesus sent the disciples out in pairs. This seems unlikely, however, because Simon would surely have commented upon it. Rather, when the disciples returned to Jesus, they were all excited at the wonders they had performed. If, however, the argument is true that a believer may become a former believer, possibly Judas did perform signs and wonders and once was saved, but ultimately, he rejected salvation.

Or, as one more possibility, Jesus testified that even non-believers may sometimes perform miracles:

> "Not everyone who says to me, 'Lord, Lord,' will enter the kingdom of heaven, but the one who does the will of my Father who is in heaven. On that day many will say to me, 'Lord, Lord, did we not prophesy in your name, and cast out demons in your name, and do many mighty works in your name?' And then will I declare to them, 'I never knew you; depart from me, you workers of lawlessness'" (Matt 7:21–23).

Deuteronomy 13 also says that a false prophet may perform miracles, but his false teaching demands that those who love God not follow him. This means that God may use anyone, even Judas or a false prophet, for his purposes. God causes all things to work together for good to those who love God and to those who are called according to his purpose (Rom 8:28).

Since the Bible says that Satan entered Judas at the Last Supper (John 13:27), it suggests that Satan had not entered Judas until then, even though Judas was previously dishonest (John 12:6). A saved believer cannot be indwelt by Satan or a demon, "for he who is in you is greater than he who is in the world" (1 John 4:4). Jesus confirmed this when he said, "How can someone enter a strong man's house and plunder his goods, unless he first binds the strong man? Then indeed he may plunder his house" (Matt 12:29). When the Jews accused Jesus of being demon-possessed, he responded, "I do not have a demon, but I honor my Father, and you dishonor me" (John 8:49). Being demon-possessed and being indwelt by the Holy Spirit are therefore mutually exclusive states. When Judas betrayed Jesus, he was indwelt by Satan and thus was not at that time saved. Before he was indwelt by Satan, although a sinner, he may have been saved.

Jesus' comment about Judas, that it would have been better if he never had been born, is evidence of hell's reality. Jesus would never have said that if Judas' fate after death were not a painful punishment.

APOCRYPHA

Muslims cite the *Gospel of Barnabas*, which says that Jesus never died on the Cross. They say Allah substituted Judas for Jesus at the last moment. This is how Jesus was able to appear to be dead and also manage "post-Resurrection" appearances. The first mention of this book is from the fifth century, and there is no evidence to support its authenticity. The

Gospel of Judas is another apocryphal work, purporting to record conversations between Jesus and Judas Iscariot. Its Gnostic author does not even pretend that Judas wrote the book. It is inauthentic.

WAS JUDAS WELL-MEANING?

Many have tried to justify Judas by making him a Zealot, like his fellow disciple, Simon. The argument is that Judas was a member of the *Sicarii* dedicated to expelling the Romans forcefully from Judaea. The idea is that he wished to promote Jesus as a leader of this movement. When Jesus refused to accept the role of rebel chief, Judas betrayed him to the High Priest, hoping to goad Jesus into action. When the plan tragically misfired and Jesus died, Judas' remorse drove him to suicide.

The problem with this tale is that it lacks biblical support. Simon, although a Zealot, understood Jesus' message and chose loyalty to the Master over devotion to a political party. The *Sicarii* emerged as a political movement in AD 40–68, seven to thirty-five years after Judas' death. Scripture portrays Judas as a man voluntarily given to greed and sin, not as a misguided idealist. Lacking contemporary evidence, this thesis is weak.

The tragedy of Judas' betrayal is similar to the Sanhedrin's rejection of Jesus. As trained rabbis, they had all the evidence they needed to know that Jesus was, as he claimed, the expected Messiah. Theirs was the unforgivable sin: the conscious, deliberate, persistent rejection of the Holy Spirit (Mark 3:29, Luke 12:10). Judas' sin led to suicide and hell. The Sanhedrin's sin led to the annihilation of Israel in AD 70, the end of the Old Covenant, the Diaspora of the Jews, and to hell. Judas personally heard Jesus say, "I am the way, and the truth, and the life; no one comes to the Father but through me" (John 14:6). Judas consciously chose to reject that truth.

> A man's own worth by himself is priced.
> Judas, for silver, sold himself, not Christ.[3]

---

3. Paraphrase of Hester H. Cholmondeley, "Betrayal."

MATTHIAS, THE THIRTEENTH DISCIPLE

AFTER JUDAS ISCARIOT'S BETRAYAL and suicide, Peter understood that God wanted the Eleven to choose someone to take Judas' place. After Jesus' Ascension on May 13, AD 33, he said:

> "So one of the men who have accompanied us during all the time that the Lord Jesus went in and out among us, beginning from the baptism of John until the day when he was taken up from us—one of these men must become with us a witness to his Resurrection." And they put forward two, Joseph called Barsabbas, who was also called Justus, and Matthias. And they prayed and said, "You, Lord, who know the hearts of all, show which one of these two you have chosen to take the place in this ministry and apostleship from which Judas turned aside to go to his own place." And they cast lots for them, and the lot fell on Matthias, and he was numbered with the eleven apostles (Acts 1:21–26).

This is Scripture's only mention of Matthias. Since Peter wanted a candidate who had witnessed Jesus' ministry from his baptism by John all the way to his Ascension, Matthias, and Joseph Justus Barsabbas must have been very early followers of Jesus, earlier than most of the other disciples. Perhaps the distinction between those who were qualified to be among the Twelve was not the length of service but that Jesus called the original Twelve personally and specifically. Many others witnessed the ministry of Jesus from the baptism to the Ascension, of whom the gospels say nothing specific. It is likely, for example, that there were more people than the Twelve Apostles at the Last Supper because Jesus said that the traitor was one of the Twelve who had dipped his bread in the dish with Jesus. Since everyone at the Passover meal would have done that, by specifying that the traitor was one of the Twelve who did it, Jesus implied there were others there—probably at least John Mark, for the Upper Room was likely in his house. We also know that there were others besides the Eleven Apostles present in the Upper Room after the Ascension (Acts 1:13–14). So, we should probably imagine many unnamed people accompanying Jesus throughout his ministry, and, indeed, the gospels frequently refer to immense crowds following him. Thus, Matthias might well have been an early but initially unmentioned follower of Jesus. Eusebius wrote that Matthias was one of the seventy-two disciples Jesus sent out (Luke 10:1).[1] At any rate, Matthias was at the birth of the Church on Pentecost, Sunday, May 22, AD 33, and at the Jerusalem Council in AD 49.

SHOULD CHRISTIANS CAST LOTS?

Were the Eleven gambling or practicing superstition by drawing lots when they chose Matthias? Should Christians follow this apostolic example and make major decisions by casting lots? Is this biblical? Proverbs says, "The lot is cast into the lap, but its every decision is from the Lord" (Prov 16:33). The proverb does not advocate casting lots; it merely states that God, not random chance, guides events. God may make his will known through casting lots but casting lots will not necessarily reveal the will of God.

In Jonah, we see another example of casting lots. "And they said to one another, 'Come, let us cast lots, that we may know on whose account this evil has come upon us.' So, they cast lots, and the lot fell on Jonah" (Jon 1:7). The sailors in Jonah's ship were anxious to know God's will, but they did not care which god told them the truth. Their piety may have been the kind found in foxholes. The Bible does not say that the sailors always discovered or followed God's will by casting lots, only that, in this case, God chose to use their casting lots to steer events according to his plan. Neither of these passages makes a clear case advocating the use of lots by believers today. But the apostles were not arbitrarily playing dice.

---

1. Some manuscripts say seventy, some seventy-two. Eusebius, *Church History*, 1:12:3.

First, they were under the guidance of the Holy Spirit. The fact that miracles attended their ministries shows that they were uniquely under God's hand. The apostles may have been common human beings, but God used them for uncommon missions in uncommon ways. Believers may take lessons from the behavior of the apostles, but we cannot slavishly imitate everything the apostles did. We are called, like them, to preach to Jerusalem, Judaea, Samaria, and the world because other verses make evident that Jesus' Great Commission is for all believers. But we are not called to replace Judas Iscariot. That was a task unique in type and in time. Second, the Eleven did more than merely cast lots. They took counsel of each other and put forward two men who demonstrably met the standards of an apostle of Christ. Third, they prayed for God's selection and believed that God would answer their prayers. Fourth, they cast lots between two good choices, two godly men, chosen by godly men, selected in a godly way. So, in this case, casting lots was not like choosing between good or evil but between good and good.

All of this suggests that it would be risky to adopt casting lots as a Christian means of making decisions. If we were to follow the Eleven and cast lots to determine God's will in our lives, we would need to ensure that: (1) like the Eleven, we are taking counsel of godly companions and are under the clear guidance of the Holy Spirit, (2) we are seeking God's will in prayer, and (3) we are casting lots between two equally good options.

The risks of using lots are that we might: (1) persuade ourselves that we are under God's guidance when we really are not, (2) fail to have the good advice of many godly companions, as the Eleven had, (3) put more emphasis on casting lots than on prayer, and (4) persuade ourselves that we are casting lots between two good choices, when, really, the choices might not be equally good. In the election of Matthias, the Eleven were devoted to God, not superstition. Their casting lots was appropriate for the task God gave them. But casting lots is unlikely to be an appropriate decision tool for believers of all times.

MATTHIAS' IMPORTANCE

Was Matthias an apostle of secondary importance? No. Scripture shows that the full number of Twelve Tribes and Twelve Apostles remains important in God's eternal plan. Revelation 21:14 showed that the New

Jerusalem has twelve gates to honor Israel's Twelve Tribes and twelve foundation stones named after the Twelve Apostles, even though ten of the twelve tribes were lost in the Assyrian conquest of Israel in 722–718 BC, and the other two were lost after rejecting Christ and in the Roman desolation of Judaea in AD 66–73. Judas Iscariot, the twelfth disciple, betrayed Christ and committed suicide. In the end, God says he makes all things new (Rev 21:5), including a full restoration of the Twelve Tribes and of the Twelve Apostles as witnesses for God.

MATTHIAS IN ARMENIA AND CUSH

Armenian tradition holds that Matthias, along with Andrew, Nathanael Bartholomew, Judas Thaddaeus, and Simon the Zealot, was among the five apostles who evangelized Armenia. Supposedly, cannibals from Cush (not the Cush in Africa, Ethiopia, but an ancient province near Armenia on the Caspian Sea) imprisoned Matthias and blinded him. The risen Christ appeared to Andrew and sent him to save Matthias. Andrew went and miraculously restored Matthias' sight. Andrew triumphed over the cannibals through prayer and freed Matthias.[2]

ARMENIA'S APOSTOLIC HERITAGE

In the fourth century, Armenia's King Tiridates persecuted Christians. He tortured an evangelist, Gregory, and threw him into a pit full of serpents and corpses, where he languished for thirteen years. During Gregory's imprisonment, Tiridates fell in love with Hripsima, a virgin under the care of a Christian abbess named Gayane. Hripsima rejected Tiridates' love, so the king put to the sword all the young girls under the abbess' care. Then, Tiridates fell desperately ill. His Christian sister, Khosroviducht, had a dream in which she perceived that only Gregory could cure the king. She urged her brother to free Gregory. The king finally did so, and Gregory miraculously healed him.

Tiridates became a Christian and destroyed all the pagan temples in Armenia, except for that at Garni, which even today is one of the most beautiful ancient Greek temples still standing. Gregory invented the Armenian alphabet so that he could translate the Bible into the Armenian tongue. He composed one of the oldest translations of Scripture

---

2. The apocryphal *Acts of Andrew and Matthias*.

in the world.[3] Armenians ever after called him Gregory the Illuminator. Armenia became the first nation to embrace Christianity in AD 301, twelve years before the emperor Constantine made Rome a Christian empire by his Edict of Milan in AD 313.

THE DEATH OF MATTHIAS

According to tradition, Matthias returned to Jerusalem, where hostile Jews stoned him to death. If so, this would have been some time in the twenty-year interval between AD 49, the Jerusalem Council, and AD 70, when the Roman general Titus burned Jerusalem to the ground. It might have been in or after AD 66 when the Roman-Jewish war began because, at that time, Jerusalem was in the hands of angry Jewish factions, who might well have treated the apostle cruelly. Helena, the mother of Constantine the Great, allegedly brought Matthias' relics to Constantinople. Later, they were taken to Rome.

---

3. When this author's wife, Madlene, organized relief to Armenia after the 1988 earthquake, one aspect of the mission was to bring Bibles to the people of that then-atheist Soviet regime. Some major American donors called Madlene for assurance that their funds would be used to bring only the King James Version to Armenia. Madlene explained that the Bibles would be in the Eastern Armenian language and that the Armenian translation from Greek predated the KJV by nearly twelve centuries.

SAUL OF TARSUS, OR PAUL

He approved of the cold-blooded stoning of an innocent man. He ravaged the Church, going from house to house and throwing both men and women into prison. He breathed threats and murder against believers in Christ and obtained a license to hunt them down in another country and drag them back to Jerusalem in chains. Violent mobs rioted against him, threatened him with death, or threw him out of at least eight cities. Forty of his co-religionists vowed to fast until they saw him dead. He did four stints in jail. The authorities whipped him five times with thirty-nine lashes. He was beaten with rods three times. Once, he was stoned and left for dead. He was shipwrecked four times.[1] He argued publicly with the foremost leaders of the Church two times. So far, how would this minister fare if he were applying to your church for a pastoral post?

But Jesus called him personally and spoke to him directly four times. He paid his own way and raised funds for other believers in over twenty thousand miles and thirty-five years of ministry on two continents. He founded at least thirteen churches and probably many more. He worked healing miracles and raised a dead man to life. He assertively bridged the gap between two hostile religions. He advocated the rights of all people and both genders with world-changing effect. He led opposition to slavery, misogyny, and racism. He trained and empowered a team of talented and effective leaders who influenced thousands. And he wrote half of the books of the New Testament. How would this applicant for a pastoral post at your church fare now?

---

1. His shipwreck in Malta was his fourth, occurring after he wrote 2 Cor 11:24–27.

This was the apostle Paul, a passionate man who began his career on the wrong track, made a breathtaking reversal, influenced the world as few ever have, and did so with bold confidence in his beliefs but with total personal humility.

Other apostles may have traveled as far and endured as much as Paul, but Acts focuses on Paul exceptionally. This is not because the labors of the other apostles were less worthy or effective. It is because the book of Acts aimed not to record every act of every apostle but to show how the Way evolved from a local sect of Messianic Jews to a worldwide call for all humanity into a restored relationship with God. The two men who most contributed to this event in the Roman world were Peter and Paul. Paul was probably twenty-nine years old when Jesus called him on the Damascus Road and sixty-three years old when he died in AD 68. He spent thirty-five years in Christian ministry.

PAUL'S SEVENTEEN LETTERS

Paul's surviving writings comprise fourteen of the twenty-seven books of the New Testament. Three of his letters, two to Corinth and one to Laodicea have been lost. He may also have written the epistle to the Hebrews, although some attribute it to Barnabas, Apollos, or Luke. The following is the list of these epistles.

1. Galatians, May, AD 49, from Antioch (Syria) to the churches in Galatia (modern Turkey)
2. 1 Thessalonians, May AD 50, from Corinth (Greece) to the church in Thessalonica (Macedonia, modern Greece)
3. 2 Thessalonians, June, AD 50, from Corinth to the church in Thessalonica
4. A lost letter of warning (1 Cor 5:9), November, AD 51, from Ephesus (modern Turkey) to the church in Corinth
5. 1 Corinthians, March, AD 52, from Ephesus to the church in Corinth
6. A lost, severe letter of tears (2 Cor 2:3,4 and 7:8), May, AD 52, from Ephesus to the church in Corinth
7. 2 Corinthians, November, AD 53, from Philippi (Macedonia, modern Greece) to the church in Corinth

8. Romans, March AD 54, from Corinth to the church in Rome
9. 1 Timothy, around April AD 54, from Caesarea (Israel) to Timothy in Ephesus
10. Ephesians, AD 57–69, from Rome to the church in Ephesus
11. Philippians, AD 57–59, from Rome to the church in Philippi
12. Colossians, AD 57–59, from Rome to the church in Colossae (modern Turkey)
13. A lost letter (Col 4:16), AD 57–59, from Rome to the church in Laodicea (modern Turkey)
14. Philemon, AD 57–59, from Rome to Philemon, the head of the church in Colossae
15. Hebrews, January, AD 59, from Rome to the Jewish Christians in Jerusalem.
16. Titus, AD 66, from Corinth to Titus in Crete.
17. 2 Timothy, around April AD 68, from Rome to Timothy in Ephesus.

PAUL'S PERSONAL LIFE

Paul was supposed to be short, broad-shouldered, and somewhat bald, with closely-knit eyebrows, an aquiline nose, a thick, gray beard, and a pleasing, friendly manner. Jerome says that Paul was of the tribe of Benjamin and was born in the town of Giscalis [Gischala] in Galilee. When the Romans claimed this region [in AD 7],[2] his parents took him and their family to Tarsus in Cilicia. So, Paul was of Galilean origin. Assuming Paul was at least two years old when his family made the move to Tarsus, he may have been born in AD 5.

Around AD 33, his parents sent him to Jerusalem to study law. He would have been about twenty-nine years old. Paul says that he was brought up in Jerusalem (Acts 22:3), but since he grew up in Tarsus, by "brought up," he means educated, studying under Gamaliel, a rabbi and "a most learned man,"[3] who was a leading authority among the Sanhedrin (Acts 22:3). Paul's sister and nephew lived in Jerusalem. We know this

---

2. Josephus, *Antiquities*, 18:1–2.
3. Jerome, *On Illustrious Men*.

because when he was imprisoned there, his sister's son brought him news of the Jewish plot to ambush him (Acts 23:16).

As was common in the bilingual culture of Roman Judaea, he probably used the name Saul in Jewish circles and Paul in Greek (and Roman) society. Every respectable Jewish young man learned a trade. A Jewish proverb says, "he who does not teach his son a trade teaches him to steal." Saul's father trained him in the trade of making tents (Acts 18:3).

Paul's father was a Roman citizen, and so was Paul by inheritance. Paul described himself as a man who was duly circumcised on the eighth day after his birth (as Moses prescribed), of the nation of Israel, of the tribe of Benjamin, a Hebrew of Hebrews, and, as to the Law, a Pharisee (Phil 3:5). As a Pharisee, he was a religious conservative and believed in the Resurrection of the dead, angels, and spirits. The Sadducees, who were the more numerous members of the Sanhedrin, believed in none of these things. They were Hellenizers, imitators of the dominant Greek culture. The Pharisees were purists, conservative adherents to Jewish tradition.

THE THORN IN PAUL'S FLESH

Paul suffered from a mysterious "thorn in his flesh," a messenger from Satan meant to keep him humble, which he prayed three times for the Lord to remove. Jesus declined to do so, saying, "My grace is sufficient for you, for my power is made perfect in weakness" (2 Cor 12:7–9). There are many conjectures about what this thorn was. It may have been a physical malady. Paul's parents may have rejected him after he began following Jesus. He may have had a never-mentioned wife who rejected him for becoming a Christian. He may have been a widower and may have struggled with the desire to remarry and settle down, as opposed to following God's call on seemingly endless missionary journeys. Or he may have struggled with some other temptation or grief. Scripture simply does not say.

STONING STEPHEN

Saul first appeared in Scripture at the stoning of Stephen in AD 33, the year of the Cross. Luke described him as a young man who guarded the robes of those who executed the first martyr, Stephen. Saul was in hearty agreement with putting Stephen to death (Acts 8:1). But this was not enough for this zealous, young Pharisee. In fact, Stephen's death made things worse in Paul's view because it caused all Christians in Jerusalem except the apostles to scatter, preaching the Gospel wherever they went (Acts 8:4).

The apostle Philip did not scatter, that is, retreat in fear, but he did leave Jerusalem and evangelize in Samaria. Peter and John joined him in that effort. Then Philip converted an Ethiopian eunuch in Gaza and preached all along the Mediterranean coast as far north as Caesarea. Saul was alarmed that the Christian sect was spreading so quickly. Like a general, he thought to outflank the enemy. Breathing threats and murder against the disciples of the Lord, Saul went to the High Priest and asked for letters from him to the synagogues in Damascus, giving him authority so that if he found any followers of the Way, whether men or women, he might bring them in chains to Jerusalem. If Saul could cause havoc among the Christians in Damascus, he might stop the progress of the cult and hammer it back down.

THE DAMASCUS ROAD: JESUS SPOKE TO PAUL THE FIRST TIME

The following is a synthesis of the three accounts of Paul's Damascus Road experience (Acts 9:3–9, 22:6–11, 26:12–18). There is no contradiction between them. Luke simply changed emphasis and details in each telling without compromising the integrity of the narrative.

Saul was convinced that he ought to do many things in opposing the name of Jesus of Nazareth. He did so in Jerusalem. He not only locked up many of the saints in prison after receiving authority from the chief priests, but when they were sentenced to death, he cast his vote against them. He punished them often in all the synagogues and tried to make them blaspheme, and in raging fury against them, he persecuted them even in foreign cities.

Now, with the authority and commission of the chief priests,[4] Saul journeyed and drew near to Damascus. Suddenly, about noon,[5] he saw on the way a great light from heaven, brighter than the sun, that shone around him and those who traveled with him. When they had all fallen to the ground, he heard a voice saying to him in Hebrew, "Saul, Saul, why are you persecuting me? It is hard for you to kick against the goads." He asked, "Who are you, Lord?" The Lord said to him, "I am Jesus of Nazareth, whom you are persecuting."

Now, the men who were traveling with him stood speechless, hearing the voice but seeing no one. Those who were with him saw the light but did not understand the voice of the one who was speaking to him. Saul asked, "What shall I do?" The Lord said to him:

> Rise and stand upon your feet, for I have appeared to you for this purpose, to appoint you as a servant and witness to the things in which you have seen me and to those in which I will appear to you, delivering you from your people and from the Gentiles—to whom I am sending you to open their eyes, so that they may turn from darkness to light and from the power of Satan to God, that they may receive forgiveness of sins and a place among those who are sanctified by faith in me. Go into Damascus, and there you will be told all that is appointed for you.

Because of the brightness of that light, although his eyes were opened, he saw nothing. Those who were with him led him by the hand into Damascus. For three days, he was without sight and neither ate nor drank.

The Lord appeared in a vision to a Damascus disciple named Ananias and told him, "Get up and go to the street called Straight and inquire at the house of Judas for a man from Tarsus named Saul, for he is praying, and he has seen in a vision a man named Ananias come in and lay his hands on him, so that he might regain his sight." Ananias

---

4. Paul carried a letter to the ethnarch under Aretas, who was king of Arabia Petraea (modern Jordan) and of Damascus, although there, like Herod Antipas in Galilee and Peraea, he was a client king under Rome. An ethnarch was the ruler of an ethnic group within a kingdom or province, in this case, Syria. This ethnarch was the representative of the Syrian Jews. His job was to present Jewish petitions to the ruler of Damascus and help the ruler keep the Jews in line. Damascus was a rich target for Paul because the Jewish population of the city was numerous. In a revolt under Nero, the Romans slew 10,000 Jews there (Josephus, *Jewish Wars*, 2:25). Within this large Jewish population were some, and perhaps many, who called upon the name of Jesus (Acts 9:14).

5. Sunday, April 2, AD 34.

answered, "Lord, I have heard from many about this man, how much harm he did to your saints at Jerusalem. And here he has authority from the chief priests to bind all who call on your name." But the Lord said to him, "Go, for he is a chosen instrument of mine, to bear my name before the Gentiles and kings and the sons of Israel; for I will show him how much he must suffer for my name's sake."

So, Ananias went and laid hands on Saul, and immediately, something like scales fell from Saul's eyes. He regained his sight, got up, and was baptized. Then, he took food and regained his strength. Saul joined the other Christians in Damascus and at once began proclaiming Jesus in the synagogues, saying, "He is the Son of God." The people were amazed that this former persecutor of Christians was now preaching Christ.

ARABIA: AD 34–37

In Galatians 1, Paul said that after his conversion on the Damascus Road, he did not go immediately to Jerusalem but went to Arabia. As Paul journeyed from Damascus to Arabia, he must have passed the place on the Damascus Road where Jesus had first called him. He must have paused to reflect on that miraculous encounter. Possibly, Paul went to Arabia to meditate on the Scriptures and on how Jesus fulfilled their Messianic prophecies. Saul had a great deal of theological rethinking to do. Perhaps Paul retreated to the Mountain of God, consciously following in the footsteps of Elijah. It is not likely that by "Arabia," Paul meant Arabia Petraea (modern Jordan), the realm of King Aretas, because Paul's original mission was endorsed by a letter from the Jewish leaders in Jerusalem to King Aretas' ethnarch in Damascus. Aretas' governor in Damascus was the official who ordered Paul's arrest (2 Cor 11:32). By "Arabia," Paul probably meant the deep and vast Arabian Peninsula.

THE MOUNTAIN OF GOD

When King Ahab told his wife Jezebel how Elijah had killed the prophets of Baal with the sword (1 Kings 19:1), Jezebel threatened to kill Elijah. Terrified, Elijah fled to Beersheba and left his servant there. He then went a day's journey into the desert. An angel gave him food and drink, and he traveled another forty days and forty nights to Horeb, the Mountain of God, where Moses received the Ten Commandments.

Two mountains are candidates for being the Mountain of Moses. Mount Saint Catherine in Sinai, Egypt, rises 4,353 feet above Beersheba (850 feet above sea level), from which it is 259 miles distant. To walk from Beersheba without taking a break, would take 4.5 days.[6] Jebel al-Lawz rises 7,615 feet from Beersheba and is 309 miles distant. To make that trek with no break would take 5.3 days. The hike to either mountain from Beersheba would take about forty days if the traveler were walking for four hours per day and pausing for twenty hours per day. This might be the case if the traveler were walking only in the cool of the morning and conserving his strength for the rest of the day while fasting.

Jebel al-Lawz was more likely Elijah's destination.[7] Elijah lodged in a cave on Mount Horeb (1 Kings 19:9). There is no cave on Mount Saint Catherine in Egypt, but there is a sizable cave on Jebel al-Lawz. Furthermore, Paul stated that "Mount Sinai is in Arabia" (Gal 4:25). Paul would not have confused Sinai with Arabia since, from at least the third millennium BC, the Sinai Peninsula was under Egyptian rule. The Egyptians called Sinai *Mafkat*, meaning the "country of turquoise," which, along with copper, the pharaohs mined there from great antiquity. Therefore, Paul's retreat to Arabia, although he never states the destination, may have been to Jebel al-Lawz. But why go there?

Paul's realization that Jesus was the Messiah required him to go back to the Scriptures, just as, on the road to Emmaus, Jesus took Cleophus (Clopas) and his companion through the Scriptures to explain his role as Messiah (Luke 24:45). Paul may have journeyed to Mount Horeb, the sacred ground where God gave Moses the Law to seek understanding about Christ. Perhaps he saw himself as a second Elijah. Like Elijah, he would perform miracles through the Holy Spirit. For example, Elijah restored a child to life (1 Kings 17:22), and Paul resurrected a young man named Eutychus (Acts 20:9–12).

Unlike Elijah, Paul stayed in Arabia for about three years. It is impossible to know what he did there or with whom he stayed. Perhaps there was a community of religious recluses, similar to the community at Qumran, who congregated near the holy site of Mount Horeb. Perhaps Paul searched the Scriptures with them. Or perhaps he studied alone. This side of heaven, barring some stunning archaeological find, we may never know.

---

6. *The Walking Englishman's Walk Time Calculator*.
7. Robert Cornuke and David Halbrook, *In Search of the Mountain of God*.

An intriguing speculation is that perhaps Jesus, when he went for forty days and forty nights into the wilderness, also journeyed to Mount Horeb in Arabia. One clue to this is that during that desert sojourn, "the devil took him up to a high mountain (Matt 4:8, Luke 4:5). Jebel al-Lawz, with an elevation of 8,465 feet above sea level, fits that description. Of course, the devil also took Jesus to the pinnacle of the Jerusalem Temple (Matt 4:5, Luke 4:9), which must surely have been either an imaginative or a supernatural event; therefore, the ascent of the high mountain might also have been imaginative or supernatural and is not proof positive that Jesus was at Mount Horeb.

After Jesus' temptation, angels from heaven came and strengthened and attended him, and he was with the wild animals (Matt 4:11, Mark 1:13, Luke 22:43). Similarly, at the start of Elijah's journey into the wilderness, an angel appeared to the prophet and gave him nourishment sufficient for forty days and nights (1 Kings 19:5). So, both Elijah and Jesus fasted for forty days and nights, and both were nourished by an angel, one at the beginning and one at the end of his desert sojourn. Since the Holy Spirit "drove" Jesus into the wilderness (Mark 1:12), if the inspired destination was Mount Horeb, perhaps the Holy Spirit also led Paul to the same place.

BACK IN DAMASCUS: AD 37

Paul returned from Arabia to Damascus after three years, that is, three years after his conversion (Gal 1:18). Once again, as he traveled the Damascus Road, he must have paused at the spot where Jesus had first appeared to him. As he meditated on the last three years, no doubt the deep meaning of Christ's call was more moving than ever.

Everyone in Damascus hearing Saul was amazed, saying, "Is this not he who in Jerusalem destroyed those who called on this name and who had come here for the purpose of bringing them bound before the chief priests?" Saul kept growing in strength and confounding the Damascus Jews by proving that Jesus was the Christ (Acts 9:21–22).

ESCAPE FROM DAMASCUS

Luke wrote that "when many days had elapsed, the Jews plotted to kill him (Acts 9:23). The ethnarch under Aretas, the Syrian King, threatened to seize him (2 Cor 11:32). An ethnarch was a national ruler from the Greek words *"ethnos"* (nation) and *"archon"* (leader). This ethnarch was the Jewish liaison officer whom Aretas appointed to govern the Jewish community in his kingdom. He was just as violently opposed to Saul's Christianizing as Saul had been against Stephen. Paul's would-be assassins were watching the city gates day and night so that Saul would not escape. Saul's friends took him by night and let him down through an opening in the wall, lowering him in a large basket (Acts 9:25, 2 Cor 11:33). It was a less than triumphal exit.

FIRST RETURN TO JERUSALEM: AD 37

After escaping from Damascus, Saul went to Jerusalem to associate with the disciples, but they were all afraid of him. The disciples suspected that he had not really become a believer, but Barnabas took hold of Saul and brought him to the apostles and described to them how Paul had seen the Lord on the Damascus Road and had preached in the synagogues of Syria. Then they accepted him, and he began loudly speaking out in the name of the Lord. Saul saw Peter at this time but stayed with him for only fifteen days. He did not see any of the other apostles except for James, the half-brother of Jesus (Gal 1:18–19). Probably by this time, the other apostles were already exploring various mission fields.

In Jerusalem, Saul debated vigorously with the Hellenistic Jews (the Sadducees), who plotted to put him to death. Paul must have been very persuasive in arguing that Jesus was the Messiah since his opponents almost always had one of two responses: to believe him or try to kill him. No adversaries ever seem to have felt that they could ignore Paul or defeat him in debate.

JESUS SPOKE TO PAUL A SECOND TIME

For the second recorded time, around May 9, AD 37, Jesus spoke directly to Paul. Luke gave Paul's account:

> When I had returned to Jerusalem and was praying in the temple, I fell into a trance and saw him saying to me, "Make haste and get out of Jerusalem quickly because they will not accept your testimony about me." And I said, "Lord, they themselves know that in one synagogue after another, I imprisoned and

beat those who believed in you. And when the blood of Stephen, your witness, was being shed, I myself was standing by and approving and watching over the garments of those who killed him." And he said to me, "Go, for I will send you far away to the Gentiles" (Acts 22:17–21).

OBSCURITY IN TARSUS: AD 37–43

When the Jerusalem Christians heard of the latest Jewish plot against Paul, they took him to Caesarea. It was not the last time he would escape a death threat by being escorted there. They then sent him away to his hometown of Tarsus (Acts 9:30). Paul disappeared from history for six years.

JOURNEY TO PARADISE: AD 39

In 2 Corinthians 12:1–5, Paul wrote this enigmatic testimony:

> I must go on boasting. Though there is nothing to be gained by it, I will go on to visions and revelations of the Lord. I know a man in Christ who, fourteen years ago, was caught up to the third heaven—whether in the body or out of the body, I do not know, God knows. And I know that this man was caught up into paradise—whether in the body or out of the body I do not know, God knows—and he heard things that cannot be told, which man may not utter. On behalf of this man, I will boast, but on my own behalf, I will not boast, except of my weaknesses.

Who was this man? Since Paul wrote "I know" rather than "I knew," the man was still alive when Paul wrote this letter, which he composed in the year AD 53. Since the event occurred fourteen years before writing the letter, it happened in AD 39. Most commentators think that Paul was referring to himself in the third person. The plain language of the text suggests that Paul was speaking of someone other than himself, although who that might be remains a mystery.

PAUL'S MINISTRY BEGINS AGAIN: AD 43–44

Around AD 43, Barnabas, who must have been impressed with him from their Jerusalem meeting, went and found Paul and encouraged him to enter the ministry at Antioch. Paul agreed, and the two worked together there for a year. Antioch was the third largest and richest city in the empire, after Rome and Alexandria. Believers were first called Christians in the Antioch church (Acts 11:26).

SECOND RETURN TO JERUSALEM: AD 44

In AD 44, Agabus, a prophet, journeyed from Jerusalem to Antioch and predicted that a great famine would devastate Judaea. The Antioch Church sent Barnabas and Saul to Jerusalem with famine relief funds two years in advance of the disaster (Acts 11:27-30). Meanwhile, between Tuesday, March 29, and Thursday, April 7 (the Passover and Feast of Unleavened Bread), Herod Agrippa I, son of Aristobulus and grandson of Herod the Great, killed James, the son of Zebedee and then arrested Peter.[8] An angel released Peter from prison, and he went to the house of Mary, the mother of John Mark (Acts 12:6-17). When Jerusalem broke into an uproar at the news of Peter's escape, Herod executed the prison guards, and Peter fled. Then Herod died a grisly death from parasitic worms (Acts 12:20-23). But the word of God increased and multiplied (Acts 12:24). After that, Paul and Barnabas returned to Antioch, taking John Mark with them (Acts 12:2). In AD 45-46, the great famine struck Judaea, as predicted by Agabus and recorded by Josephus and the Roman historian Paulus Orosius.[9]

FIRST MISSIONARY JOURNEY: AD 44

The years of Paul's three great missionary journeys were the most active of his life. His achievements were astonishing. He was probably about thirty-nine years old when he embarked upon his first missionary journey in May AD 44.

After serving in the Antioch church for one year, Lucius of Cyrene, Paul, Barnabas, Simeon Niger, and Manaen were praying and fasting. All five men were teachers and prophets in Antioch. The Holy Spirit

---

8. Eusebius, *Church History*, 2:9.

9. Josephus, *Antiquities*, 20:2. Famine raged in Judaea under the procurator Cassius Fadus (AD 44-46). Orosius, in his *Histories Against Pagans*, 7:6:9, 12, placed it in the fourth year of Claudius' reign. Claudius began to reign on January 24, AD 41, so his fourth year began on January 24, AD 45.

appointed Barnabas and Paul for a special assignment. Lucius, Simeon, and Manaen laid hands on them and sent them on their first missionary journey to evangelize among the Gentiles (Acts 13:1–3). They left Antioch and embarked at Seleucia, Antioch's seaport, with Barnabas' cousin, John Mark. They sailed for Cyprus, the birthplace of Barnabas, and preached in the synagogue of Salamis.

This was not John Mark's first missionary journey; Peter and Mark had preached to Jews in Pontus, Galatia, Cappadocia, Asia, and Bithynia sometime between AD 41 and 43. Then they pushed on to Rome, founding the church there in AD 43.[10] Reading Acts, one may easily get the impression that Paul was the first to bring the Gospel to these parts of the world, but Peter and Mark preceded him. Mark had already composed his gospel in Rome in AD 43. No doubt, he brought it with him so that he, Paul, and Barnabas could use it as an inspired preaching text.

CYPRUS

The team crossed the island from east to west and reached Paphos, the residence of the Roman proconsul, Sergius Paulus. Opposed by a Jewish false prophet named Bar Jesus Elymas, Saul, who then began using his Hellenic name, Paul, fixed his gaze on him, condemned him, and caused him temporarily to go blind. Witnessing this miracle, the Roman proconsul converted, and Luke thereafter wrote of Paul as the leader of the mission, with Barnabas following.

From Paphos, they sailed to Perga in Pamphylia (Asia Minor), near Paul's birthplace, Tarsus. There, to Paul's disappointment, John Mark deserted them and returned to Jerusalem. Why did Mark go back to Judaea? Scripture is silent. Although it is conjecture, perhaps Mark felt called to disseminate his gospel rather than to pursue this missionary trip with Paul and Barnabas. After all, he had been through this line of country with Peter the year before. Maybe he felt that by leaving them a copy of his gospel, he was not deserting them at all but managing to cover more ground by splitting up. At this time, Mark probably went to Jerusalem and then on to Alexandria, where he founded the Egyptian church. Perhaps that is where Mark thought his real calling led. In any case, it would take time for Paul to forgive Mark.

---

10. Eusebius, *Church History*, 2:14–15.

PISIDIAN ANTIOCH

Paul and Barnabas carried on through the wild and bandit-infested mountains of Pisidia toward Antioch (not the city in Syria), seven days' journey from Perga on the coast. Paul preached the Gospel in the synagogue there, and many Jews accepted Christ. But on the following Sabbath, a large crowd of angry Jews rejected the Gospel and persecuted Paul and Barnabas. Shaking the dust of Pisidian Antioch off their feet, they turned to the Gentiles, and the Gospel went out to the whole region of Antioch.

ICONIUM AND LYSTRA

The pair proceeded to Iconium (modern Konya), four days' journey to the east, where they met with hostility from the native Jews. So, they walked eighteen miles south to Lystra. In Lystra, Paul healed a man lame from birth, and the citizens proclaimed Barnabas and Paul to be the gods Zeus and Hermes. They assumed that since Paul was the more talkative one, he must be Hermes, the messenger of the gods and that Barnabas, the strong, silent one, must be Zeus, the king of gods. The priest of Zeus brought oxen to sacrifice to them, but Paul and Barnabas tore their robes and refused to accept blasphemous worship. As they preached the Gospel, the Jews from Antioch and Iconium caught up with them and incited the crowd, who stoned Paul and left him outside the city for dead. Surrounded by Christian disciples, he rose and staggered back into the city.

DERBE AND HOME

The next day, he and Barnabas set out for Derbe, forty miles to the east. Paul must have had great fortitude to travel forty miles and preach the day after having been stoned nearly to death. They made many converts in Derbe. Then, they returned to Lystra, Iconium, and Antioch, strengthening the new churches and appointing elders. They returned to Perga, where they preached, and then went to Attalia, a coastal town, from which they took ship to Syrian Antioch. Home again, they reported to their church how the door of faith had been opened to the Gentiles. They remained with the disciples there "no little time" (Acts 14:28).

THIRD RETURN TO JERUSALEM: AD 47

Paul took the Greek (Gentile) Christian Titus on a journey to Jerusalem "because of a revelation" (Gal 2:1–2). Paul said in Galatians that this journey was "after" fourteen years, probably meaning after his conversion, which would put it in AD 47. This trip could not have been the one in Acts 11:28–30 because Luke placed it before Herod Agrippa's murder of James in AD 44.

The "revelation" Paul referred to was probably Agabus's prophecy. Two years before the famine, in March AD 44, Agabus had prophesied a famine in Judaea (the "revelation"), and the Antioch church had sent Paul and Barnabas to Jerusalem with famine relief. The famine occurred in AD 45–46. On this trip back to Jerusalem, Paul and his team probably wanted to see to what extent Agabus' revelation had come true and how effective their famine relief had been.

This trip to Jerusalem also cannot be the same as the trip to attend the Jerusalem Council two years later since Paul says he took this trip to Jerusalem "because of a revelation" (Gal 2:2). Paul went to the Jerusalem Council not because of a revelation but because of dissent in the Antioch church (Acts 15:2). Also, Paul's meeting with Peter, John, James, and Barnabas was private on this trip (Gal 2:2), while the Jerusalem Council's debates were public (Acts 15:5).

ECUMENICAL CHRISTIAN THEOLOGY

Paul took advantage of this trip to set before Peter, John, and James (the half-brother of Jesus) the Gospel that he had presented to Gentiles on his first missionary journey. Paul wanted to make sure that he was "not running or had not run in vain" (Gal 2:2).

Paul did not doubt that he understood the Gospel correctly. He stated that he had received it directly from Christ, that he did not have to consult with anyone about its interpretation, and that he did not need to ratify it with those who were apostles before him (Gal 1:15–17). So, why did Paul, when he did not feel the need to get advice from the other apostles in AD 37 during his trip back to Jerusalem in AD 44, want to set his presentation of the Gospel before Peter, John, and James?

It was because Paul had affirmed a discovery that Peter had first made when Peter presented the Gospel to the Gentile household of Cornelius, namely that the Gospel did not require Gentiles to become

Jews to be Christians, and it did not require Jews to become Gentiles to become Christians. Each group of people could remain in their cultural nest and still be brothers and sisters in Christ because "[they had] been crucified with Christ. It is no longer [they] who live, but Christ who lives in [them]. And the life [they] now live in the flesh [they] live by faith in the Son of God" (Gal 2:20).

Peter, James, and John entirely agreed with Paul. They felt no need to add anything to his message (Gal 2:6), and they gave Paul and Barnabas the right hand of fellowship. This theological issue was further tested on that same trip to Jerusalem when some Judaizers spied on Titus, who was a Gentile Christian from Antioch. They saw that he was uncircumcised. They tried to compel his circumcision, but Paul and Barnabas refused to submit to their demand, and James, Peter, and John agreed with them.

Paul and Barnabas had proven themselves in many ways, not the least of which was bringing funds to the Jerusalem church before the famine. James, Peter, and John only asked Paul to remember to help the poor of Jerusalem, which was the very thing he wished to continue doing (Gal 2:10).

Paul never forgot the poor of Jerusalem. He encouraged the churches in Philippi and Corinth to raise money for their support. No doubt, Paul felt a deep sense of guilt for his early, fierce persecution of those people who now were his brothers in Christ. He wrote, "for I am the least of the apostles, and not fit to be called an apostle, because I persecuted the Church of God" (1 Cor 15:9).

Paul's commission to preach to Gentiles and Peter's commission to preach to Jews were primary, not exclusive, assignments. Paul was not actually the first missionary to the Gentiles. Philip, Peter, and John were, in Samaria, to the Ethiopian eunuch and to the household of Cornelius, the Roman centurion. Probably by the time of this trip to Jerusalem, the other apostles had already been on missionary journeys, probably making Gentile converts, too. Paul's commission was to preach primarily to the Gentiles, as that of Peter and the other apostles was to preach primarily to the Jews (Gal 2:9), but all the apostles preached with great effect to both Gentiles and Jews. The main lesson from this trip to Jerusalem was that "there is neither Jew nor Greek [Gentile], there is neither slave nor free, there is no male and female, for you are all one in Christ Jesus" (Gal 3:28). And, importantly, it was not necessary for Gentiles to become Jews or Jews to become Gentiles for all to become Christians.

DEBATE WITH JUDAIZERS AND OPPOSITION TO PETER: AD 49

Paul and his companions returned to Antioch sometime in AD 47, where he remained "no little time" until around May of AD 49. Judaizers from Jerusalem arrived in Antioch and tried to persuade the Gentiles there that they had to become Jewish to be Christian. Paul and Barnabas debated this with them. After seeing the door of faith opened to the Gentiles during their first missionary journey and having settled the matter in Jerusalem with Peter, John, and James with regard to Titus, Paul must have been astonished that the Judaizing argument could still carry on.

Probably between March 30 to April 15, AD 49 (Passover), Peter visited Antioch, and a dispute arose between him and Paul. Peter agreed that Christian Jews were free of the law, but he refrained from eating with Gentiles because he thought it unwise to offend the Judaizers, who were associates of James, the Lord's half-brother. Peter probably thought it was not a big issue because the Gentile Christians would probably not care about eating the Passover meal with Peter anyway. Only the Jewish Christians would be eager to do so. He possibly also thought that what he, Paul, John, and James had agreed upon in Jerusalem was that Paul's department was the Gentiles and Peter's department was the Jews. But Paul's argument went far beyond that.

Paul meant that when evangelizing, the apostles did not need to persuade converts to abandon their cultural heritage; they could become Christians just as they were (so long as they did not drag idolatrous or immoral traditions into the church). Peter's example in Antioch would have influenced Gentiles and Jews to reach the opposite conclusion and either create opposing camps within the church or repel many from the church altogether. Paul opposed Peter's actions publicly and to his face. It must have come as a shock to see the last-called of the apostles rebuke the first of the apostles. Yet, Peter humbly accepted Paul's reproof. Then Peter sailed back to Caesarea and, from there, returned to Jerusalem, probably between April 15–20.

THE EPISTLE TO THE GALATIANS

The Judaizers seem not to have accepted the matter as settled because the Antioch church decided to send Paul and Barnabas to Jerusalem to confer with the apostles and the elders there on this question. At this time, Paul wrote his fiery letter to the Galatians, affirming that Gentiles were free of the Law in Christ. The passionate arguments of Paul in this epistle probably reflect the emotion he displayed in his debates with the Judaizers. The book of Galatians theologically tracks with the book of Romans, but Galatians seems like Romans written in a bad mood.

Paul wrote Galatians to show that Gentile Christians need not be circumcised; that is, they need not become Jews to become Christians. The Jerusalem Council officially settled this issue, siding with Paul. If the Jerusalem Council had already occurred, Paul would not have needed to write Galatians. Paul could simply have forwarded the decree of the Jerusalem Council to the Galatians and said, "Read it and weep."

The fact that Paul wrote Galatians before the Council illustrates that Paul knew his position was right. He said he received his guidance from Jesus directly, not from being an understudy to other apostles. And the apostles at the Council would agree with him. Paul was one of the most influential authors of all time. His writing career began with this epistle.

The book of Acts does not explicitly record Paul and Barnabas visiting Galatia. Galatia was named after a tribe of Gauls (Celts), who, in the third century BC, migrated from what is now France, invaded the Balkans and Asia Minor, and eventually settled in what is now central Turkey. By the first century BC, these Gauls had become so Hellenized that the Greeks and Romans called them "Greek Galatians," or, modernizing the epithet, "Greek Frenchmen." The emperor Augustus turned Galatia into a Roman province, including in Galatia proper the regions of Pamphylia,[11] "Lycaonia, Isauria, and portions of Phrygia and Pisidia."[12] The first missionary journey of Paul and Barnabas took them to the island of Cyprus and then across the Mediterranean Sea to Perga in Pamphylia (Acts 13:13), to Antioch in Pisidia (not Syria, Acts 13:14), to Iconium (modern Konya) in Phrygia (Acts 13:51), to Lystra and Derbe in Lycaonia (Acts 14:6), back along the same route to Antioch in Pisidia (Acts 14:21), back to Perga (Acts 14:25), and from Attalia by ship back to their home church of Antioch in Syria (Acts 14:26). When Paul wrote Galatians, therefore, he was addressing all the churches that he and Barnabas founded on this journey, all of which were located in what Paul's contemporaries would have recognized as "greater Galatia."

---

11. Smith, *Dictionary of Greek and Roman Geography*.
12. Cheetham, "The Province of Galatia," *The Classical Review*, 396.

The term "Galatian Church," therefore, is shorthand for the cluster of churches in the Galatian region on the first missionary journey.

Paul and Barnabas traveled south from Antioch to Jerusalem through Phoenicia and Samaria. They told Christians all along the way how Gentiles were coming to Christ, and the brothers rejoiced. Evidently Paul was in no doubt about how this question would be settled. He had no intention of waiting for the apostles in Jerusalem to affirm his position. He freely gave out his views along the way.

THE JERUSALEM COUNCIL: AD 49

When the Council convened, some Christian Pharisees continued to insist that circumcision was required for believers. It is important not to let the phrase "Christian Pharisees" slip by unnoticed. It is amazing that many Pharisees, formerly the implacable enemies of Jesus, had become Christians. Nicodemus, Joseph of Arimathea, and Paul were the first of them. Luke also records that many priests became Christians (Acts 6:7). But even after becoming Christians, some Pharisees still had a tendency toward legalism. Old habits die hard.

Paul and Barnabas argued against the Judaizing Christian Pharisees. After much debate, Peter sided with Paul and Barnabas. James, Jesus's half-brother, agreed.[13] The Jerusalem Council officially recognized that Christianity was more than a Jewish sect; it was a universal religion, embracing Jews and Gentiles.

The Council decided that Gentiles were acceptable as Christians without circumcision but that they should refrain from eating meat offered to idols, from eating blood and strangled animals, and from fornication. All these rituals were associated with the worship of pagan gods. The Council further affirmed that Christian Jews were free to continue observing the Law of Moses but that, like Christian Gentiles, they might also consider themselves free from the Law and under the New Covenant of grace. The Council wrote a letter to this effect and charged a certain Judas Justus Barsabbas and Silas (Silvanus) to go to the Gentile brethren in Syria and Asia Minor, promulgating the Council's decree.

---

13. This was not James, the son of Zebedee, for Herod Agrippa I had murdered him in AD 44.

SECOND MISSIONARY JOURNEY: AD 49–51

With the letter from the Jerusalem Council in hand and, no doubt, with copies of his epistle to the Galatians, Paul asked Barnabas to return with him to all the young churches they had planted in Asia Minor to see how they were. They had been on their own for five years. Doubtless, he wanted to ensure that the Judaizers had not shaken their faith.

Barnabas suggested bringing his cousin, John Mark, but Paul sharply disagreed to take the one who had deserted them in Pamphylia. Mark may seem in this account to be an inexperienced boy, not up to the rigors of evangelism, but Mark had already accompanied Peter to Rome by this date and had composed his gospel.[14] He may also already have founded the church in Egypt. At any rate, Barnabas returned with Mark to Cyprus, and Paul took Silas back to Asia Minor. Silas was a Roman citizen, like Paul, a fact that would become relevant when they crossed over to Europe.

Paul and Silas walked from Antioch in Syria to Derbe and Lystra. On the way, the two apostles would have had to pass by Saul's hometown of Tarsus. Whether they stopped to greet Paul's family or whether, knowing Paul's family shunned him for becoming a Christian, they passed silently by can only be imagined.

ENLISTING TIMOTHY

A few years before, Paul had healed a man who had been lame from birth in Derbe and Lystra. The people had tried to worship Barnabas and Paul as Zeus and Hermes, and the Jews of Iconium had stoned Paul and left him for dead. This time, in Lystra, they met a disciple named Timothy, the son of a Jewish Christian mother and Greek father. This family must have remembered the ignominious treatment Paul had suffered before, but rather than despise him for it, they admired him.

Paul wanted to take Timothy on their missionary journey, so Paul had Timothy circumcised. This was not because Timothy's salvation depended on it but because Timothy wanted to evangelize among the Jews. This was not a reversal of the Council's decision about Judaizing. As the son of a Greek Gentile, Timothy could not have entered synagogues for missionary purposes without being circumcised, and in the

---

14. Eusebius, *Church History*, 2:14–15.

living conditions of the first century, sooner or later, his physical state would have been observed. This willing self-sacrifice by Timothy shows how devoted he was to the cause.

COME OVER AND HELP US

As the missionaries visited the young churches, they shared the decree of the Jerusalem Council, and the churches grew. Then the Holy Spirit forbade them from preaching any more in Asia Minor (Turkey). As they passed through Galatia and Phrygia and reached Mysia, on the coast of the Aegean Sea, they wanted to go north to the populous and prosperous province of Bithynia on the Black Sea, but the Spirit of Jesus prevented them, so they came to Troas, the ancient city of Troy. There, Paul dreamed of a man from Macedonia urging him to come over to Europe and help them. At this point in the narrative (Acts 16:10), Luke changed from the pronouns "he" or "they" to the pronoun "we." Evidently, Luke joined Paul's mission at Troas. It may be that Luke had completed and published his gospel in AD 49 and brought a copy with him when he joined Paul, at which point he began composing the book of Acts.

PHILIPPI

Around October AD 49,[15] they sailed from Troy to the Greek island of Samothrace and then to Neapolis in Thrace. From Neapolis, they walked to Philippi, a leading Roman city in Macedonia.[16] As there was no synagogue there, on their first Sabbath, they went to the banks of the Krenides River, which they thought might be a place of prayer. There, they met Lydia, a seller of purple fabrics from Thyatira, a city in Asia Minor. Lydia became Paul's first convert in Europe.[17] She and all her household were

---

15. Navigation between September and March was perilous in the Mediterranean (Acts 27:9), but this trip was a short one across the Aegean Sea. The ship's captain could have timed it to avoid bad weather, and this may have been why they stopped at the island of Samothrace en route, to break up the trip and minimize risk.

16. Philip II, the father of Alexander the Great, founded Philippi in 356 BC. In 42 BC, at the Battle of Philippi, Marc Antony and Octavian (the future emperor Augustus) defeated Brutus and Cassius, the assassins of Julius Caesar and defenders of the Roman Republic. This was an important city.

17. If the Roman Christians we were present at the birth of the Church on Pentecost, AD 33, brought their faith back to Rome, and if Peter and Mark had evangelized Rome in AD 43, Lydia would not have been the first convert in Europe, just Paul's first

baptized, and they gave lodging to Paul and his followers. Since this household of new believers is denoted as Lydia's household, Lydia seems to have been the first leader of the Philippian church. This undermines the frequent claim that Paul was a misogynist.

In Philippi, Paul commanded a demon to come out of a slave girl whose masters had profited from her fortunetelling. Angered, the girl's masters dragged Paul and Silas in front of the city authorities and accused them of teaching unlawful doctrines. The city magistrates had them stripped, beaten, and jailed. They then warned the jailer to guard them well. The jailer threw them into the innermost cells and locked their feet in stocks.

About midnight, despite painful injuries, Paul and Silas were singing hymns. The other prisoners were listening to them. Then, an earthquake struck, broke open the prison doors, and ruptured the prisoners' bonds.[18] At this, the jailer nearly committed suicide, knowing that the penalty for losing his prisoners would be death. If he had tried to escape his fate by running away, the authorities would have killed his family. Suicide would be an honorable remedy that would spare him a lingering death and save his loved ones. However, Paul called out loudly for the jailer not to harm himself, for all his prisoners were there. Paul witnessed to the jailer. He and his whole household believed and were baptized that night.

In the morning, the magistrates ordered the prisoners released. Paul indignantly informed them that he and Silas were Roman citizens and that the magistrates had punished them without a trial. For this, the magistrates might have faced severe punishment. Terrified, they begged Paul and Silas to leave Philippi. Haughtily taking their time, Paul and Silas went to stay with Lydia and then departed for Amphipolis, Apollonia, and Thessalonica, where they found a synagogue of Jews.

THESSALONICA

They preached in Thessalonica, and a number of Jews, Greeks, and prominent women in the city believed. But other Jews became angry, and they dragged Jason, who was hosting Paul and Silas, before the authorities, complaining that he was helping these renegades to proclaim

---

convert there. She may have been the first convert in Greece.

18. The bonds were probably stocks, not chains, as an earthquake would probably not have broken chains.

another king, Jesus, in place of Caesar. They stirred up a crowd and extorted a pledge from Jason not to support the preaching of Paul and Silas anymore. The Christians of Thessalonica smuggled Paul and Silas out of the city by night. They made their way to Berea, further south, near Mount Olympus.

BEREA

In Berea, around January of AD 50, they preached in the synagogue again. The Berean Jews were more noble-minded than those of Thessalonica, and they eagerly searched the Scriptures to check if what Paul was teaching about Jesus fit the Messianic prophecies. Many Jews and Greeks believed. But the Jews from Thessalonica pursued them to Berea and incited a mob. The brethren sent Paul, Luke, and some others to Athens. Silas and Timothy remained in Berea, but Paul left Timothy instructions to return to the church in Thessalonica to encourage them after all the trouble the Thessalonian Jews had made in their own city and in Berea (1 Thes 3:2). After that, Silas and Timothy were to join Paul in Corinth as soon as they could.

ATHENS

Paul and Luke were alone in Athens.[19] The city was full of idols, including one to the "Unknown God." Paul preached in the Athenian synagogue and marketplace, and the numerous philosophers of Athens brought him to Ares Hill (the Areopagus) to hear what philosophy he espoused. Paul's sermon was elegant and persuaded some to believe, including Dionysus the Areopagite and a woman named Damaris and

---

19. It might seem that because Luke stopped using the pronoun "we," which he adopted in Acts 16:10, and reverted to the pronoun "they" at this time, Luke did not accompany Paul to Thessalonica. Luke resumed using the pronoun "we" in Acts 20:5 when Paul sailed back to Macedonia after his third visit to Corinth. This begs the question of who recorded Paul's eloquent speech in Athens. Paul may have recited the details from memory to Luke later as he composed the book of Acts, but Luke's vivid account of the Athenian story in Acts 17:20–34 seems like an eyewitness account. If Luke was in Athens, he may have made an insignificant pronoun shift between Act 17:1 and 20:5, purely as a literary decision. Luke was Paul's Boswell, so he probably accompanied Paul all the way from Philippi to Thessalonica to Berea to Athens to Corinth to Ephesus to Jerusalem, back to Ephesus, back to Philippi, and finally back to Corinth, and thence to Macedonia.

others with them, although most of the Athenians seemed only mildly interested. Paul left Athens without being persecuted or thrown out, for once, and proceeded to Corinth, farther south.

CORINTH

In Corinth, around January AD 50, Paul met Aquila and his wife Priscilla, Christian Jews from Rome. Possibly, this couple had been converted to Christianity in Rome by Peter in AD 43, seven years before. In any case, they were forced to leave Rome by a decree that the emperor Claudius made in the ninth year of his reign, AD 49. Claudius was weary of the persecution of Christian Jews by non-Christian Jews, so he expelled all Jews, of whatever persuasion, from Rome.

Paul had a family trade: he was a tentmaker. Since Aquila and Priscilla were in the same trade, Paul stayed and worked with them. Paul preached in the Corinthian synagogue every Sabbath. Silas and Timothy reached Corinth from Macedonia around February AD 50.

Then, violent opposition of the Jews forced Paul to start preaching in a house next to the synagogue. This house was owned by a Jewish Christian named Titus Justus. No doubt to the horror of the non-Christian Jews, Crispus, the leader of their synagogue, and his whole household became Christians. They presumably went next door to join the church in Justus' home. Paul remained in Corinth for one year and six months (Acts 18:11).

ILLYRICUM

At some point during this sojourn, Paul must have made a side trip to Illyricum, the Roman province west of Greece on the Adriatic Sea (modern Albania, Montenegro, Bosnia, Herzegovina, and coastal Croatia) because he wrote, "From Jerusalem and all the way around to Illyricum I have fulfilled the ministry of the gospel of Christ" (Rom 15:19). Obviously, the trip occurred before he wrote Romans in AD 54, and there is no other place in Paul's itinerary when he was so near to Illyricum or had the time to go. If Paul had walked to Illyricum, it would have taken about thirty-three days each way. If he had sailed from Corinth, it would have taken about eight days each way. Thus, if he had sailed in good weather, the whole trip might have taken a month or less. If he went overland in the winter, it would have taken over two months. We know nothing about Paul's work there except for this passing remark.

JESUS SPOKE TO PAUL A THIRD TIME

In Corinth, around February 20, AD 50, Jesus spoke for the third recorded time to Paul, saying, "Do not be afraid, but go on speaking and do not be silent, for I am with you, and no one will attack you to harm you, for I have many in this city who are my people" (Acts 18:9–10).

1 AND 2 THESSALONIANS

In AD 50, Paul sent Timothy back to Thessalonica to check on the church's status and strengthen their faith (1 Thess 3:1–2). Timothy brought back a very encouraging report. Despite the riotous behavior of the Thessalonian Jews, the church in Thessalonica had remained faithful to the Gospel, even though Paul had presented it "in the midst of much conflict" (1 Thes 2:2). Paul gladly wrote 1 Thessalonians to them. He sent greetings from himself, Silas, and Timothy, so the courier had to be someone else.

After reading 1 Thessalonians and after receiving a fake, alarming letter from someone pretending to be Paul (2 Thes 2:2), the Thessalonians had further questions. Probably, they wrote Paul a letter or sent a messenger asking them. The questions included whether Jesus had already come a second time, something about the resurrection from the dead, and something about a "man of lawlessness." Reading 2 Thessalonians is like hearing one half of a phone conversation. Paul reminded the Thessalonians of things he had already told them, but we do not know what he told them. He said they knew what was restraining the "man of lawlessness," but we do not know what was restraining him, much less who "the man of lawlessness" was. Presumably, the Holy Spirit was restraining him, but certain passages of 2 Thessalonians are frankly a mystery without a solution. In this letter, Paul again sent greetings from himself, Silas, and Timothy, suggesting that the courier was someone else.

GALLIO

The Jews complained about Paul to Gallio, the Roman proconsul of Achaia (Greece). Junius Annaeus Gallio was the brother of Seneca, the

Roman Stoic philosopher, playwright, and advisor to the emperor Nero. Gallio ignored the complaints of the Corinthian Jews, saying:

> If it were a matter of wrongdoing or vicious crime, O Jews, I would have reason to accept your complaint. But since it is a matter of questions about words and names and your own law, see to it yourselves. I refuse to be a judge of these things" (Acts 18:14–15).

FOURTH RETURN TO JERUSALEM: AD 51.

Paul remained many days longer in Corinth after this hearing. He had his hair shaved in the nearby village of Cenchreae because he had made a vow of some kind. Then he, Aquila, Priscilla, Timothy, Silas, and Luke sailed for Ephesus. In Ephesus, Paul reasoned with the Jews in the synagogue. He declined to stay there a long time but promised to return. He and Luke left Aquila and Priscilla in Ephesus and sailed to Caesarea at the end of summer AD 51. For the fourth time, Paul returned to Jerusalem. He was in time to celebrate the Jewish Fall holy days.

APOLLOS IN EPHESUS: AD 51

At this time, Apollos, a powerful preacher of the Gospel, left Alexandria in Egypt and headed for Ephesus. He arrived in Ephesus and met Aquila and Priscilla there. He just missed Paul.

> [Apollos] was an eloquent man, competent in the Scriptures. He had been instructed in the way of the Lord. And being fervent in spirit, he spoke and taught accurately the things concerning Jesus, though he knew only the baptism of John. He began to speak boldly in the synagogue, but when Priscilla and Aquila heard him, they took him aside and explained to him the way of God more accurately. And when he wished to cross to Achaia (Greece), the brothers encouraged him and wrote to the disciples to welcome him. When he arrived, he greatly helped those who through grace had believed, for he powerfully refuted the Jews in public, showing by the Scriptures that the Christ was Jesus (Acts 18:24–28).

THIRD MISSIONARY JOURNEY: AD 51–54

From Jerusalem, Paul returned to Antioch. After a brief rest there, he began his third missionary journey. He walked through Galatia and Phrygia. Again, he must have passed by his hometown of Tarsus. Whether he paused to greet his family or, knowing their aversion to his Christian faith, walked sadly by can only be imagined. He then returned to Ephesus, a trek of about 710 miles. He probably walked because the time of year was October and November of AD 51, a season when storms made it too dangerous to sail (Acts 27:9).

EPHESUS

Apollos had moved on to Corinth, but Aquila and Priscilla were awaiting Paul in Ephesus. He again joined them in earning a living by making tents so that he could pay his own way and not burden the faithful. He began in Ephesus by teaching twelve believers who, until then, had only known the baptism of John. Paul baptized them in the Holy Spirit (Acts 19:1–6). Then he taught in the synagogue for three months, where he spoke boldly. But some in the synagogue became stubborn and spoke evil of the Gospel before the congregation, so Paul withdrew and took his disciples with him. He then taught daily in the hall of Tyrannus from eleven in the morning till four in the afternoon for two years, from about November AD 51 to about February AD 53. The identity of Tyrannus is uncertain. He was probably a teacher with a private school or lecture room.

While in Ephesus, God performed many miracles through Paul. Even handkerchiefs and aprons that he touched healed the sick when they touched them. Seven sons of the chief Jewish leader, Sceva, attempted to imitate Paul's exorcisms, but a demon-possessed person beat and wounded the would-be exorcists, saying, "I recognize Jesus, and I know about Paul, but who are you?" Then, the man who had the evil spirit jumped on them and overpowered them all. He gave them such a beating that they ran out of the house naked and bleeding.

Paul's teaching so triumphed over his phony rivals that the Ephesians turned away from superstitions and sorcery. They burned books of magic worth 50,000 pieces of silver. In 2024, the metallic value of this was about $598,333. But money had greater purchasing power in the first century than it has today. Since a piece of silver was about a day's wages, this was a value equivalent to more than 136 years of work. Converting this sum to the average day's wages in the United States in 2024, the current equivalent purchasing power would be about $11.4 million.

BETWEEN EPHESUS AND CORINTH

This is a phase of Paul's Third Missionary Journey that can be difficult to follow because the details of Paul's actions and travels are embedded throughout Acts and 1 and 2 Corinthians. Mixed in with Paul's actions and travels are the actions and travels of Apollos, Timothy, Titus, Luke, Erastus, Sosthenes, Chloe's people, Stephanas, Fortunatus, and Achaicus (who may be Chloe's people). The following summary of events will aid the reader in following Paul's story, as well as the turbulent story of the newly planted Corinthian church.

- Paul traveled from Antioch to Ephesus between September 25 to October 24, AD 51 (Acts 18:23, 19:1).
- Apollos was in Corinth at that time (Acts 19:1).
- Timothy, Titus, and probably Luke ("the brother who is praised by all the churches for his work in the gospel") either went with Paul from Antioch to Ephesus or they joined Paul in Ephesus (1 Cor 4:17, 2 Cor 8:18, 12:18).
- Someone from Corinth brought news of jealousy, quarreling, factionalism, litigation, adultery, incest, and other kinds of immorality in the Corinthian church. Probably, the messenger was Apollos. This stands to reason because if Apollos was in Corinth when Paul arrived in Ephesus (Acts 19:1) and then he was in Ephesus refusing Paul's request for him to go back to Corinth (1 Cor 16:12), Apollos must have traveled from Corinth to Ephesus.
- Paul wrote a lost warning letter to Corinth (1 Cor 5:9). Timothy took it to them (1 Cor 4:17). Since traveling alone might be dangerous, it is reasonable to suspect that Titus went with him.
- Paul's lost first letter did not fix the problems. The Corinthians wrote Paul a lost letter back with questions about proper sexual mores (1 Cor 7:1), entrusting it to Timothy, Chloe's people, Stephanas, Fortunatus, Achaicus, and Sosthenes, the synagogue leader in Corinth (Acts 18:17, 1 Cor 1:1, 11, 16:17).

- Paul wrote a second letter, 1 Corinthians, in part answering the Corinthians' lost letter to Paul and in part addressing the generally scandalous practices in the Corinthian church. Timothy took 1 Corinthians to Corinth (1 Cor 4:17, 16:10), accompanied by Chloe's people, Stephanas, Fortunatus, Achaicus, and perhaps Sosthenes.[20] Apollos refused to return to Corinth at this time (1 Cor 16:12). Apparently, he was fed up with the Corinthian mess.

- The Corinthian church did not respond well to 1 Corinthians. Timothy was probably the messenger who brought this bad news back to Paul in Ephesus.

- Paul wrote a lost, painful letter of tears and anguish to Corinth (2 Cor 2:4, 7:8, 12). Probably, Timothy brought this back to Corinth.

- After sending the lost letter of tears and concluding, on reflection, that Corinth needed personal intervention, Paul made a second, quick, and painful trip to Corinth (2 Cor 12:14, 13:1). This is evident because Paul could not have made a third trip without making a second one.

- Paul returned from Corinth to Ephesus. This is evident because Paul could not have left Ephesus after his second trip to Corinth (2 Cor 12:14, 13:1) and before his third trip to Corinth (Acts 20:1–3) without first returning from Corinth to Ephesus.

- From Ephesus, Paul sent Titus and probably Luke to Corinth to help steady the church on the right course until Paul should return (2 Cor 8:18, 12:18).

- Paul sent Timothy and Erastus ahead of him to Macedonia (Acts 19:22).

- Paul traveled to Troas, hoping to meet Titus there, but Titus missed the rendezvous (2 Cor 2:12–13).

- Paul went on to Philippi and met Timothy (and Erastus) there (2 Cor 1:1).

---

20. From Ephesus, Paul sent greetings to the Corinthians from himself and Sosthenes (1 Cor 1:1). Perhaps this implies that Sosthenes remained in Ephesus with Paul for some time since Paul would not need to send Sosthenes' greetings if Sosthenes accompanied the epistle back to Corinth. On the other hand, perhaps Sosthenes did accompany 1 Corinthians back to Corinth, but Paul included his greetings in the letter to add Sosthenes' authority as leader of the Corinthian synagogue (Acts 18:17) to the epistle.

- Titus arrived in Philippi, bringing Paul news of the apparently improved state of the church in Corinth (2 Cor 7:6–7, 14).
- Paul wrote 2 Corinthians from Philippi, adding greetings from Timothy (2 Cor 1:1, 9:2–5).
- Titus, probably Luke, and other brothers carried 2 Corinthians to Corinth (2 Cor 8:17–18, 9:3).
- Paul promised that he would come again to Corinth for a third time (2 Cor 12:14, 20–21, 13:1).
- In Corinth, Titus collected funds for the Jerusalem church, while Paul collected funds in Macedonia (2 Cor 8:6).
- Paul arrived in Corinth and remained there for three months (Acts 20:2–3).
- In Corinth, Paul added the funds Titus had collected for the Jerusalem church to those he had collected in Macedonia (Rom 15:25–26).
- In Corinth, Paul wrote Romans and sent greetings to Prisca (Priscilla) and Aquila and many others (Rom 16:3) from Timothy, Lucius,[21] Sosipater, Paul's kinsman, Tertius, Paul's scribe, and four others (Rom 16:21–23).

TROUBLE IN CORINTH

While in Ephesus, Paul received troubling news from Corinth, probably brought to him by Apollos. Members of the church there were indulging in jealousy, quarreling, factionalism, litigation, adultery, incest, and other kinds of immorality. He probably wanted to travel immediately to Corinth to correct them, but since this was around November AD 51, the sailing weather was too dangerous. Even if Paul had been willing to risk the winter storms, most sea captains would not do so. So, from Ephesus, Paul wrote a lost warning letter to the Corinthian Church. It had to travel overland so it would reach Corinth only by the end of AD 51. Timothy was the messenger. Since traveling alone was risky, it is reasonable to suspect that Titus went with him.

---

21. This Lucius may have been Lucius of Cyrene (Acts 13:1) or some otherwise unknown person with this common Roman name. He was probably not Luke the Evangelist because his name in Greek was Loukas, not Lucius.

Paul's lost first letter did not fix the problems. The Corinthians wrote Paul a lost letter back with questions about proper sexual mores, entrusting it to Timothy, Chloe's people, Stephanas, Fortunatus, Achaicus (who may have been Chloe's people), Sosthenes, the synagogue leader in Corinth, and probably Titus. Paul probably only received this delegation from Corinth by February AD 52. The news prompted him to write 1 Corinthians (which, despite its name, was actually Paul's second letter to Corinth). This grand epistle scolded the church in Corinth for its licentious behavior and acknowledged Apollos' ministry there. He referred to Apollos as his co-worker, who was watering the seed of faith that Paul had planted. Paul also defined moral sexual behavior (1 Cor 7) and expressed many lofty theological concepts.

JESUS SPOKE TO PAUL A FOURTH TIME

In 1 Corinthians, written in Ephesus around March, AD 52, Paul wrote:

> I received from the Lord what I also delivered to you, that the Lord Jesus on the night when he was betrayed took bread, and when he had given thanks, he broke it, and said, "This is my body, which is for you. Do this in remembrance of me." In the same way, he also took the cup after supper, saying, "This cup is the new covenant in my blood. Do this, as often as you drink it, in remembrance of me." For as often as you eat this bread and drink the cup, you proclaim the Lord's death until he comes (1 Cor 11:23).

This is a beautiful summation of the Eucharist. The account is also remarkable because Paul says that he did not learn this from Peter or John, who were present at the Last Supper, but that Jesus taught him this personally.

BACK TO CORINTH

Since the weather was now fair, Paul sent Timothy with 1 Corinthians to Corinth, accompanied by Chloe's people, Stephanas, Fortunatus, Achaicus, and probably Sosthenes (unless he remained for some time with Paul in Ephesus). Apollos refused to return to Corinth at this time. Apparently, he was fed up with the Corinthian mess.

Unfortunately, 1 Corinthians was still not well received. Timothy returned to Ephesus and reported this to Paul, probably around May AD 52. Paul responded with a lost, severe, tearful letter to the Corinthians. Since the sailing weather was still fine, the letter probably reached Corinth before June AD 52. Probably Timothy was the courier again.

Paul realized that he needed to revisit all his churches in Greece, and he made plans for a sweeping journey through Macedonia, Greece, back to Jerusalem, and ending up in Rome (Acts 19:21). Unwilling, however, to wait that long to intervene in Corinth, and probably concluding, after sending three letters, that letters alone would not fix the problems there, Paul made a second, quick round trip to Corinth around June, AD 52.

The proof that Paul made this second, quick trip to Corinth is as follows. Since 2 Corinthians says that Paul was planning to come to Corinth a third time (2 Cor 10:2, 12:14, 20–21, 13:1), there had to have been a second time. From this comes the inescapable inference that Paul made a second, quick trip to Corinth between his first visit there (Acts 18:1) and before his third visit there (Acts 20:2–3). In 2 Corinthians, however, written about eighteen months after this quick trip, Paul made apparently contradictory statements about traveling to Corinth.

> I wanted to come to you first so that you might have a second experience of grace. I wanted to visit you on my way to Macedonia and to come back to you from Macedonia and have you send me on my way to Judea. Was I vacillating when I wanted to do this? Do I make my plans according to the flesh, ready to say yes, yes, and no, no at the same time?.. I call God to witness against me, it was to spare you that I refrained from coming again to Corinth . . . for I made up my mind not to make another painful visit to you . . . and I wrote to you as I did so that when I came, I might not suffer pain from those who should have made me rejoice . . . for I wrote to you out of much affliction and anguish of heart with many tears (2 Cor 1:15–23, 2:1–4).

Paul wrote that before writing 2 Corinthians that he was planning to go to Corinth to give them a second blessing of grace (outreach). Since his first outreach to Corinth was his first trip there, it is obvious that if he went to Corinth again, that would be his second outreach. His original idea was to go to Macedonia and from Macedonia to go to Corinth again. In 1 Corinthians, he said he would come to Corinth again soon (1 Cor 4:19–21, 11:34, 16:2), but he specified that it would be only after he passed through Macedonia (1 Cor 16:5). He also said that he would not come quite yet because he did not want to make just a quick, passing visit: "I do not now want to see you in passing. I hope indeed to remain a certain time with you if the Lord permits. I will remain, however, in Ephesus until Pentecost" (1 Cor 16:7-8).

But then Paul sent 1 Corinthians to Corinth and received an unsatisfactory response. He shot off an anguished letter of tears (2 Cor 2:4). He did this in lieu of making a second painful visit to Corinth (2 Cor 2:1). But then he changed his mind. He decided he must make a personal intervention in Corinth without delay. So, he went to Corinth a second time, returned to Ephesus, went to Macedonia, returned to Corinth a third time, and then returned, via Macedonia and Asia, to Jerusalem. Explaining this change in his plans, he wrote, "Did I not use lightness in thus planning? Or do I plan according to the flesh so that with me there should be yes, yes and no, no?" (2 Cor 1:17).

In this epistle, written after his promise in 1 Corinthians to follow a certain itinerary and after changing that itinerary, Paul was excusing his seeming inconsistency. He followed a course of action different from what he originally planned (2 Cor 2:1). Yet the circumstances made his revised plan the right one. After the second trip to Corinth, Paul returned to Ephesus, completed his two-year mission there, and then resumed his original plan to travel back through Macedonia and Achaia to Corinth again and thence back to Jerusalem (but via Macedonia again, as a Jewish plot changed his original plan once again).

SENDING OUT HIS TEAM

From Ephesus, Paul sent Timothy and Erastus to Macedonia (Acts 19:22) to prepare the way for his next grand journey. He then sent Titus to Corinth to help steady the church on the right course until he could return. He also instructed Titus to raise funds for the Jerusalem church and meet him in Troas afterward. This rapid sequence of letters and trips to Corinth implies how concerned Paul was for this wayward church.

Around AD 53, Paul apparently sent Aquila and Priscilla back to Rome to see how the church there had survived Claudius' decree expelling all Jews and to lay the groundwork for his planned visit there (Acts 19:21, Rom 15:22-24). This is inferred because when Paul wrote Romans from Corinth in AD 54, Aquila and Priscilla were already back in Rome (Rom 16:3). They probably felt it was safe to return despite the edict of AD 49. While Claudius' edict would expire with his death on October 13, AD 54, even before he died, government inefficiency being what it always is, the decree probably had relaxed. This happened with a similar decree by Tiberius in AD 19, which became a "dead letter" before Tiberius' death.[22]

ARTEMIS OF THE EPHESIANS

Before Paul could leave Ephesus in November AD 53, a riot erupted. The temple in Ephesus, which was four times the size of the Parthenon in Athens, contained a famous statue of Artemis, the Greek goddess of the hunt. Devout pilgrims bought silver facsimiles of her image until Paul's preaching undermined this cult. Demetrius, the head of the silversmiths' guild, roused the populace. He gathered the tradesmen and made the following speech:

> Men, you know that from this business, we have our wealth. And you see and hear that not only in Ephesus but in almost all of Asia this Paul has persuaded and turned away a great many people, saying that gods made with hands are not gods. And there is danger not only that this trade of ours may come into disrepute but also that the temple of the great goddess Artemis may be counted as nothing and that she may even be deposed from her magnificence, she whom all Asia and the world worship (Acts 19:25–27).

Demetrius' hearers were enraged, and they began to shout, "Great is Artemis of the Ephesians!" The city was filled with confusion. The mob dragged Paul's Macedonian traveling companions, Gaius and Aristarchus, into the theater. Paul wanted to address the crowd, but his disciples would not let him. Possibly, this was when Aquila and Priscilla risked their necks to save Paul (Rom 16:4). Many of the agitators were swept away by the hysteria but did not even know why they had come together. The Jews in the crowd pushed a Jew named Alexander forward so that he could address the mob. Perhaps he was Alexander the coppersmith, who Paul says did him great harm (2 Tim 4:14). He may have had a metals trade in connection with Demetrius. Given the great harm he may have done to Paul, he was either a non-Christian Jew or he was a Christian Jew who later betrayed Paul. In any case, when the mob heard

22. Bruce, "Christianity Under Claudius," *Bulletin of the John Rylands Library*, 317.

that Alexander was a Jew, they drowned him out, crying out with one voice for about two hours, "Great is Artemis of the Ephesians!" At last, the town clerk quieted the crowd, saying:

> Men of Ephesus, who is there who does not know that the city of the Ephesians is temple keeper of the great Artemis, and of the sacred stone that fell from the sky? Seeing then that these things cannot be denied, you ought to be quiet and do nothing rash. For you have brought these men here who are neither sacrilegious nor blasphemers of our goddess. If, therefore, Demetrius and the craftsmen with him have a complaint against anyone, the courts are open, and there are proconsuls. Let them bring charges against one another. But if you seek anything further, it shall be settled in the regular assembly. For we really are in danger of being charged with rioting today, since there is no cause that we can give to justify this commotion (Acts 19:35–40).

With that, he dismissed the assembly.

TROAS

After this, Paul and Timothy traveled to Troas, where he expected to meet Titus, who was not, however, there. Possibly, this was because the riot caused Paul to leave Ephesus earlier than expected, and so he arrived before the planned rendezvous. Possibly, it was because Titus, in winter, had to make the slower overland journey from Corinth back east and simply did not make the rendezvous in time. Paul preached in Troas for a little, but concerned at missing Titus, he and Timothy pushed on to Macedonia.

JESUS SPOKE TO PAUL A FIFTH TIME

Sometime around AD 53, Paul prayed for the Lord to remove the "thorn in his flesh." He said that it was a messenger of Satan, sent to harass him, to keep him from becoming conceited. Three times, he pleaded with the Lord to make it leave him, but Jesus replied, "My grace is sufficient for you, for my power is made perfect in weakness" (2 Cor 12:9).

WRITING 2 CORINTHIANS

In Philippi, Titus finally caught up with Paul and brought him good news about the apparently improved state of affairs in the Corinthian church (2 Cor 7:6–7, 14). Gratified, Paul wrote 2 Corinthians, a letter milder in tone and full of theological insights. (What we call 2 Corinthians was really his fourth letter to Corinth.) In this letter, Paul warned the Corinthians not to be deceived by "super-apostles," that is, false teachers who presented a Gospel different from what they had accepted from Paul. He pointed out that he was in no way inferior to such teachers since he had performed the signs of a true apostle among them, including signs, wonders, and mighty works. He also implied that the "super-apostles" were hustlers looking for financial support because, in contrast to them, Paul did not burden the Corinthians financially (2 Cor 11:5–9, 12:11–13). Since it was around November AD 53, Paul must have sent this epistle overland. Titus, probably Luke, and other brothers carried 2 Corinthians to Corinth. Timothy was probably not the courier because Paul sent Timothy's greetings to Corinth in the letter (2 Cor 1:1). In Corinth, Titus resumed collecting alms for the Jerusalem church, while in Macedonia, Paul did the same (2 Cor 8:4–6).

PAUL'S THIRD VISIT TO CORINTH

Paul continued traveling further west, revisiting and strengthening the churches in Thessalonica and Berea. He then finally returned to Corinth. He remained there for about three months, between January to April AD 54 (Acts 20:2–3). There, he met Titus and received the funds for the Jerusalem church (Rom 15:25–26). He probably received news from Aquila and Priscilla about the state of the church in Rome, prompting him to write the Book of Romans. When the sailing weather was fair, at the end of March or in early April AD 54, Phoebe, a deacon of the church in Cenchreae, took the epistle to the Romans from Corinth (Rom 16:1) to Aquila and Priscilla.

BACK TO MACEDONIA

Learning of a Jewish plot to kill him, rather than sailing for Syria, Paul sailed from Corinth back to Macedonia. He sent Sopater of Berea,

Aristarchus and Secundus of Thessalonica, Gaius of Derbe, Timothy, Tychicus, and Trophimus of Asia ahead of him to Troas (Acts 20:4).

Paul and Luke reached Philippi in April. There, they collected more funds for the Jerusalem church. They then sailed away after Passover, on April 17, 22 Nisan, AD 54. They arrived in Troas after five days, on April 22, where they remained for seven days (Acts 20:6).

RAISING EUTYCHUS

On their last day in Troas, April 29, Paul and the Trojan church ate together, and afterward, Paul spoke until midnight. A young man named Eutychus, sitting on a third-story windowsill, dozed off during Paul's sermon, fell to the ground, and died. Paul resurrected Eutychus and then continued to talk to the gathering until daylight, leaving the congregation greatly comforted. There can have been few sermons in the history of the Church quite as dramatic as that (Acts 20:7–12).

TO MILETUS

Paul, Luke, Sopater, Aristarchus, Secundus, Gaius, Timothy, Tychicus, and Trophimus then sailed to Assos, where they awaited Paul with a ship. Paul walked overland, arriving on May 1. The team then made a short sailing trip to Mytilene. The next day, they sailed to Chios, arriving there on May 2. The following day, they sailed to Samos, arriving there on May 3. The next day, May 4, they reached Miletus. Since Paul was in a hurry to reach Jerusalem before Pentecost, and also because the Jews of Ephesus had plotted to kill him, he bypassed Ephesus and sent for the elders of the Ephesian church to meet him at Miletus. The distance between Ephesus and Miletus is about thirty-nine miles, so it would have taken two days for Paul's messenger to reach Ephesus and two days for the elders to reach Miletus. This meeting, therefore, occurred after four days of travel on May 6 (Acts 20:13–38).

JESUS SPOKE TO PAUL A SIXTH TIME

Paul told the Ephesian elders to be on guard against deceivers and quoted Jesus, saying, "It is more blessed to give than to receive" (Acts 20:35). This saying of Jesus is recorded nowhere else in the Bible, so probably

Paul received it by special revelation. It is also possible that he learned it from one of the other apostles, although he had previously insisted that he received his learning from Jesus directly, not from them (Gal 1:1, 19, 2:6, 9, 1 Cor 9:1).

BACK TO JERUSALEM

After praying and bidding an emotional farewell, Paul sailed to Cos on May 7, to Rhodes on May 8, and then to the seaport of Patara on May 9. In Patara, they boarded a ship bound for Phoenicia, sailing south of Cyprus; they reached Tyre around May 11. Paul's team stayed in Tyre for seven days between May 12–18 (Acts 21:1–6). After that, they proceeded to Ptolemais (Acre) and stayed there one day, May 19 (Acts 21:7). Paul then walked to Caesarea, on Judaea's Mediterranean coast, which was a journey of two days. He thus arrived on May 21 and stayed "for many days" at the house of Philip, the Evangelist (not the apostle, but one of the seven deacons chosen to care for the poor and widows in the Church).

Here, a prophet named Agabus, the same one who had correctly foretold the famine in Judaea fourteen years earlier, came from Judaea to Caesarea and prophesied that the Jews would bind Paul if he went to Jerusalem. Skeptics claim that Agabus was a false prophet because he said that the Jews would bind Paul, whereas it was the Romans who did so. In fact, the Jews did bind Paul before the Romans took him into custody (Acts 24:6).

Despite his companions' pleading not to go into harm's way, Paul was determined to press on. He and his team (and probably Agabus) walked from Caesarea to Jerusalem, a sixty-eight mile, two-day journey, arriving there on May 28, 5 Sivan, the Eve of Pentecost, as he had planned. He stayed at the home of Mnason (Acts 21:16).

PENTECOST

On Pentecost, May 29, 6 Sivan, AD 54, in Jerusalem, Paul delivered the alms he had collected in Greece and Macedonia for the Jerusalem church. The brothers and sisters received him gladly, and the day after arriving, Paul and his team visited James, Jesus' half-brother, and all the elders. He told the brothers of all that God was doing among the Gentiles, and they praised God (Acts 21:17–20).

The Jewish-Christian leaders told Paul that because thousands of Jews had put their faith in Jesus, many accused Paul of teaching the Jews in the Diaspora to forsake Moses and not to circumcise their sons. They suggested that Paul join four other men who were under a vow and that he pay for all to shave their heads, purify themselves, and make offerings at the Temple. Their recommendation was political, meant to keep the peace. It was not a compromise of the decision made by the Jerusalem Council five years ago. Paul agreed to this, and seven days later, he completed his vow on June 5.

But Jews from Asia Minor recognized him in the Temple and incited some non-Christian Jews to riot. Having seen Trophimus the Ephesian with Paul in Jerusalem, they falsely accused Paul of bringing an uncircumcised Gentile into the Temple. Paul's team of non-Jewish disciples must have been conspicuous in Jerusalem, consisting, as they did, of Luke, Sopater of Berea, Aristarchus and Secundus of Thessalonica, Gaius of Derbe, Timothy, Tychicus and Trophimus of Asia (modern Turkey), and probably Titus.

A JEWISH RIOT

A mob seized Paul and dragged him outside the Temple to kill him, but the commander of the Roman cohort, Claudius Lysias, stopped them and brought the crowd to order. Paul appealed to Lysias and obtained permission to address the Jews in their own language. He told them the story of his conversion and of his mission to bring salvation to the Gentiles.

The Jews erupted in anger and resumed their murderous threats. Probably persuaded by the mob's rage that Paul must have been guilty of something, Lysias seized Paul and planned to question him under torture. Paul, however, stated that he was a Roman citizen. And his citizenship was superior to that of Lysias, for Lysias had purchased his citizenship for a large sum, while Paul was born a Roman. Afraid of committing false arrest, Lysias unchained Paul and allowed him to stand trial before his accusers, the Jewish Council.

PAUL'S JERUSALEM TRIAL

During Paul's trial, Ananias (Annas), the High Priest, ordered Paul to be struck on the mouth.[23] This was obviously out of order in a legal trial. Angrily, Paul said to him, "God is going to strike you, you whitewashed wall! Are you sitting to judge me according to the law, and yet contrary to the law you order me to be struck?" (Acts 23:3).[24] What then transpired was dramatic.

> Those who stood by said, "Would you revile God's high priest?" And Paul said, "I did not know, brothers, that he was the high priest, for it is written, 'You shall not speak evil of a ruler of your people.'" Now, when Paul perceived that one part was Sadducees and the other Pharisees, he cried out in the council, "Brothers, I am a Pharisee, a son of Pharisees. It is with respect to the hope and the resurrection of the dead that I am on trial." And when he had said this, a dissension arose between the Pharisees and the Sadducees, and the assembly was divided. For the Sadducees say that there is no resurrection, nor angel, nor spirit, but the Pharisees acknowledge them all. Then, a great clamor arose, and some of the scribes of the Pharisees' party stood up and contended sharply, "We find nothing wrong in this man. What if a spirit or an angel spoke to him?" And when the dissension became violent, the tribune, afraid that Paul would be torn to pieces by them, commanded the soldiers to go down and take him away from among them by force and bring him into the barracks (Acts 23:4–10).

JESUS SPOKE TO PAUL A SEVENTH TIME

Lysias took Paul into custody to save his life. This was polite custody, not incarceration, for Lysias did not dare to keep a fellow Roman citizen in chains (Acts 22:29). That night, Jesus spoke to Paul directly for the fourth

---

23. This was Ananias ben Nebedeus (Josephus, *Antiquities of the Jews*, 20:5:2), not the defrocked High Priest Ananias (Annas), who was the father-in-law of Joseph Caiaphas and who joined in the trial of Jesus in AD 33. This Ananias served from AD 46–58. Although Paul had been in Jerusalem in AD 47 and in AD 51, probably, as a Jewish Christian, he did not meet the High Priest either time. This is why Paul did not recognize that Ananias was the High Priest.

24. Paul was echoing Jesus' rebuke of the Sadducees when he called them whitewashed tombs, beautiful on the outside but filled on the inside with dead people's bones and filth (Matt 23:27).

time. He said, "Take courage, for as you have testified to the facts about me in Jerusalem, so you must testify also in Rome" (Acts 23:11). Jesus did not say that Paul would be the first to take the Gospel to Rome, because he was not. When Paul finally reached Rome for the first time in AD 57, he found many Christians already there (Acts 28:14). Peter had founded the Roman Church in AD 43, eleven years before. And Roman Jews present at the birth of the church on Pentecost in Jerusalem probably brought the faith back to Rome as early as AD 33 (Acts 2:10).

ESCAPE TO CAESAREA

The next day, more than forty Jews conspired to kill Paul. The son of Paul's sister heard of the plot.[25] He told his uncle Paul in the Roman barracks. The would-be assassins swore they would neither eat nor drink until they killed Paul. Paul lived for another fourteen years, so either they broke their vow, or they died of fasting.

Paul asked a centurion to inform Lysias of the plot. Lysias reacted immediately, ordering two of his centurions to assemble 470 cavalry, infantry, and spearmen to accompany Paul out of Jerusalem. This was a huge escort for a political prisoner. Pontius Pilate never deployed any comparable force to deal with Jesus or his followers. It suggests how intense the rage of the Jews must have become and how much the Romans feared civil unrest in troublesome Judaea. Lysias ordered the military detachment to take Paul to Caesarea, the seat of the Roman government on the Mediterranean Sea.

They did not wait until the next day but set out urgently for the coast at 9 p.m. They arrived in Antipatris, thirty-seven miles, the halfway point, at around 9 a.m. the following morning. Probably considering that the remainder of the journey would be safe, the Roman infantry and spearmen returned to their barracks in Jerusalem. The remaining seventy cavalry accompanied Paul the rest of the way to Caesarea. Cavalry trots at about eight miles per hour, so they made the thirty-five-mile ride in a little over four hours, arriving in Caesarea after noon.

---

25. Paul's sister lived in Jerusalem.

IN THE CUSTODY OF FELIX

In Caesarea, Paul passed into the custody of Antonius Felix, procurator of Judaea (AD 52–60), the top Roman official on station. The next day, the High Priest Ananias (Annas), a lawyer, and other representatives of the Jerusalem Council came to Caesarea to accuse Paul. Since this was a twenty-two-hour walk, assuming no breaks, the Jewish accusers must have set out from Jerusalem no later than the same day that Paul left Antipatris. They must have been outraged that Paul had flown the coop, and so they lost no time. After listening to the complaints of the Jewish elders, Felix decided to call for Claudius Lysias to hear his side of the story before making a decision. He then dismissed the frustrated Jewish leaders.

Felix and his Jewish wife Drusilla (daughter of Herod Agrippa I) conversed with Paul privately. Paul's teachings of righteousness, self-control, and God's judgment discomfited Felix. Perhaps Felix was conscious that he was not a model of righteousness and self-control and, therefore, he may have feared God's wrath.

Hoping for a bribe from Paul, Felix did not hand Paul over to his Jewish accusers, but Paul offered no money. So, Felix kept Paul in custody for two years until the arrival of his successor as governor of Judaea, Porcius Festus. During this time, Paul's friends were free to visit and minister to him. Felix frequently sent for Paul and talked with him, perhaps fishing for that bribe or perhaps tentatively exploring the doctrine of the Gospel.

1 TIMOTHY

During this two-year interval, Paul must have sent Timothy back to Ephesus to take charge of the church there because while in Caesarea, Paul wrote the epistle of 1 Timothy, offering Timothy pastoral advice (1 Tim 1:2–3). Some suppose that Paul wrote 1 Timothy from Philippi to Timothy in Ephesus. The basis for this view is this verse: "As I urged you when I was going to Macedonia, remain at Ephesus so that you may charge certain persons not to teach any different doctrine" (1 Tim 1:3). However, as shown above, after the riot in Ephesus Paul traveled with Timothy to Troas and back to Philippi in Macedonia. He returned to Corinth, and Timothy was with him since when he left Corinth, he sent Timothy and others ahead of him to Troas (Acts 20:4–5). Therefore, in Paul's swing from Ephesus to Philippi and to Corinth, Timothy was with Paul and was not in Ephesus. When Paul pushed on from Troas to Jerusalem, Timothy was almost certainly still with him since (1) on this trip, Paul bypassed Ephesus (Acts 20:16), (2) Timothy and Trophimus were part of the same missionary team (Acts 20:4), and Trophimus ended up in Jerusalem with Paul (Acts 21:29). So, when Paul was leaving Ephesus for Macedonia, he took Timothy with him. The meaning of 1 Tim 1:2–3 must be that as Paul and Timothy were departing Ephesus, Paul was ordaining him to return in the future to take charge of the Ephesian church. Timothy had the opportunity to do this only during Paul's incarceration in Caesarea, and so that is when Paul wrote 1 Timothy to Timothy in Ephesus.

IN THE CUSTODY OF FESTUS

In AD 56, Porcius Festus replaced Felix as procurator. Three days after he arrived in Judaea, Festus traveled from Caesarea to Jerusalem, where the Jewish leaders laid their complaints about Paul before him. They were still exercised about Paul, even after his being jailed for two years. They wanted Festus to send Paul to Jerusalem, ostensibly to question him further, but really because they planned to ambush and kill him.

Festus was too shrewd to fall into that trap. He told the Jewish elders that he was keeping Paul in custody at Caesarea, and if they wished, they could send some men of authority there to present their accusations. After eight or ten days, Festus returned to Caesarea. The Jews went with him. The day after they arrived, Festus held a meeting of Paul and his Jewish accusers. They brought many serious charges against him, none of which they could prove. Paul said, "Neither against the law of the Jews, nor against the Temple, nor against Caesar have I committed any offense." Festus asked Paul if he would go to Jerusalem to stand trial. Paul insisted that he was in Caesar's tribunal and that he had appealed to Caesar. Festus said, "To Caesar, you have appealed. To Caesar you shall go" (Acts 25:12), following the Roman habit of washing his hands of Jewish religious disputes (as did Pilate and Gallio).

After some days had passed, King Herod Agrippa II (the son of Herod Agrippa I and the great-grandson of Herod the Great) and his sister, Bernice, visited Festus. After staying in Caesarea for many days, Agrippa asked to hear Paul, and Festus arranged an audience. He thought it was a good idea because it might inform him of what to write about Paul when he sent him to Nero since, so far, Festus had discerned no crime that Paul had committed. Paul told the story of his conversion and proclaimed the Gospel. As he was speaking, Festus said with a loud voice, "Paul, you are out of your mind; your great learning is driving you out of your mind." Paul replied, "I am not out of my mind, most excellent Festus, but I am speaking true and rational words." Paul then appealed to King Agrippa to verify his testimony. "I am persuaded that none of these things has escaped [the king's] notice, for this has not been done in a corner. King Agrippa, do you believe the prophets? I know you believe," said Paul. Agrippa replied, "In a short time, would you persuade me to be a Christian?" Paul answered, "Whether short or long, I would to God that not only you but all who hear me this day might become such as I am, except for these chains." Then, the king, Bernice, Festus, and all who were with him rose and agreed that Paul had done nothing to deserve death or imprisonment. Agrippa said to Festus, "This man could have been set free if he had not appealed to Caesar" (Acts 26:32). Festus then made plans to send Paul to Rome to meet Nero.

VOYAGE TO MALTA

Paul and his companions (including Luke and Aristarchus, a fellow prisoner and other unnamed prisoners) embarked on a ship for Italy under Julius, a kindly Roman commander of the Augustan Cohort, and several soldiers under his command, around August 24, AD 56. Julius, like Cornelius, bore one of the most ancient and influential family names in Rome. Julius was either somebody or he was related to somebody. Aristarchus was a disciple from Thessalonica. He was apparently also arrested and sent to Rome with Paul, although under what charge Scripture does not say (Acts 27:2, Col 4:10).

They made port in Sidon, Lebanon, where they met friends, probably around Yom Kippur ("the Fast"), August 28, 1 Tishri (Acts 27:9). They put out to sea again from Sidon, but because the wind was against them (coming out of the west), they sailed to Cyprus, reaching its lee shore around September 3. Since they could not sail into the west wind, they tacked north across the open sea from Cyprus to Cilicia (modern Turkey and Paul's home province), reaching the coast around September 9. They followed the coastline westward, tacking to and fro as they headed into the wind. They followed the shore from Cilicia to Pamphylia to Myra,[26] on the southwest coast of modern Turkey. They put into port there around September 28.

In Myra, Julius found a grain ship from Alexandria, Egypt, and he transferred his charges to it. This would have been one of the largest vessels to ply the Mediterranean, carrying stores of grain from the fertile Nile Valley to the ever-hungry populace of Rome. As a centurion on official business, Julius would have been able to commandeer berths for himself, his soldiers, and his charges. The sailing season in the Mediterranean normally ended by October, so the captain of this ship was flirting with luck. The profits he would gain in Rome were immense, and he probably thought he had a good chance of slipping through to Italy before the winter storms began.

The Alexandrian ship put to sea around October 2. It sailed westward to Cnidus, a city at the tip of a fingerlike peninsula that juts out into the Aegean Sea on the southwest coast of Turkey, just north of the island of Rhodes, arriving around October 10. The wind, however, continued to blow against the freighter out of the west. The captain no doubt had hoped to sail from Cnidus northwest to Greece, island hopping all across the Aegean Sea. There, having made it halfway to Rome, he could winter snugly in any of the excellent safe harbors, such as Piraeus. But the wind prevented him from sailing west, so, in frustration, he chose another tack. He sailed southwest from Cnidus to Crete, setting out around October 18.

The ship reached Salmone on the far eastern tip of Crete around October 21. But the wind continued to blow out of the west. Sailing upwind, the ship tacked back and forth along the southern coast of Crete until it reached the port of Fair Havens, probably around October 23. Since it was now fifty-seven days past Yom Kippur ("the Fast") and well into the dangerous winter sailing weather, Paul warned the ship's captain and crew not to press on but to spend the winter in Fair Havens (Acts 27:9-10). Julius and the ship's captain (who was also its owner) ignored Paul's warning and decided to sail for Phoenix farther west on the south coast of Crete and spend the winter there. They probably realized that Paul was right. It was time to give up trying to reach Greece. But they probably did not like the idea of wintering in Fair Havens because it was not a very secure port. It was wide open to the east wind, and just north of it was the Messara Valley. If, during the winter, the dreaded northeasterly storms came crashing

---

26. Myra is the city where Saint Nicholas (Santa Claus) was born in the third century AD.

down through that valley, they might batter the ship to pieces or rip it free of its moorings and drive it helplessly across the open sea into the Gulf of Sidra off Libya and into the dreaded shoals of Syrtis, the graveyard of ships. It may be that "Fair Havens" was a humorously ironic name given to the port by sea captains who knew it was anything but. The ship put out from Fair Havens about October 26.

At first, the decision of Julius and the captain seemed a propitious one. The wind swung out of the west and now blew gently from the south, allowing the ship to follow the coast of Crete placidly toward Phoenix. They continued on this course until around October 28. Then, around October 29, a terrible storm moved in from the northeast, blowing the ship off course. It scudded before the wind to the island of Cauda, about twenty-three miles south of Crete, alone on the open sea. They managed to get under Cauda's lee shore. They had so far been pulling the ship's boat behind the freighter. In the lee of Cauda they managed, with some difficulty, to pull in the ship's boat and to haul it out of the water, securing it on deck. This would prevent the boat's line from getting tangled in the freighter's rudder. If that happened, they might be unable to steer. It would also keep the boat secure in case they needed it to abandon ship.

The storm continued to drive them along, and they lowered the sails and cast out a stern anchor to slow the ship down because the fear of being driven all the way to the shoals of Syrtis continued to haunt them. Then, they threw some of the ship's cargo overboard, suggesting that the ship was beginning to take on water and sink. The storm did not abate, and on November 1, the crew jettisoned some of the ship's tackle. The word tackle in Greek is *skeué*, which means equipment. This does not, therefore, mean that the crew began to throw over gear essential to navigate the ship but that they began to jettison non-essential furniture. When neither the sun nor the stars appeared for many days, and the storm raged on, they abandoned all hope of being saved.

The crew had eaten nothing for many days (and with the seasickness that even tough sailors experience in bad storms, no wonder). Paul told them that an angel of God had come to him in the night and told him that they would all be saved because Paul must stand before Caesar. He urged them to take heart because he had faith that God would do exactly as promised. He added that they would soon run aground on some island.

After midnight on November 14, the sailors suspected they were approaching land. They took soundings with a lead line and found twenty fathoms. They threw a lead line again and found fifteen fathoms.

They were sure they were approaching land. Fearing that they might run up on the rocks, they threw out four anchors off the ship's stern to slow their speed and lessen the possible impact.

Paul noticed that some of the crew, thinking they could escape the ship and reach the beach, were lowering the ship's boat into the sea under the pretense of laying anchors down from the bow. He warned the centurion, Julius, and his soldiers that "unless these men stay in the ship, you cannot be saved." The centurion, his soldiers, and his prisoners were not qualified to manage the ship. They needed all hands on deck to ensure their survival. At Julius' command, the Roman soldiers cut away the ropes of the ship's boat and let it go, bobbing in the waves.

As day dawned, Paul urged everyone to take some food. They had eaten nothing in the fourteen days since they had secured the ship's boat on the lee shore of Cauda. They needed their strength, and he promised that all 276 men aboard would be saved. They were encouraged and ate. Then, they lightened the ship further to soften the impact of running aground by throwing the cargo of Egyptian grain overboard.

SHIPWRECK

Paul and everyone aboard the Egyptian freighter were shipwrecked, and all hands survived. This was Paul's fourth shipwreck. In 2 Corinthians 11:25, he wrote, four years before, in AD 52, "Three times I was shipwrecked; a night and a day I was adrift at sea."

Just before the shipwreck, Paul's ship was "being driven about . . . in the Adria" (Acts 27:27).[27] The ESV translates this as "being driven across the Adriatic Sea." A glance at a modern map shows that the Adriatic Sea extends from Venice to Lecce on the heel of the Italian boot on its western shore and to Albania on its eastern shore. This is a long way from Malta, the traditional site of Paul's shipwreck. The Adria in ancient parlance, however, was not the same as the modern Adriatic Sea. Ptolemy speaks of the Adria as extending from Crete[28] in the east to Sicily in the west.[29] Given this, Luke's reference to the body of water across which they had been driven would be accurate, although, on a

---

27. This author's translation.
28. Ptolemy, *Geography*, 3:15:1.
29. Ptolemy, *Geography*, 3:4:1.

modern map, we would say that the ship had been driven across the Ionian or the Mediterranean Sea, not the Adriatic.

ON MALTA

The Maltese showed kindly hospitality to the shipwrecked mariners. They kindled a fire because it had begun to rain and was cold. As Paul gathered a bundle of sticks for the fire, a snake fastened onto his hand and hung there. Thinking that this species of snake was lethal, the Maltese natives expected him to swell up and fall down dead. They suspected that he was a murderer because, having survived a shipwreck, Justice had nevertheless condemned him to die. When he shook the snake off into the fire and survived with no ill effects, however, they decided Paul must be a god. This perhaps fulfilled Jesus' prophecy that his apostles would suffer no ill effects, even from the deadly bite of serpents (Mark 16:18).

Some doubt has been cast upon the identity of Paul's shipwreck site because there are now no vipers on Malta, and there is no archeological evidence that there ever were. This has given rise to the theory that Paul did not land on Malta but on the island of Meleda, now called Mjlet, off the coast of Croatia.[30] The Greek name for the island on which Paul beached is Melite (Acts 28:1). The horned viper (*Vipera ammodytes*) lives on Mjlet and throughout southern Europe and parts of the Middle East. It is the most dangerous of European vipers because of its large size, long fangs, and highly toxic venom. The island of Mjlet was so overrun by poisonous snakes until 1911 that mongooses were introduced to eliminate them. But for Paul's ship, driven by a northeast gale, to make its way northwest from Crete halfway up the modern Adriatic Sea to Mjlet seems unlikely.

There are better explanations. Possibly there was a venomous snake native to Malta in Paul's day that went extinct, and the evidence of its existence is as yet undiscovered. Possibly, Paul encountered the European cat snake (*Telescopus fallax*), a venomous rear-fanged colubrid (not a viper) that lives on Malta. Its mouth is too small to bite humans easily, but it can do so if handled. Possibly, Paul encountered a viper not native to Malta that had stowed away on the Alexandrian grain ship and had nestled among the sticks Paul gathered. That the Maltese seemed to recognize the snake and knew of its toxicity does not mean that the snake

---

30. Meinardus, "St. Paul Shipwrecked in Dalmatia," 145.

had to be native to Malta. Many ships put into the harbor at Malta and many animals had no doubt stowed away on some of them and landed on the island. The Maltese may simply have recognized what they had seen before. Or possibly the snake Paul encountered was not venomous at all. The Greek word for this snake is *echidna*, which may mean either viper or serpent. The Bible does not say the snake bit Paul. It says it "fastened on his hand" and was "hanging from his hand" (Acts 28:3–4). So, it is possible that the people simply assumed, as people often do, that this snake was deadly and that, naturally, Paul would bloat and die. In conclusion, the problem of which snake Paul encountered after his shipwreck does not undermine the identification of his shipwreck site with Malta, which it almost certainly was.

Publius, the chief man in Malta, hosted Paul and his team. Paul healed Publius' father of fever and dysentery, and then Paul healed many others during his three-month stay on the island (Acts 28:7–10).

VOYAGE TO ROME

Julius then transferred Paul and his other charges to another Alexandrian ship, the *Castor and Pollux*, which had wintered in Malta. They sailed to Syracuse in Sicily, then to Reghium in southern Italy, and finally to Puteoli on the Bay of Naples. Finding fellow Christians there, the group stayed with them for seven days. Julius, the centurion, must have been exceptionally lenient.

Paul and his entourage then walked north to Rome. Along the Appian Way, Christians came out from Rome to meet them at the village called Three Taverns. On seeing the welcoming party, Paul thanked God and took courage. He reached Rome around March 8, AD 57. He was allowed to stay there by himself under the light guard of one soldier. Three days after reaching Rome, Paul proclaimed the Gospel to the Roman Jews on Saturday, the Sabbath, March 10 (Acts 28:17–29). On the next Sabbath, March 17, Paul addressed the whole congregation of Roman Jews at Paul's place of lodging. After hearing him from morning to evening, they rejected the Gospel. So, Paul turned to preaching to the Gentiles in Rome (Acts 28:23–28).

ROME: AD 57–59

Paul remained in Rome under house arrest for two years. Even so, he preached the Gospel boldly and without hindrance (Phil 1:12). He had a relative in Rome, Herodian (Rom 16:11). From Rome, he wrote the books of Ephesians, Philippians, Colossians, Philemon, and a lost letter to the church of Laodicea. Paul's letter to the Philippians says that while in a Roman prison, he converted even members of Caesar's household (Phil 1:13, 4:22). Mark arrived in Rome sometime during Paul's stay this time. Also with him were Timothy, Luke, Onesimus, Aristarchus, and Demas (Phlm 1). Peter also arrived in Rome between AD 57–59 and resumed leadership of the Roman church, which he had founded. Silas joined him and perhaps acted as his scribe (1 Peter 5:12). All these details suggest that Paul was not in a dungeon with dripping walls infested with rats. He was under reasonably comfortable house arrest, surrounded by colleagues.

PHILEMON AND ONESIMUS

While in Rome, Paul encountered Onesimus, a slave who had run away from his master, Philemon, the head of the church in Colossae (Phlm 1:1). While imprisoned, Paul led Onesimus to the Lord (Phlm 1:10) and wrote a letter to Philemon, pleading with him to free Onesimus. Paul sent Epaphroditus to Philippi and Tychicus to Ephesus, armed with copies of Paul's letters to the churches in Greece and Asia, namely Ephesians, Philippians, Colossians, and a lost letter to the Laodiceans (Eph 6:21, Phil 2:25, Col 4:7, 16).[31] Since Paul asked the Colossians and the Laodiceans to read each other's letters, it seems that he wanted all the churches to read all four letters.

The letter to Philemon was different. It was personal. Philemon had a decision to make: punish Onesimus for running away or forgive him and set him free. Paul was sure Philemon would comply with Paul's plea on Onesimus' behalf since Paul had led Philemon to Christ (Phlm 19). Onesimus may have been less certain. He must have spent many an anxious hour as, at Paul's command, he traveled with Epaphras back to Colossae. Since the letter is published in our Bible, we can be sure that Philemon

---

31. Paul says the Colossians should read the letter "from Laodicea." He does not mean that the Laodiceans wrote a letter to the Colossians. He means that his letter to Laodicea would be delivered there first, after which the Laodiceans were meant to share the letter for Laodicea with Colossae.

complied with Paul's request and freed Onesimus. If he had not done so, he surely would not have made Paul's letter public. Onesimus eventually succeeded Timothy as the bishop of the church at Ephesus.

Paul wrote in his letter to Philemon that he was "an old man and a prisoner for Jesus Christ." He was probably between fifty-two and fifty-four years old. He would survive another ten to twelve years.

NERO'S VERDICT

This was the early period of Nero's reign before the emperor went mad and began persecuting Christians. At this time, after January AD 59, Luke, who was with Paul in Rome, completed his book of Acts. Since Luke states that Acts was his second book, Luke obviously had completed his first book, the Gospel of Luke, before this date.

Mark and Luke were together in Rome during Paul's first imprisonment (Col 4:10–14, Phlm 1:24). It is hard to imagine that they failed to read each other's books and shared their experiences of composing Scripture under the Holy Spirit's auspices.

Nero acquitted Paul, possibly because the young emperor wanted to distance himself from the anti-Jewish policy of his late uncle, Claudius. If so, that benevolent spirit would last for only five years.

Paul's movements after this are less certain. If Paul wrote the book of Hebrews, dictating it to Luke as his scribe, this is probably when he did so. He says he had released[32] Timothy on some mission away from Rome and hoped he would return in time to rejoin him on his travels and ultimately go with him back to Jerusalem (Heb 13:23).

ITALY, SPAIN, ILLYRICUM, ASIA MINOR, CRETE, AND GREECE

Since Paul's acquittal probably occurred in January AD 59, the sailing weather would be bad until Spring, so he probably evangelized nearby. Hippolytus said he evangelized in Italy and Illyricum.[33] After that, he probably traveled to Spain, as he wrote that he hoped to do (Rom 15:24).

---

32. The word "released" in Greek is sometimes translated as "set free," as if Timothy were liberated from jail. There is no record, however, of Timothy in prison, so probably by "released," Paul just means "sent away."

33. Hippolytus, *List of the Apostles and Disciples*.

From there, he probably returned to the churches in Greece. He went to Crete and founded churches there, leaving them in the care of his fellow worker, Titus (Titus 1:5). He then went to Ephesus. At some point, Aquila and Priscilla had returned to Ephesus from Rome (2 Tim 4:19). Paul probably visited the churches in Asia Minor, including Miletus (2 Tim 4:20), and then returned to Philippi, Thessalonica, and Corinth. From Corinth, Paul wrote his letter to Titus in Crete, probably between September 11, AD 60 and September 14, AD 64 (Titus 1:5).[34] While in Corinth, Paul sent Artemas or Tychicus from Corinth to Titus, asking him to leave Crete and meet Paul in Nicopolis (Greece) if he could (Titus 3:12). All this probably happened in the good Spring sailing weather, around March or April of AD 65.

Paul did not simply trudge around the world conducting missions solo. He trained disciples to whom he delegated the task of making disciples and sent them around the world. They included Silas, Timothy, Titus, Aquila, Priscilla, Tychicus, Epaphroditus, Phoebe, and doubtless many more.

THE NERONIAN PERSECUTION

The Great Fire of Rome broke out between July 18–26, AD 64. Taking advantage of the land that the fire cleared, the emperor Nero claimed a large plot on which he proposed to build a luxurious golden palace. The resentful mob of common Romans spread the rumor that Nero had set the fire himself with this result in mind. Their mutinous mood was lethal, and it terrified Nero. He tried every possible means to mollify them. When nothing worked, he hit upon the scheme of blaming the Christians in Rome for setting the fire. Even the anti-Christian Roman historian Tacitus realized this was a lie. To impress the surly crowd, Nero began a merciless persecution of Christians. Tacitus described this as follows.

> Neither human help nor imperial munificence nor all the modes of placating Heaven could stifle scandal or dispel the belief that the fire had taken place by order. Therefore, to scotch the rumor, Nero substituted as culprits and punished with the utmost refinements of cruelty, a class of men loathed for their vices,

---

34. The clue is that Paul asked Titus to meet Paul in winter in Nicopolis, which is in Western Greece between the Ambracian Gulf and the Ionian Sea. This suggests that Paul was positioning himself for a return to Illyricum, to the north, when the Spring weather came.

whom the crowd styled Christians. Christus, the founder of the name, had undergone the death penalty in the reign of Tiberius by sentence of the procurator Pontius Pilatus, and the pernicious superstition was checked for a moment, only to break out once more, not merely in Judaea, the home of the disease, but in the capital itself, where all things horrible or shameful in the world collect and find a vogue. First, then, the confessed members of the sect were arrested; next, on their disclosures, vast numbers were convicted, not so much on the count of arson as for hatred of the human race. And derision accompanied their end: they were covered with wild beasts' skins and torn to death by dogs, or they were fastened on crosses and, when daylight failed, were burned to serve as lamps by night. Nero had offered his Gardens for the spectacle and gave an exhibition in his Circus, mixing with the crowd in the habit of a charioteer or mounted on his car. Hence, in spite of a guilt that had earned the most exemplary punishment, there arose a sentiment of pity due to the impression that they were being sacrificed not for the welfare of the state but for the ferocity of a single man.[35]

All this terror served to make the populace more sympathetic to the Christians and more inimical to Nero.

Meanwhile, Paul returned to Asia Minor, ending up in Ephesus and finally Troas.[36] In AD 66, the Jews launched their ill-fated war of independence against Rome. Caught up in the reverberations of this turmoil, Paul was arrested at Troas, probably unexpectedly, which would explain why he left his cloak and books with Carpus (2 Tim 4:13). His captors left him no time to pack. The fact that he was arrested so far from Rome implies that Nero's persecution of Christians spread far beyond the capital city. Titus, Crescens, Tychicus, Trophimus, Carpus, Demas, and Alexander, the coppersmith, were possibly all with Paul when he was arrested. Alexander the coppersmith did Paul great harm, opposing Paul's message and that of Timothy, too. Titus went to Dalmatia, Crescens to Galatia, and Tychicus to Ephesus, no doubt, to carry on the mission of proclaiming the Gospel and working with Timothy. Erastus remained in Corinth. Mark was also with this team somewhere in Asia Minor (modern Turkey).

35. Tacitus, *Annals*, 15:44.
36. This largely unrecorded interval is a little over four years, so Paul had plenty of time to make a return circuit, or even multiple circuits, of all the churches in Asia, Macedonia, Achaia (Greece), and Illyricum and even a return trip to Rome and Spain if he chose.

From Troas, Paul was taken to Ephesus, the capital of the province of Asia. Paul left Trophimus, who was ill, at Miletus (2 Tim 4:20). When Paul made his first defense in his second Roman incarceration, no one came to his support. Demas, whom Paul called his fellow-worker in his letter to Philemon (Phlm 1:24), and who joined in sending greetings in Paul's letter to the Colossians (Col 4:14), had deserted him for love of the world and had gone to Thessalonica (2 Tim 4:10). Everyone deserted him, except Luke.

SECOND ROMAN INCARCERATION

This time in Rome, Paul was imprisoned, possibly in the Mamertine prison, where Nero had also incarcerated Peter.[37] This was very different from the relatively comfortable house arrest of his first imprisonment. At this time, Paul wrote his last epistle, 2 Timothy. In it, he begged Timothy to rejoin him and to bring Mark. The rift between him and Mark, arising at the start of Paul's second missionary journey seventeen years before, had mended. Of his non-Roman followers, Luke was with him, but Eubulus, Pudens, Linus, Claudia, and other brothers in Rome were also with him, possibly also as prisoners of Nero (2 Tim 4:21).

PAUL'S DEATH

In 2 Timothy, Paul poured out his heart in this profound and moving epistle. He knew that this time, the Romans would not set him free. He knew he was going to die.

> I am already being poured out as a drink offering, and the time of my departure has come. I have fought the good fight, I have finished the race, I have kept the faith. Henceforth, there is laid up for me the crown of righteousness, which the Lord, the righteous judge, will award to me on that day, and not only to me but also to all who have loved his appearing (2 Tim 4:6–8).

Jerome says that Paul suffered martyrdom on the same day as Peter.[38] As a Roman citizen, Paul died a dignified death by the sword, while Peter, a non-citizen, died upside down on a cross. Their deaths occurred

---

37. De Montor, *The Lives and Times of the Roman Pontiffs*, 26.
38. Jerome, *On Illustrious Men*.

near the end of Nero's reign in AD 68.[39] Nero committed suicide on June 9 of that year.[40] Had Nero delayed the execution but for a few months, Peter and Paul would have survived his evil reign.

PAUL'S EPILOGUE

Back in 51 BC, still five years before his famous shipwreck in Malta and seventeen years before his execution, Paul wrote a catalog of what he already had suffered for Jesus:

> Five times I received from the Jews the forty lashes minus one. Three times, I was beaten with rods; once, I was stoned; three times, I was shipwrecked; I spent a night and a day in the open sea, and I have been constantly on the move. I have been in danger from rivers, in danger from bandits, in danger from my own countrymen, in danger from Gentiles; in danger in the city, in danger in the country, in danger at sea, and in danger from false brothers. I have labored and toiled and have often gone without sleep; I have known hunger and thirst and have often gone without food; I have been cold and naked (2 Cor 11:24–27).

"I am an ambassador in chains," wrote Paul (Eph 6:20). He preached the Gospel for thirty-five years.[41] If he began studying under Gamaliel at the age of twenty-nine, he probably died at the age of sixty-four. As he wrote in Second Timothy, penned shortly before his execution, Paul had fought the good fight, finished the course, and kept the faith.

---

39. Finegan, *Handbook*, 380.

40. Finegan, *Handbook*, 379.

41. Hippolytus says, "Paul entered into the apostleship a year after the assumption of Christ; and beginning at Jerusalem, he advanced as far as Illyricum, and Italy, and Spain, preaching the Gospel for five-and-thirty years. And in the time of Nero, he was beheaded at Rome and was buried there." Hippolytus is off by one year. Paul ministered for thirty-five years, from AD 33–68, not from a year after the assumption of Christ but from the year of the assumption of Christ.

ABOUT THE AUTHOR

I GREW UP EXPOSED to Christianity, but in my late teens, I concluded that the Bible was a compilation of myths and, compared to the *Mahabharata* and *Arabian Nights*, rather inferior ones. I felt too smart to be a Christian. So, I sought truth elsewhere. But, after traveling the world and diving deeply into the great religions, I grew tired of being a seeker after truth. I wanted to be a finder of it. My family urged me to read the Bible and visit a church. I did so gingerly. I visited a mega-church in southern California with chorus lyrics projected on a big screen. The meandering tunes and euphoric devotees made me want to reach for a pinch of salt.

The pastor, however, preached salvation through Christ alone. He promised that if I would walk to the altar and repent before God in Jesus' name, I would receive the Holy Spirit. I doubted him, but I was rational. Faith is the daughter of doubt. I had crossed the Himalayas and met the Dalai Lama. I had trekked through a steaming Java jungle to meditate at a Sufi shrine. I could walk down this air-conditioned aisle and prove or disprove the pastor's claim.

At the altar, I prayed a rather impudent prayer. "God, I know you exist. If this is the way to know you personally, I accept it." If I had been God (which, fortunately for all of us, I am not), I would have responded to my impertinence by reducing me instantly to a grease spot. Instead, a light flickered on in my heart. I had been in the occasional midnight chant in Asia, and I attributed this sensation to mere ambience. But it lasted. It lasted until today and will last beyond the horizon of time. I was saved. The problem was that my mind was far behind my heart. My overly "educated" brain possessed clear and convincing proof that the Bible was philosophically and scientifically wrong. Either the Bible or my brain had to give. So, I began to devote myself to proving or disproving the Bible.

To my ongoing humiliation, the battering rams of "enlightenment" kept splintering against the impervious gates of Scripture. Everywhere I turned—archaeology, paleontology, astronomy, history, physics, mathematics, and philosophy—the Bible proved right, and I proved wrong. I burned with shame to think how many Christians I had "defeated" in debate and how smugly superior I had felt to them. How could God have any desire to love me, who had been such an arrogant fool? The answer came when I found I could comfortably witness to Muslims, Hindus, Buddhists, and skeptics because I had once embraced their positions.

In the summer of 2008, my church asked me to teach an adult theology class for three Sundays. I was nervous. I did not know the Bible well enough to teach it. During those first three Sunday lessons, I was shed rivers of sweat. By the third, I learned that no substitute teacher had been found, and I ended up teaching the Bible, verse by verse, repeatedly, from then until Sunday, May 29, 2016. In the course of doing this, I grappled with every problem and seeming contradiction in the Bible that I could find. From apparent discrepancies in chronology and with science to the arcane mystery of Solomon's Sea, I discovered, through 8,000 hours of research and teaching and 1,005 GB of writing original course material, that the Bible is totally inerrant.

I was blessed to have a class of devoted and highly educated adults. Among them were a trained and professional theologian, philosophers, educators, mathematicians, physical scientists, a rocket scientist (literally), and Bible students of many decades. They were of inestimable help in correcting and guiding me as I presented and tested my lessons. As iron sharpens iron, so we sharpened each other. I turned my original course material into many books on theology, of which this is one.

In May 2022, I earned a master's degree in Theology with High Distinction at Liberty University's Rawlings School of Divinity, Lynchburg, Virginia. I live in rural Massachusetts. I am now earning my Ph.D. in Bible Exposition at Liberty. I host a website, www.thebiblehistoryguy.com, and I appear regularly on Real America's Voice streaming TV network as the Bible History Guy. My aim is to continue to teach and to keep writing.

BIBLIOGRAPHY

Allen, David L. *Lukan Authorship of Hebrews*. Nashville: B&H Academic, 2010.
"The Acts of Andrew." Translated by M. R. James. *The Apocryphal New Testament*. Oxford: Clarendon, 1924. http://www.earlychristianwritings.com/text/actsandrew.html.
"The Acts of Andrew and Matthias." *Fathers of the Church*. New Advent. https://www.newadvent.org/fathers/0820.htm.
"The Acts of John." Translated by M. R. James. *The Gnostic Society Library: Gnostic Scriptures and Fragments*. http://gnosis.org/library/actjohn.htm.
"The Acts of Philip." *The Gnostic Society Library*. http://gnosis.org/library/actphil.htm.
"The Acts of Timothy." *The North American Society for the Study of Christian Apocryphal Literature*. https://www.nasscal.com/e-clavis-christian-apocrypha/acts-of-timothy.
"Biography of Saint Luke." *New Advent*. https://www.newadvent.org/cathen/09420a.htm.
Appell, Victor S. "Why Do Some Jews Have One Seder and Others Have Two Seders?" *ReformJudaism.org: Jewish Life in Your Life*. https://reformjudaism.org/learning/answers-jewish-questions/why-do-some-jews-have-one-seder-and-others-have-two-seders.
Augustine of Hippo. "De Adulterinis Conjugiis 2:6-7." *Evidence Unseen*. https://www.evidenceunseen.com/bible-difficulties-2/nt-difficulties/john-acts/jn-753-811-does-this-belong-in-the-bible/#_ftn13.
Bereford, James. *The Ancient Sailing Season*. Boston: Brill, 2013.
Beyer, David W. "Josephus Reexamined: Unraveling the Twenty-Second Year of Tiberius." In *Chronos, Kairos, Christos II*. Macon: Mercer University Press, 1998.
Bromberg, Irving L. *Kalendis Calendar Calculator*. Toronto: University of Toronto. http://individual.utoronto.ca/kalendis/kalendis.htm
Bruce, F. F. "Christianity Under Claudius." *Bulletin of the John Rylands Library* 44 (March 1962) 309–326.
Caldwell, Zelda. "Three of the Oldest Images of Jesus Portray Him as the 'Good Shepherd.'" *Aleteia* (Sunday, March 27, 2019). https://aleteia.org/2019/05/12/three-of-the-oldest-images-of-jesus-portrays-him-as-the-good-shepherd/.

BIBLIOGRAPHY

Cassius Dio. *Roman History*. https://penelope.uchicago.edu/Thayer/e/roman/texts/cassius_dio/home.html.

Casson, Lionel. *Speed under Sail of Ancient Ships*. https://penelope.uchicago.edu/Thayer/E/Journals/TAPA/82/Speed_under_Sail_of_Ancient_Ships*.html#ref42a

Cheetham, S. "The Province of Galatia." *The Classical Review*, vol. 8, no. 9. www.jstor.org/stable/693143.

Cholmondeley, Hester H. "Betrayal."

Clement of Alexandria. *Stromata ("Miscellanies")*. https://www.newadvent.org/fathers/0210.htm.

Cornuke, Robert and David Halbrook. *In Search of the Mountain of God: The Discovery of the Real Mt. Sinai*. Nashville, TN. Broadman & Holman, 2000.

De Montor, Artaud. *Lives and Times of the Roman Pontiffs, from St. Peter to Pius IX*, Vol. 1. Paris: D & J Sadlier, 1869.

De Voragine, Jacobus. "Chapter 9: On St. John the Apostle and Evangelist." In *The Golden Legend*. New York: Fordham University Press. https://sourcebooks.fordham.edu/basis/goldenlegend/

Elwell, Walter A. *Encountering the New Testament: A historical and Theological Survey*, 3rd Edition. Grand Rapids: Baker Academic, 2013.

Eusebius. *Church History*. New Advent, LLC. https://www.newadvent.org/fathers/2501.htm.

Finegan, Jack. *Handbook of Biblical Chronology*, Revised Edition. Peabody: Hendrickson, 1998.

Gottheil, Richard, et al. "Babylonian Captivity." In *Jewish Encyclopedia: The Unedited Full-Text of the 1906 Jewish Encyclopedia*. https://jewishencyclopedia.com/

Gottheil, Richard, et al. "Captivity, or Exile, Babylonian." In *Jewish Encyclopedia*. https://www.jewishencyclopedia.com/articles/4012-captivity.

Herodotus. *The History of Herodotus*, Book IV. Translated by George Rawlinson. http://classics.mit.edu/Herodotus/history.4.iv.html.

Hippolytus. "List of the Apostles and Disciples." Translated by J. H. MacMahon. *North American Society for the Study of Christian Apocryphal Literature*. https://www.nasscal.com/e-clavis-christian-apocrypha/list-of-the-apostles-and-disciples-by-pseudo-hippolytus-of-thebes/

Hirsch, Emil G. "Festivals." In *Jewish Encyclopedia: The Unedited Full-Text of the 1906 Jewish Encyclopedia*. https://jewishencyclopedia.com/

Irenaeus. *Against Heresies*. https://www.newadvent.org/fathers/0103.htm.

Jerome. *On Illustrious Men*. https://www.newadvent.org/fathers/2708.htm.

Josephus. *Antiquities of the Jews*. https://www.biblestudytools.com/history/flavius-josephus.

———. *War of the Jews*. https://www.biblestudytools.com/history/flavius-josephus.

Justin Martyr. *First Apology* and *Dialogue with Trypho*. http://www.earlychristianwritings.com/justin.html.

Kitto, John, et al. *The Journal of Sacred Literature and Biblical Record*, Vol. 11. London: John Crockford, 1860.

Larson, Frederick E. *Star of Bethlehem*. http://www.bethlehemstar.net.

Merrill, Elmer Truesdell. "The Expulsion of Jews from Rome under Tiberius." *Classical Philology*. Vol. 14, No. 4 (1919) 365–372.

Moseley, James Allen. *Bethlehem Star*. https://www.youtube.com/watch?v=5Z-hZWAvpIE&t=827s.

———. *The History of Daniel: Truth in Exile*. Petersham: Winterwood, 2019.
———. *The History of Jesus, the Son of Man*. Petersham: Winterwood, 2019.
———. *The History of Revelation: Beyond the Veil*. Petersham: Winterwood, 2019.
"The Muratorian Canon, Fragment III, Robert-Donaldson Translation." *Early Christian Writings*. http://www.earlychristianwritings.com/text/muratorian.html.
Nollet, James A. "Astronomical and Historical Evidence for Dating the Nativity in 2 BC." In *Perspectives on Science and Christian Faith*. Dec 2012, Vol. 64 Issue 4, 211-219.
O'Kane, Murray. *Little Lives of the Great Saints*. Charlotte: TAN, 2009.
Orosius, Paulus. *Histories Against the Pagans*. http://attalus.org/info/orosius.html.
Papias of Hierapolis. "Fragment X." In *Exposition of the Sayings of the Lord*. http://www.earlychristianwritings.com/text/papias.html.
Plutarch. *Parallel Lives*. https://penelope.uchicago.edu/Thayer/e/roman/texts/plutarch/lives/home.html.
"Roman Empire Population." *UNRV Roman History*. http://www.unrv.com/empire/roman-population.php.
"Saints Thaddaeus and Bartholomew." *The Armenian Prelacy*. https://armenianprelacy.org/2020/11/25/saints-thaddeus-and-bartholomew/.
Schechter, Solomon, et al. "Holy Days." *Jewish Encyclopedia: The Unedited Full-Text of the 1906 Jewish Encyclopedia*. https://jewishencyclopedia.com/
Schnabel, Eckhard J., et al. *Revelation: An Introduction and Commentary*. Downers Grove: InterVarsity, 2018.
Schnelle, Udo. *Apostle Paul: His Life and Theology*. Nashville: Baker Academic, 2012.
Shelton, W. Brian. *Quest for the Historical Apostles: Tracing Their Lives and Legacies*. Grand Rapids: Baker Academic, 2018.
Smith, William. *Dictionary of Greek and Roman Geography*. London: Walton and Maberly, 1854. http://www.perseus.tufts.edu/hopper/text?doc=Perseus:text:1999.04.0064:entry=attaleia-geo&highlight=attalia.
Stanford Geospatial Model of the Roman World. "Orbis." https://orbis.stanford.edu/
Starry Night Pro Software. http://www.starrynight.com/
Steinman, Andrew. "When Did Herod the Great Reign?" *Novum Testamentum*. Vol. 51, No. 1 (2009) 1–29.
Strong, James. *Strong's Exhaustive Concordance to the Bible*. Peabody: Hendrickson, 2009.
Suetonius. *Lives of the Twelve Caesars*. https://www.gutenberg.org/files/6400/6400-h/6400-h.htm.
Tacitus. *Annals*. https://penelope.uchicago.edu/Thayer/e/roman/texts/tacitus/home.html.
———. *Histories*. https://penelope.uchicago.edu/Thayer/e/roman/texts/tacitus/home.html.
Talmud. "Yoma 3b." https://www.sefaria.org/Yoma.39b?ven=William_Davidson_Edition_-_English&vhe=William_Davidson_Edition_-_Vocalized_Aramaic&lang=bi
Tertullian. *The Acts and Martyrdom of the Holy Apostle Andrew*. https://www.tertullian.org/fathers2/ANF-08/anf08-95.htm.
———. *Prescription Against Heresies*. https://www.newadvent.org/fathers/0311.htm.
Walking Englishman's Walk Time Calculator. https://www.walkingenglishman.com/walktime.aspx.
WordsRated, https://wordsrated.com/bible-sales-statistics/

www.ingramcontent.com/pod-product-compliance
Lightning Source LLC
Chambersburg PA
CBHW070310230426
43663CB00011B/2072